Design Thinking

Design Thinking is a set of strategic and creative processes and principles used in the planning and creation of products and solutions to human-centered design problems.

With design and innovation being two key driving principles, this series focuses on, but not limited to, the following areas and topics:

- User Interface (UI) and User Experience (UX) Design

- Psychology of Design

- Human-Computer Interaction (HCI)

- Ergonomic Design

- Product Development and Management

- Virtual and Mixed Reality (VR/XR)

- User-Centered Built Environments and Smart Homes

- Accessibility, Sustainability and Environmental Design

- Learning and Instructional Design

- Strategy and best practices

This series publishes books aimed at designers, developers, storytellers and problem-solvers in industry to help them understand current developments and best practices at the cutting edge of creativity, to invent new paradigms and solutions, and challenge Creatives to push boundaries to design bigger and better than before.

More information about this series at https://link.springer.com/bookseries/15933.

Interfaceless

Conscious Design for Spatial Computing with Generative AI

Diana Olynick

Apress®

Interfaceless: Conscious Design for Spatial Computing with Generative AI

Diana Olynick
Winnipeg, MB, Canada

ISBN-13 (pbk): 979-8-8688-0082-5
https://doi.org/10.1007/979-8-8688-0083-2

ISBN-13 (electronic): 979-8-8688-0083-2

Managing Director, Apress Media LLC: Welmoed Spahr
Acquisitions Editor: James Robinson-Prior
Development Editor: James Markham
Coordinating Editor: Gryffin Winkler

Cover image designed by eStudioCalamar

Distributed to the book trade worldwide by Apress Media, LLC, 1 New York Plaza, New York, NY 10004, U.S.A. Phone 1-800-SPRINGER, fax (201) 348-4505, e-mail orders-ny@springer-sbm.com, or visit www.springeronline.com. Apress Media, LLC is a California LLC and the sole member (owner) is Springer Science + Business Media Finance Inc (SSBM Finance Inc). SSBM Finance Inc is a Delaware corporation.

For information on translations, please e-mail booktranslations@springernature.com; for reprint, paperback, or audio rights, please e-mail bookpermissions@springernature.com.

Apress titles may be purchased in bulk for academic, corporate, or promotional use. eBook versions and licenses are also available for most titles. For more information, reference our Print and eBook Bulk Sales web page at http://www.apress.com/bulk-sales.

Any source code or other supplementary material referenced by the author in this book is available to readers on GitHub (https://github.com/Apress). For more detailed information, please visit https://www.apress.com/gp/services/source-code.

Paper in this product is recyclable

To you.

Table of Contents

About the Author

Diana Olynick stands at the crossroads of design, engineering, and spatial computing innovation. As a registered professional engineer, she brings a blend of technical acumen and design creativity to the XR field with over a decade of experience. Beyond academia, Diana's voice has resonated globally, with invitations to speak at several esteemed international conferences. She has dedicated herself to educating the next generation, guiding them through the intricacies of spatial computing and conscious design. Her ability to deconstruct and demystify complex XR topics for a wide audience sets her apart. In a rapidly evolving digital landscape, Diana is a leader fostering the transformative potential of interfaceless. Diana's educational contributions can be found at `www.dianaolynick.com`.

About the Technical Reviewer

 **Jerry Medeiros** is a seasoned professional with over a decade of hands-on experience in immersive technology, focusing on games and extended reality. With a robust background in artificial intelligence, Jerry brings a unique perspective to the intersection of technology and interactive experiences. Holding a bachelor's degree in game development with a specialization in interaction design, as well as a master's degree in computer science with research expertise in artificial intelligence, Jerry is well-versed in cutting-edge technologies and their applications.

Acknowledgments

First and foremost, my deepest gratitude goes to my family: Sara, my mom, Stephen, Gani, and Penny. Their unwavering belief in my ability to convey this pivotal message to the world was the anchor of my inspiration. And to my two faithful dogs, who patiently awaited their cuddles as I poured my heart into these pages, thank you for the silent comfort. Together, their collective support was the beacon that guided me through the long nights and challenging moments of this journey.

To the diligent teams, editors, and managers who helped bring this vision to life, Welmoed Spahr, James Robinson-Prior, James Markham, Gryffin Winkler, Shonmirin Vareichung, and everyone else involved in the project working so hard to make this a reality—thank you. To every expert, colleague, and friend who offered insights—your contributions have been invaluable.

As you've journeyed through this book on spatial computing and generative AI, I invite you to a brief moment of reflection. Consider the last interfaceless interaction you had. How did it shape your experience of the digital world?

To those picking up this book in the distant future, I hope its contents have not just informed but have also been a testament to the commitment of our era toward conscious, ethical design.

A heartfelt acknowledgment to the developers, designers, and visionaries behind the algorithms that power our digital age. While these algorithms operate silently, they are born from human ingenuity and aspiration. Their interfaceless interactions are evidence not just of technological advancement but of our collective human drive to innovate and improve.

ACKNOWLEDGMENTS

During the writing of this book, a chance interaction with a new piece of generative AI solidified the urgency and relevance of this work for me—a machine-generated piece of music that stirred human emotion just as poignantly as any human composition.

But most importantly, dear reader, thank you. By engaging with this content, you've made this work truly alive. And I hope, in some way, it empowers you to shape the future of spatial computing with intentionality and care.

Introduction: The Challenge of Conscious and Interfaceless Design

What if there was another way to interact with technology? What if it could understand us effortlessly, be intuitive, and feel natural? This is where interfaceless design comes in—a vision of technology that understands and adapts to us seamlessly creating interactions while being invisible in the background.

Although it is a very exciting journey, reaching this future comes with its set of challenges. How do we teach machines to comprehend not just our words but our intentions, emotions, and the context in which we exist? How can we ensure that technology respects our privacy, individuality, and humanity? How do we design technology that enhances our lives without becoming intrusive?

Finding answers to these questions requires a combination of technological expertise, psychological understanding, and design principles. This is where the Mindful Spatial Design Framework (MSDF) comes into play—a paradigm that brings together these fields to guide us toward a mindful approach in creating technological experiences from our own awareness and empowerment. The most important nuance of the framework: You are invited to actually create your own!

This framework is proposed as a general guide to assist designers and technologists in the creation of experiences that truly resonate with humans. It places an emphasis on mindfulness and empathy, urging designers to consider how their creations can impact the emotional well-being of individuals. The foundation of this framework lies in computing principles, where technology is not merely seen as a tool but as an integral part of our surroundings.

To properly address the transitioning away from flat screens, we first take a look at spatial computing as the 3D canvas, where our actions and context get translated into digital information. In this scenario, the aim of moving to an interfaceless design is to eliminate the 2D intermediary and allow us to interact directly with our environment just as we do it naturally in the physical world. Arriving at this goal implies a broader understanding of generative AI as most of us are understanding it today. Currently, most of us might think that generative AI models are here to allow us to create more and better images and written text. However, when it comes to spatial computing, the implications of its use are far more reaching than just generating images, text, or sound. Let's imagine a scenario where a human, immersed in a 3D spatial computing environment, makes a gesture or interacts with an object. Instead of a traditional predefined response as the ones dictated by traditional UIs, the system would use a generative AI to create a response. This could be in the form of altering the environment's soundscape, generating a new object, or even generating a visual pattern in real time. This type of interaction is immediate, fluid, and doesn't rely on predetermined 2D interface commands or set, static, limiting "user" journeys.

Generative AI models, especially those like GANs (Generative Adversarial Networks), are designed to generate data which also includes behaviors. When applied to spatial computing, generative AI can be used to dynamically generate content in real time based on the human's interactions with their surroundings.

Finally, since this kind of implementation could increasingly become concerning due to the potential issues with data privacy and ethics, conscious design is imperative for any implementation: to protect human rights and society at large while using technology mindfully and responsibly.

Within the pages of this book, we also delve into the history of AI and its pivotal role in shaping its path. Moreover, we explore approaches for harnessing AI's potential within design while providing valuable insights into mindful design principles. Through engaging case studies showcasing implementations, readers are guided on how to bring these principles to life using preliminary models of AI while foreseeing the most advanced and upcoming possibilities in its evolution.

An important note to keep in mind is that throughout the book I don't refer to "user(s)" but "human(s)." The reason is because the term "user" already has a connotation of an individual that is isolated from the process and someone that we are trying to find data from, with the goal of integrating that data into the design process, mostly for business purposes. This approach has taken design to the direction of imposing onto the "user" a specific interaction journey they need to follow rather than how they can cocreate and actively participate from the full human perspective, which is the purpose of conscious and mindful design.

Finally, whether you are a designer venturing into frontiers, a technologist interested in the future of human-computer interaction, or even a futurist intrigued by the convergence of AI and design, this book aims to ignite your imagination, challenge your perspectives, and equip you with the necessary knowledge to be at the forefront of this thrilling frontier.

So step into our vision for a future where design transcends interfaces and becomes synonymous with experiences. Welcome to an era defined by interfaceless design.

CHAPTER 1

Setting the Stage for the Interfaceless Future

Interfaces are part of our day to day, playing an important role, connecting us with technology and shaping our interactions. The objective of interfaces is to simplify the process while making it more accessible.

Many experts agree that we are moving toward a future where interfaces become almost invisible, and as technology evolves rapidly, this envisions immediate interactions without any intermediaries.

The fast pace of this transformation and evolution sparks our imagination and invites us to reflect on our current interactions with the tools and technologies from today. Have you noticed that we have been admired and mesmerized by newer and newer technological discoveries and inventions, promising us a significant reduction in time for our daily activities (sometimes called efficiency) and helping us make better things? Now, the question is, with all the technology we have so far, how are you doing with your efficiency? Do you have more time right now compared to years ago as a result of using so many new and "efficient" tools that swear to help you work less? Are we having more and more availability to do the things that we want, perhaps working only two hours daily or by projecting only models where we can walk, run, travel, explore, meditate, cook, and have plenty of family time thanks to supporting technology?

D. Olynick, *Interfaceless*, Design Thinking, https://doi.org/10.1007/979-8-8688-0083-2_1

Nowadays, every time we are waiting for a service to be delivered, say at the doctor's or dentist's office, at the restaurant, at the park, everywhere, most likely you will see in a stagnant mode, humans glued to the screen of their mobile device. Swiping left, up, tapping, clicking, dragging, pinching... our days go by with a computer in our hands, and we cannot resist the urge to "be connected." Social media use has proliferated and augmented even more our behaviors, and more and more cases are reported of increased anxiety and depression in younger demographics. Advertisements have made their way in all the places we go digitally, and now we are not the consumer anymore but also the product. When we think of the progression of humanity under these terms, what comes to mind? What will the future of humanity look like?

This concern and the potential dangers of extinction posed by humanity, where technology can become smarter than humans due to a lack of values and the fact that humans are depending more and more on materialistic views of evolution, are other reasons why we need to rethink from our own individuality as creators our role and responsibility in all this panorama. Even if you don't have children, which are an immediate potential perpetuation of our species that you can see directly in your life, there is a sense of empathy that still exists in each human being that helps us propel this new approach to technology in a holistic and moral way.

Imagine a world where technology seamlessly integrates into our lives, eliminating the need for interfaces. This concept is truly remarkable. Just think about a reality where technology effortlessly adapts to our instincts, where a simple thought or gesture can initiate a series of actions without relying on screens or buttons. The shift going from a mobile device to a head-mounted device (HMD) is inevitable. It is parallel to the shift needed to happen going from a desktop to a mobile device. In just a couple of years, it became a necessity, and this change went from merely connecting us voice to voice through a phone call to offering us the entire world accessed in one tap.

Spatial computing is also part of a technology that not only involves interacting digitally through an HMD but also without it. A good example of this is a smart home, where, through voice commands, appliances, lights, temperature regulators, and other devices can be seamlessly controlled without relying on traditional interfaces.

When we discuss a world driven by interfaces, we must acknowledge the role played by artificial intelligence (AI). The desire to create machines of human-like thinking, emotions, and reactions has been around long before modern computers were even born. From those room filling machines to today's AI algorithms that not only understand but also anticipate and tailor experiences according to our preferences, this journey has been remarkable.

In this changing world, one thing becomes abundantly clear: technology is the driving force propelling us into the future, and design serves as our guiding map in this journey. The Mindful Spatial Design Framework (MSDF) perfectly captures the essence of this dynamic. As we move toward a future where the boundaries between humans and technology become less defined, the importance of design becomes more critical.

A Brief Overview of the Current Interface Paradigm

In the most basic sense, an interface is the communication point between two entities of systems. Its name derives from "inter" (Latin root) meaning "between or amid" and "facies" meaning "form or appearance," or the face or front, that one entity presents to the other one for interaction and vice versa. The space where interactions occur between humans and machines is what is called an interface in computing (Figure 1-1).

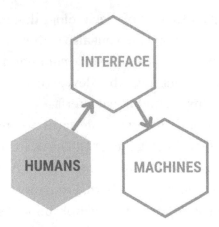

Figure 1-1. *Interface Paradigm*

From this type of interaction, we can distinguish two types of interfaces: software (auditory or visual elements called screen-based like windows, icons, menus, pointers) and hardware (mouse, keyboard, touchscreen). Interfaces matter profoundly because they guide the user experience as well as being a reflection of human psychology and technological capability; that is to say, they need to fulfill both purposes.

While the current approach has allowed us to effectively utilize the capabilities of technology, it does have some limitations. Firstly, users need to learn the language and limitations of the machine in order to adapt. Secondly, screen-based interactions sometimes divert our attention away from engaging with our surroundings.

Moreover, this paradigm assumes that users have both cognitive abilities. For example, individuals with physical impairments may face challenges when using traditional interfaces, and navigating them can also be difficult for those with learning impairments.

Lastly, the screen-based paradigm has limitations when it comes to creating experiences that are aware of their context of use. In this paradigm, there is a distinction between the world and the digital space. Spatial computing is a technology that strives to bridge this gap and unite these two realms. As we evolve in the era of spatial computing and generative AI, it becomes clear that the current interface paradigm needs to evolve in order to embrace these emerging technologies and the thrilling possibilities they bring for interaction.

The Evolution of the "Interfaceless" Philosophy

The idea of "interfaceless" is not completely new as early humans began interacting with their surroundings without the need of switches or buttons. In fact, the use of gestures and voice commands was the early form of interaction (Figure 1-2).

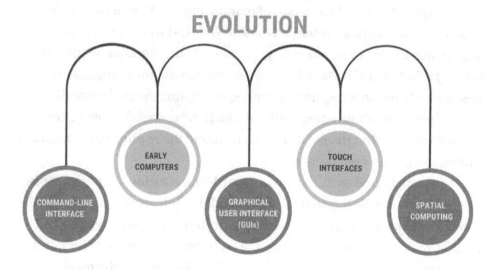

Figure 1-2. *Interfaceless Philosophy Evolution*

With the introduction of the first computers, the systems for interaction were designed depending on the type of device and its capabilities (that is one of the reasons that 2D interfaces do not make sense for more advanced computing devices). So in the first computer models, we could see the use of physical interfaces like the command line and punch cards, which were like writing a letter by hand, while command-line interfaces were like using a specific code or language to speak. As the computers evolved, the interfaces also changed giving advent to the graphical user interfaces or GUIs, featuring more visual and graphic displays with cursor, icons, and windows. From here, another switch happened from button devices to smart touch–based screens.

At the outset of mobile devices as well, the use of voice commands and virtual assistants, like Alexa and Siri, marked the beginning of spatial interactions and reduction of manual inputs. Next, it is the more proliferated use of head-mounted devices (HMDs) with virtual reality, augmented reality, or mixed reality, not only for the video game industry but any other field of work, education, or entertainment at large, allowing gesture and motion recognition features, facilitating the understanding of human gestures or movement without touch. Now, we are moving next to Brain-Computer Interfaces (BCIs) that facilitate the reading of the human's intention through neural signals.

As we might presume, the move toward "interfaceless" experiences is not only technological, practical, and functional but also philosophical, since it's about creating real human-centric, intuitive, and, therefore, natural ways of interaction, making the technology the result of human intent without being intrusive or even evident. Remember the magic carpet from *Aladdin*, and other fairy tales, that could take you where you wanted to go without telling you? That's where we are going…

The evolution toward an "interfaceless approach" leads to profound transformations. It also presents designers with numerous design challenges. In the following sections, we will explore the intricacies of designing for interfaceless experiences and discuss frameworks such as our Mindful Spatial Design Framework (MSDF) that assist in overcoming these obstacles.

The Origins and Development of AI

In the early dreams of artificial intelligence (AI), we can see humans always wanting to simulate other intelligences perceived in nature or to create life itself (Figure 1-3). AI and its early beginnings are rooted in formal math and logic with some theories developed by computer scientist Alan Turing who imagined machines talking in the same way we talk to our family or friends, in natural language. From there, AI was born as a formal discipline in 1956 when the term "artificial intelligence" was officially coined during the Dartmouth Conference in 1956, marking the beginning of AI as a recognized field.

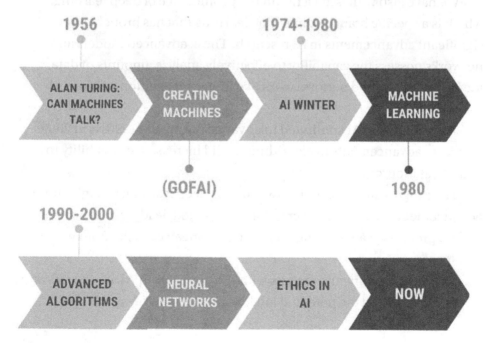

Figure 1-3. *AI Development*

In its early stages, AI research primarily focused on creating machines of emulating human thinking and effectively solving complex problems while also learning new tasks. This phase is often referred to as "Good Old Fashion Artificial Intelligence" (GOFAI) where AI systems were manually programmed with predetermined rules and logical instructions.

The initial decades of AI research saw both successes and setbacks. There were achievements such as developing computer programs for playing chess and establishing principles for AI. However, there were also periods commonly known as "AI winters" characterized by reduced funding and decreased interest in applications.

However, in the 1980s a breakthrough emerged for the field with machine learning. This approach shifted the focus from coding rules to developing algorithms that could learn from data and make decisions based on it, as if instead of trying to teach a robot every dance step, it would see you dance and learn on their own!

We have also witnessed a rise in the prominence of deep learning, which is a specific branch of machine learning that has brought about significant advancements in AI research. These advanced models and networks possess the capability to effectively analyze amounts of data, identify patterns, and perform tasks like image recognition and speech processing.

The progress of AI continued to advance during the 1990s and 2000s thanks to advancements in algorithms as did increased accessibility to digital data sources.

The progression of neural networks and deep learning brought more advancements in application creations supported, leading to expansions in data processing and storing, Internet, and speed capacity from games to healthcare.

The most prominent concerns with the advances in AI are related with ethics, privacy, and the potential job loss impact to fairness.

As of now, AI is continuing to advance, merging with other technologies, becoming more human centric, and empowering more of its capabilities and autonomy. This is the right time, with the current proficiencies, to advance toward technology that is more empathetic and supportive for humans. Interfaceless design is here now to move toward that future where machines and humans don't interact separately but integrate for human cocreation.

The Inception and Evolution of Generative AI

Unlike traditional AI models that strictly interpret and classify existing data, generative AI (GenAI) has the capacity to produce novel content. While it is grounded in the patterns and structures learned from its training data, GenAI can extrapolate and recombine these patterns to create content that, while inspired by the original dataset, is unique in its own right. This ability to generate rather than merely interpret represents a significant shift in AI's developmental trajectory.

As AI evolved at utilizing neural networks of mid-brain structures, generative models became more and more sophisticated, like the magic felt pens that initially can create only line drawings and eventually can create realistic photos of full landscapes with trees, animals, and buildings at high-definition quality.

Generative AI, a subset of broader AI techniques, has demonstrated its prowess in a myriad of applications. It's been instrumental in areas of graphic design, such as creating realistic images, and in the field of music, where it's been used for composition. In the pharmaceutical sector, for example, while AI—including traditional machine learning models and newer generative techniques—has been assisting in the discovery and optimization of drug molecules, generative AI's capability to generate novel molecular structures offers fresh perspectives. A notable and concerning application of generative AI, especially GANs (Generative Adversarial Networks), has been the production of deepfakes: computer-generated images or videos that can convincingly replace someone's appearance, presenting challenges related to misinformation and ethical implications.

Moreover, advancements in natural language processing techniques like GPT (a subset of transformer models) have opened up possibilities for generating AI-driven text. These models possess the capability to generate paragraphs and long written text, showcasing the immense potential of AI (Figure 1-4).

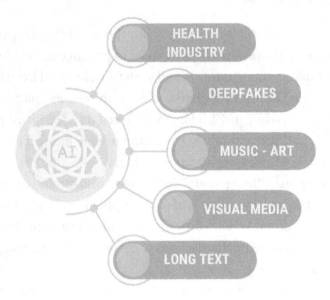

Figure 1-4. Evolution of GenAI

With all the recent years' iterations and advancements in its capacities, GenAI has become a now foundational and basic need in applications previously built and new ones coming up. We see more and more different platforms adding integration with GenAI features to be more and more competitive in the market. GenAI is, at the moment, a very powerful tool to craft personalized, anticipatory, and intuitive interactions without traditional interfaces. Picture this: your favorite apps can now know what experiences you love to do, and you just think, and they bring to your space the playground without even asking.

Important Breakthroughs and Milestones

With the emergence of touchscreen devices, we saw the shift from buttons and keys to a direct command in the digital environment, marked as well by the change from cell phones with buttons to make phone calls to direct gestures on the screen to explore the Internet (Figure 1-5).

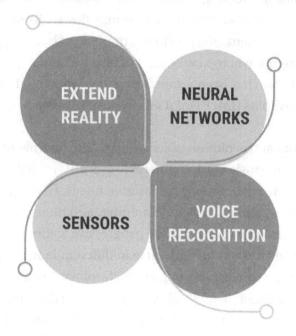

Figure 1-5. Breakthroughs and Milestones

Following on, and thanks to advanced voice recognition systems, we can now talk to Siri or Alexa to help us find a restaurant or to send a message to a friend while we are driving. With the rise of predictive and contextual human experiences, these systems can now anticipate needs based on the environment, past actions, and behavior. We are getting close to the time when your devices suggest you grab an umbrella before going out because they know it is going to rain.

Another important milestone is extended reality, a term that includes virtual reality, augmented reality, and mixed reality. Virtual reality allows the experience of immersion through an HMD, and it was popularized in the 1980s by Jaron Lanier, a computer scientist who founded the Visual Programming Lab (VPL), showcasing a VR headset. Augmented reality is a technology that facilitates the overlay of digital objects in the physical space. The term was first credited to Tom Caudell in the early 1990s, showcasing a solution for a system he was building for Boeing at the time to support their assembly flows. Mixed reality is a more recent development referring to the merging of both physical and digital environments, where new objects of physical and digital nature coexist. This medium has been around since the 1990s, but it wasn't until Microsoft, with its HMD: HoloLens in the 2010s, made its use more popular.

The inception and evolution of sensors and the Internet of Things (IoT) also simultaneously mark an interesting era of smart devices that can understand the environment and human needs, creating seamless interconnectedness among devices, machines, and humans.

In terms of conscious design, these progressive technologies and devices have paved the way for wider use in different industries. Every time there is a milestone and breakthrough in technology, there is a tendency to continue using the same methods of input, interaction, and output to facilitate development, but the consequences of this approach are far more reaching. We are now at the stage where it is imperative to understand how to properly balance automation with human control, ensuring that devices are not intrusive but supportive of human evolution.

Introduction of Conscious Designing

Design in its essence involves solving problems. It requires understanding an issue, empathizing with the people facing that issue, brainstorming solutions, creating prototypes, and testing and refining those solutions. This traditional process continues until a solution is reached that meets the needs of humans and that aligns with business objectives while being technologically feasible (Figure 1-6).

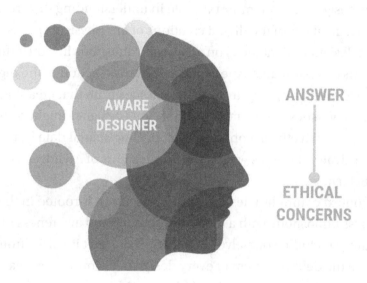

Figure 1-6. *Conscious Design Paradigm*

The impact of design can be seen everywhere. Whether it's the chair you are currently sitting on or the app you use on your smartphone. It shapes how we interact with our environment. Good design often goes unnoticed; it seamlessly improves our lives without drawing attention. On the other hand, poor design stands out glaringly. It can lead to frustration, confusion, and inefficiency.

As technologies like AI continue to advance, the field of design is evolving rapidly with it. One notable approach gaining popularity is conscious or mindful design. Since some might use these terms interchangeably, I will reveal their differences so we can effectively apply them in our design thinking process.

While conscious design focuses on awareness, it is not only about presence but way broader implications like societal, environmental, ethical, and even future-oriented decisions. In spatial computing, conscious design plays an important role in understanding the present and long-term effects of the digital creations of our physical spaces. A conscious designer might focus on answering questions like the ethical implications of a particular experience at the cross section of the digital and physical mediums, long-term societal issues from that creation, as well as privacy issues. For instance, a conscious designer might be ready to answer potential ethical concerns by collecting spatial data from users' homes or private spaces, as well as the implications of AR advertisement in societal behaviors.

The context of mindful design is more specific. It is rooted in the mindfulness philosophy with a focus on presence and awareness of the surroundings including ourselves in time and space. It involves from this perspective the deliberateness of every design decision with a clear and defined emphasis on intentionality and purpose. In the context of spatial computing, mindful design has the function of supporting designers in the creation of experiences that help humans regain control over their own healthy behaviors during the experience, coming back periodically to themselves and ensuring that there is no overwhelm, heavy cognitive load, or distraction, through intuitive interactions that are harmoniously integrated.

Note that both conscious and mindful designs work together to support the design practice to offer an integral and holistic experience to humans, taking care not only of the outside factors but also of the internal needs of humans.

14

Some of the questions conscious design invites designers to propose are related to how the design influences the humans for whom the design was created. Is it overwhelming for the mind? Is it challenging for more than one individual or for groups? What ethical and societal considerations does it involve? It revolves around being aware of how our design choices impact others. It not only involves considering aesthetics and functionality but also the emotional cognitive and psychological effects that design has on users.

Summary

In this chapter, we discussed the current interface paradigm on how interfaces have evolved over time from physical inputs to touchscreen to the absence of manual inputs. The way technology has been evolving hints to a future where interfaces would become almost invisible, integrated seamlessly into our surroundings. We then discussed the origins and development of AI from rule-based logic to becoming self-learning machines. Breakthroughs and milestones were addressed by studying key developments that set the stage for today's design capabilities.

CHAPTER 2

Exploring Generative AI and Its Transformative Power

Imagine you are an artist and all of a sudden you receive a gift: it is a magic box. You open it and discover that if you ask it to draw or create a unicorn, voila! It sketches one for you! It also reads data about the unicorn and can improve it and make many iterations on it. Figure 2-1 illustrates some of the processes behind generative AI (GenAI) which enable it to assess and create data and content.

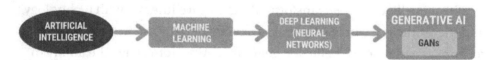

Figure 2-1. *Generative AI*

Remember the early artists? From making strokes on the wall of a cave using red ochre 65,000 years ago... then moving to paper, fabrics, and now digital media to spatial. Just as painters moved from caves to canvases, the world of design has seen many iterations and has evolved with technology, with GenAI becoming the latest brush in the designer's toolkit. This form of intelligence not only imitates human creativity but also takes it to new heights, returning designs that were once only imaginable.

D. Olynick, *Interfaceless*, Design Thinking, https://doi.org/10.1007/979-8-8688-0083-2_2

As we look closer into the concept of interfaceless design and the role of technology in it, it is essential to study the workings of this subtype of AI. GenAI is a transformative tool that is molding the basic foundations of creativity and design. We might think of it as if traditional design tools were bicycles and GenAI rocket ships, taking us to new planets or worlds of supercharged creativity. We all get excited when these types of breakthroughs appear in the world helping us to create even better experiences. However, a deeper study is necessary to not only learn to use the tools but deliberately use it in the most ethical and responsible way.

While AI comes with great abilities, it is with human intuition and empathy that we need to approach the tools and their outputs.

In this chapter, we will explore the beginnings and evolution of GenAI and why its use became so quickly proliferated, understanding its place in the design landscape, comparing traditional methods with GenAI-powered ones, and getting familiar with platforms and the dos and don'ts of its use.

Unpacking Generative AI

Artificial intelligence has transformed the way we interact with technology and the world as a whole. Unlike AI systems that rely on predetermined responses and reactive behavior, generative AI systems have the ability to generate content on their own, to propose solutions and make decisions.

Generative AI refers to any AI model that goes beyond predefined responses by producing outputs, and that's why the term "generative" reflects its capacity for creating (Figure 2-2).

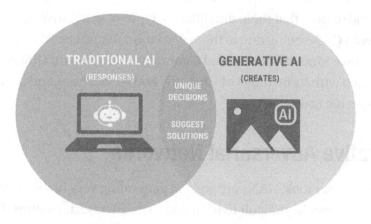

Figure 2-2. *Traditional AI vs. Generative AI*

Imagine you have a box of felt color pens, but they are not the common pens; they are special because they have some magic in them. They are able to draw without your own hand guiding them and directing them. You could say to them, "please draw me a cat with a Victorian hat," and they would begin the task at hand, returning a very realistic scene with a cat in it, wearing the Victorian hat.

Before the magical felt color pens learned to draw by themselves, they had some training on it though. They have studied many, many images to learn to recognize patterns and understand what distinguishes a cat from a dog. The training received and the system that governs their magic are called Generative Adversarial Networks (GANs), a subcategory of machine learning.

The way GANs work involves two parts: a generator and a discriminator. As the word indicates, the job of the generator is to draw new cats with the magical color felt pens every time you ask for it or, as a matter of fact, to create anything you ask for. The discriminator, in turn, acts as the teacher of the color felt pens and decides whether a creation is good or not, much like passing or not passing the drawing test. The generator uses that feedback, and it gets considerably better over time learning from the corrections or mistakes provided by the teacher (the discriminator). Sounds cool, right?

It's good to note that there are different types of generative AI models, with GANs being one of them, Variational Autoencoders (VAEs), Autoregressive Models, Flow-Based Generative Models, and Diffusion Models, each with its own sets of strengths and weaknesses and particular uses for specific tasks.

Generative Adversarial Networks

Let's take a closer look. GANs are great at generating very high-quality data as images, but can be difficult to train due to its adversarial nature. The word "adversarial" means that the generator is always trying to create data that is as realistic as possible, acting, for example, as a fake moneymaker, while the discriminator is always trying to discern between real money and counterfeit money (the one created by the generator), acting just like a detective. In this interaction, the generator aims to excel at deceiving the discriminator, while the discriminator aims to excel at revealing the generator, where the term "adversarial" comes from.

Variational Autoencoders

Variational Autoencoders (VAEs) are a type of generative model that work by encoding an input (like an image) into a compact latent space and then decoding from this space to produce an output. The unique aspect of VAEs is the way they handle this latent space: they assume it follows a specific probabilistic distribution, usually Gaussian. During training, the model learns to enforce this distribution, which allows it to generate entirely new samples from the latent space during inference.

VAEs excel at tasks requiring manipulation of this latent space, or interpolation, and they are generally easier to train than GANs. However, a known drawback is that the images they generate can be less sharp and sometimes appear blurred.

Applications of VAEs are diverse:

- *Video Game Design*: Developers often require a plethora of faces for their characters. VAEs can generate a variety of facial features, making them valuable in this domain.

- *Anomaly Detection*: This involves identifying patterns that do not conform to expected behavior. In a manufacturing context, for example, VAEs can be trained on images of "complete products." When a "defective product" image is encountered, the VAE's reconstruction will differ significantly from the original, triggering anomaly detection.

- *Recommendation Systems*: By analyzing patterns in data, like how frequently and when someone watches certain types of movies, VAEs can suggest new content that aligns with those preferences.

Autoregressive Models

To understand Autoregressive Models, let's study another cool example. Have you ever played the "broken telephone" game? It is a game where you say a word to, let's say, a friend next to you, and your friend has the task to deliver the same word to the next friend, and so on. At the end, the last person is asked what word was delivered. I remember laughing at the outputs sometimes when I was a little girl. Autoregressive Models are like this game, but instead of playing with your friends, you are playing with a very smart robot that is trying all the time to guess what the next word is, based on all the previous words it has heard so far, and in fact, this robot is so good at the game, its accuracy improves pretty fast, and its outputs are of great quality. The problem, though, is that the robot can only concentrate in the order the words come one by one, and it cannot go back and listen again or skip ahead. For example, in the sentence "despite being of tiny structure, the hamster...," the robot could foresee the hamster would run in the wheel or eat some nuts. But if the sentence is completed as "was able to lift the door cage," the robot would be confused because it didn't know that the hamster was strong. Despite the challenges, the robot is so good at creating speech that sounds like human real talk, creating new stories, and even translating sentences. This is the system used by OpenAI with its GPT models.

Flow-Based Generative Models

Flow-Based Generative Models, as distinct from Variational Autoencoders (VAEs) and simpler statistical models, offer a unique approach to data generation. While both Flow-Based Generative Models and VAEs learn to generate new data samples, they differ significantly in their approach and the intricacies of their operations.

At its core, a VAE is designed to compress data into a low-dimensional space and then decode it back into its original form, often with slight variations, thereby generating new samples. On the other hand, Flow-Based Generative Models utilize a sequence of invertible transformations, known as "Normalizing Flows," to transform simple distributions into complex ones. This sequence ensures a deterministic relation between inputs and outputs, providing a predictable yet flexible generation process.

The colored blocks analogy helps elucidate this. Think of VAEs as machines that first squash the blocks into a mold (latent space) and then expand them back, whereas Flow-based models methodically reshape the blocks step by step.

Compared to simpler statistical models that may also be employed for similar tasks, both VAEs and Flow-based models bring a more profound level of intricacy and flexibility, enabling them to capture and replicate more complex data distributions. This allows them to be more effective in tasks such as image synthesis, data augmentation, and other applications where capturing nuanced patterns and structures in the data is essential.

Diffusion Models

And finally, let's take a look at the Diffusion Models. Let's pretend we are playing with a box of Lego blocks. You want to build a mansion for the hamster earlier, but you don't know where to begin. Since we are all about magic, you have a magic wand and you decide to use it to facilitate the construction of the hamster's mansion step by step. You then wave the magic wand, and the legos move a little, but still everything looks very random. You wave it again and again, and now the mansion is starting to take shape. Finally, it's there, finished, before your eyes! You realize the magic wand can help you build mansions with a lot of details and complexity. This is what is called the "long-range dependencies" in Diffusion Models, defining what they can handle. The magic wand also has its own struggles because you need to wave the wand many times before something is finished. Despite this, the magic wand is extremely helpful because it can help us build mansions for our hamsters we have never seen before. They can be used in image and speech synthesis, data augmentation, and super resolution (increasing the resolution of low-quality images as an example).

In today's world, we see that there is also the possibility to create music and video using generative AI. For music, Variational Encoders, Transformer Models (a type of Autoregressive Model), and Recurrent Neural Networks (RNNs) (especially the ones with LSTM, Long Short-Term Memory) are used due to the ability to capture temporal dependencies. For video, usually GANs, Variational Encoders, and Autoregressive Models are used.

Now that we have set the foundations, let's discuss how GenAI is transforming the design process. The future of design invites us with promises of innovation, transformation, and endless possibilities.

How Generative AI Is Revolutionizing the Design Process

GenAI is not a trend in technology but a significant advancement in artificial intelligence that encourages proactive creation. It enables us to visualize, narrate, and bring our ideas to life.

Now that we have this understanding, let's shift our focus to the design ecosystem and explore how GenAI is transforming it (Figure 2-3).

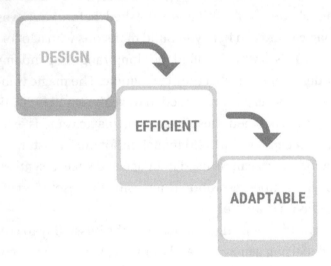

Figure 2-3. *Design Process with AI*

The Old vs. the New

Traditionally, the design process has been a balance of creativity, technical expertise, and intuition. Designers would meticulously sketch, prototype, test, refine, and iterate their ideas. While each stage was fulfilling in its way, it also presented challenges such as time constraints, limited resources, or even the boundaries of imagination. However, with the advent of GenAI, this paradigm has been redefined. The way we approach design and the speed at which we materialize our visions is evolving at a rapid pace.

One notable impact of GenAI is its ability to democratize creativity. The design process is no longer limited to those with training or years of experience. Through model utilization, even beginners can now create designs that would have previously required time and effort from experts.

This doesn't downplay the importance of expertise; in fact, it expands the impact of creativity. It ensures that design becomes more inclusive, easier to access, and not constrained by barriers.

Additionally, GenAI offers a platform for research and exploration. With its ability to generate design iterations quickly, designers or creators now have a range of options at their disposal. They can easily visualize design paths, select the elements from each one, and further refine them. This type of extensive exploration was not possible on such a scale before. The abundance of possibilities that GenAI brings forth accelerates the cycle of innovation. The ability of GenAI to analyze extensive datasets (groups of data) ensures that designs are not only being created with visual appeal but also contextually and functionally relevant. GenAI is at the point that can identify preferences and patterns, allowing richer feedback data into the design process, iterating more effectively, and returning experiences that are customized for each human based on their specific needs.

With this tremendous shift in capabilities also comes a considerable transformation in the role of traditional designers. In the future, designers would see themselves partially creating, more exactly cocreating, with AI and curating, carefully making more impactful and relevant decisions. In the new era of AI, designers will be more dedicated to the bigger picture of design, refining and aligning outputs with real human purpose and intent, all while iterating options with the help of AI, requiring designers to develop other skills related to analytical thinking and intuition blending art and science.

Speed and Efficiency

Efficiency in the design process can face various obstacles, such as time-consuming manual tasks, revisions, client meetings, and more. It often involves iterations that can slow down the project timeline, particularly when unexpected issues or changes arise.

The emergence of AI has brought about changes in the design process, leading to a new era of innovation and creativity. Unlike design methods that are often linear and limited, GenAI allows for a more dynamic, iterative, and human-focused approach. By utilizing machine learning algorithms and data analysis, GenAI empowers designers to swiftly create, test, and refine designs with speed and efficiency.

AI tools that automate tasks can also generate design options offering real-time feedback and streamline communication between different stakeholders. This allows designers to dedicate their time and energy to imaginative aspects of the project, ultimately improving overall productivity.

Adaptability and Personalization

AI has the ability to adapt designs that are based on feedback in real time and human preferences. To amplify the workings of this capability, let's discuss some of its components.

Before an adaptation can take place, there is a need for information and data, that is, obtaining the recurrent data from the humans on the needs, preferences, feedback, interaction, and the holistic approach previously discussed. This data might, for instance, come from gazes, gestures, movements, from human time spent in specific activities, elements or objects of the experience, repeated interactions, direct feedback on the most enjoyable features and reasons for it, emotional responses and degree of awareness of the environment and themselves.

When the process of data collection is executed, then a real-time processing system takes place, where humans interact with the design and AI processes this data. All this processing is backed up with powerful hardware that can process vast amounts of data extremely quickly. One example of such platforms and equipment at the moment is Nvidia cloud solutions (a technology company that specializes in Graphics Processing Units (GPUS)) with tools accessible even from browsers powered by cloud computing.

Using models like neural networks, especially the ones called "reinforcement learning models" or "feedback neural networks," the activity of providing behavioral feedback is facilitated. For instance, if a human frequently changes their screen from bright to muted tones, the AI model learns this preference and suggests in future interactions the auto-adjusting to muted tone mode.

As this process continues, more feedback is added into the model, creating what is called the "continuous feedback loop," consistently modifying and refining its decisions, so the more feedback that is added, the better it gets at understanding what the human prefers. In a more advanced version of this process, very individualized and customized profiles are created, making the same environment appear different for each human visiting simultaneously, customized independently for each participant. At this point, having enough data, GenAI will create specific iterations or options that are completely catered for each specific human interacting in the experience, even changing the space altogether if that is required, generating unlimited permutations, based on the previous data gathered, analyzed, and learned.

At the stage of deployment and rendering, and as the decision on changes is made, the AI system renders and deploys almost instantly the experience, using back-end processing and efficient front-end rendering tools. Processes like validation, safety checks, and collaboration with other systems or platforms could take place here to keep the system safe and updated.

While the technicalities of the complete adaptability and personalization process can be challenging to implement, it's worth mentioning that designers need to have a foundational view of how the process works, but not necessarily are called to implement it, as it is the case in the current design process where the scope of work goes so far as to creating a prototype and handing it to the development team for further processing.

Comparison of Traditional vs. AI-Powered Design Results

Figure 2-4 illustrates how AI-powered design compares with traditional design in each of the design metrics.

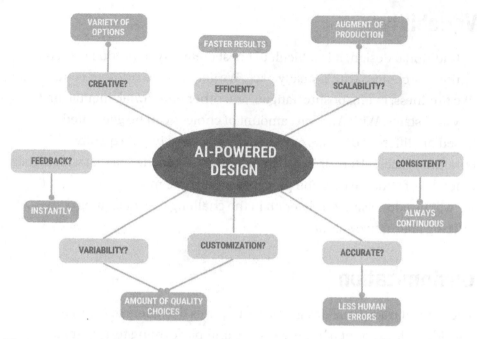

Figure 2-4. *Traditional vs. AI-Powered Designs*

Time Efficiency

Since human designers have to go through the iterative process themselves, it requires more time to arrive at the conceptualization, drafting, refining, and finalizing aspects of design. Through the processing of vast amounts of data, AI-powered designs offer faster results, making the decision process more immediate and cost effective. It is like jumping from drawing manually a sketch vs. obtaining a magic device that can instantly return the same or even more detailed drawing.

Variability

In traditional design, it is difficult to boost creativity to produce different options or choices with a steady pace. We get affected by other conditions like tiredness, overexposure, fatigue, and other emotional, mental, or physical states. With AI, a vast amount of choices can be generated based on different datasets or parameters, enhancing the quality of the curation process. Here, it is also beneficial to acknowledge that with higher amounts of data the curation process can become more complex, and we will be addressing this later on in the challenges of designing with AI, offering alternative solutions.

Customization

The current traditional design model requires designers to invest a considerable amount of time assessing and performing tests to try to understand human intentions, but this approach might not be as adaptive. AI-powered designs can be personalized, and with the data backup systems, future iterations can happen on their own, rather than through repetitive human intervention.

Accuracy and Consistency

Due to a diverse number of factors, humans cannot be as accurate and consistent as efficiently programmed machines, so oversights or human errors can be minimized, leading to fewer inconsistencies in the design process. With the use of algorithms, this concern is reduced due to their programming for error detection and self-correction. Imagine if you play a game and sometimes forget the rules, but the computer can maintain consistency, remembering the rules every try and winning again and again.

Scalability

Traditional designs require more time and human resources and can be most expensive. AI-powered designs can augment the production rates while minimizing impacts, which makes it very attractive for companies to implement, facilitating a variety of different scaled processes across different platforms and projects.

Creativity

In traditional design, we see how humans bring forward unique perspectives, creating emotional connection. Although AI designs could provide a wide variety of options, they might also lack the human spirit, soul, and emotion that connects with other humans. In this regard, it can be comparable to when our parents used to read stories at bedtime using all their range of expressions compared with that of a robot reading the story trying to gain the same appeal. Both experiences could be fun, but mom's stories feel more special.

Feedback and Iteration

Finally, traditional design involves discussions, meetings, and plenty of time to arrive at a final decision. This is contrasted with AI-powered designs, where feedback is analyzed instantly, facilitating the decision-making for design teams.

As we deepen into the history of design, it becomes clear how much it has evolved with the emergence of GenAI. These changes are noticeable in the process as in the final outcomes.

Overview of Generative AI Platforms

As we continue to explore the world of GenAI and its profound impact on the field of design, it becomes essential for us to familiarize ourselves with the platforms that harness this technology. Previously, we have discussed the principles, processes, and comparisons related to AI-driven designs. Now let's delve into the tools that enable innovation. Today, there is a range of GenAI platforms offering designers various options tailored to their specific needs and requirements.

The rapid growth of generative AI has naturally given rise to a market where different platforms strive to provide designers with design tools. This vibrant ecosystem serves as evidence that the world recognizes the potential of AI not as a tool, but as a transformative force in the design industry.

Traditionally, design tools have always been manual—whether it's painters using brushes or architects relying on compasses. However, with digitalization came software like Adobe Photoshop, Illustrator, and Sketch, revolutionizing how designers conceptualize and bring their ideas to life. Now, with this new wave of evolution, newer platforms are being created deeply rooted in GenAI, pushing boundaries even further. At this stage, it's of interest to note that some platforms or systems offer a back-end support, that we can categorize as foundational technologies for the general works to take place, while other ones are focused on the front end, the actual applications to produce the final results or visual designs. Let's zoom in on this.

Common Back-End Systems (Foundational Tech)

Neural Network–Based Platforms

These systems are somewhat like the brains behind many platforms, taking data, identifying patterns, and producing outputs based on the newly learned trends. Part of this classification are GANs.

As discussed previously in the section "Unpacking Generative AI," these are the engines behind many of the AI creations we are seeing these days, consisting of two neural networks, the "creator" and the "judge," in adversarial positions. If a developer looks to train the models from scratch, then a dataset would be needed from platforms like Kaggle. The networks are possible to be obtained through some frameworks like PyTorch, TensorFlow, or Keras. There are also pretrained models to use, for instance, Nvidia's StyleGAN is one of them. Bear in mind that these processes are computationally intensive, and powerful GPUs are required.

Recurrent Neural Networks (RNNs)

These systems are often used for sequential tasks, like language translation by Google Translate, speech recognition with AI assistants like Alexa and Siri, stock price prediction, video analysis, or music generation where it is essential to have an orderly structure of data, which means that, unlike traditional neural networks, these ones have the capability of retaining some memory from previous inputs, providing more accuracy in decision-making.

Highlighted Front-End Platforms (Apps)

OpenAI's GPT Series

These models are framed for natural language processes, and they are being used more frequently to power story generators and chatbots, enhancing customer experiences and producing written content based on text inputs popularly called prompt crafting (Figure 2-5).

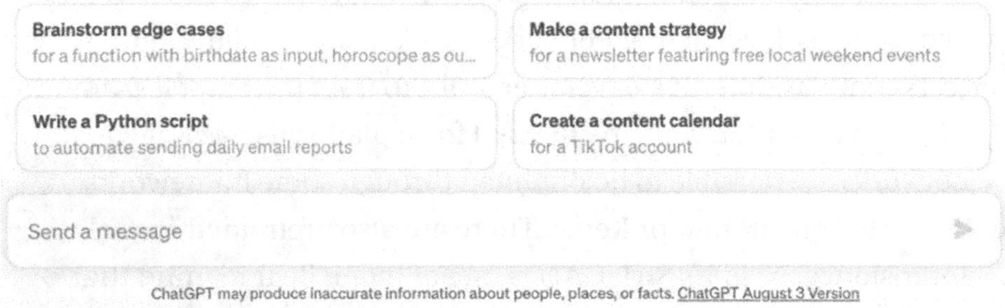

Brainstorm edge cases for a function with birthdate as input, horoscope as ou...	**Make a content strategy** for a newsletter featuring free local weekend events
Write a Python script to automate sending daily email reports	**Create a content calendar** for a TikTok account

Send a message   ➢

ChatGPT may produce inaccurate information about people, places, or facts. ChatGPT August 3 Version

Figure 2-5. *OpenAI's GPT Series*

RunwayML

Based on its ability to generate text-to-image and image-to-image, which means you write text describing your desired output or upload an image to obtain another image plus a description, RunwayML (Figure 2-6) also uses a model to produce video based on text inputs, images, or videos. Because of the use of high computational power, at the moment, the video production is rendered in short seconds at the time.

Figure 2-6. *RunwayML*

Midjourney

This is a platform currently working from inside another platform: Discord. In Midjourney (Figure 2-7), it is possible to obtain images based on text inputs or prompts, upload images to obtain descriptions that can then be converted into new images as inspired from the original one, upload and blend different images at once to produce new combined image choices from the originals, and adjust ratios or iterate on previous images generated in the chat editor. This is one of the best generators so far for images, and its quality is sometimes indistinguishable from real-life photography.

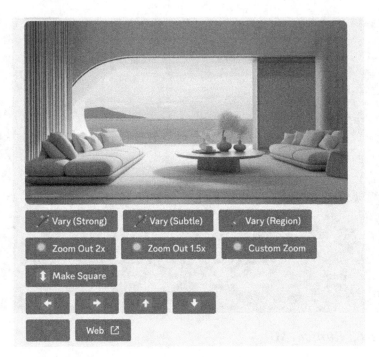

Figure 2-7. *Midjourney Interface*

DALL E

DALL E (Figure 2-8), developed by OpenAI, is a variation of the GPT 3 model that focuses on generating images based on text descriptions. While it shares a transformer architecture with models used for natural language processing, DALL E has been trained extensively using image data. This unique training allows it to produce a range of images from depictions of objects to entirely unique creations.

Figure 2-8. *DALL E Interface*

Adobe Firefly

Adobe Firefly utilizes AI technology to streamline and automate the design process, enabling designers to work with efficiency and creativity. Its main goal is to simplify the design process for professionals and enable them to produce top-notch content. Firefly relies on cutting-edge Generative Adversarial Networks (GANs).

Adobe Firefly (Figure 2-9) significantly streamlines the time-consuming process of creating aspects within a design. Moreover, it offers customization options that designers can fine-tune. For web designers, it offers automated assistance in creating layouts for web pages, eliminating the need for arrangement of elements. Logo designers can benefit from Firefly's ability to generate a range of logos based on specific brand attributes, allowing them to find the perfect design more quickly. Additionally, graphic designers can rely on Firefly to automate the creation of assets, freeing up their time and energy and focusing on higher-level aspects of their designs.

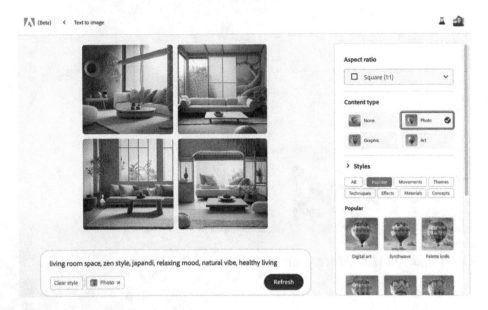

Figure 2-9. *Adobe Firefly Interface*

Adobe Sensei

Adobe Sensei is a technology developed by Adobe for their cloud
applications. It combines the power of AI and machine learning
to optimize workflows, automate repetitive tasks, and make digital
experiences easier to create. You can find Adobe Sensei seamlessly
integrated into applications, like Photoshop (Figure 2-10), Illustrator,
Adobe XD, and Premiere Pro.

Figure 2-10. *Photoshop AI*

What truly sets Adobe Sensei apart is its ability to learn from human behavior over time, continuing to improve based on how humans interact with it.

Sensei, the assistant developed by Adobe, goes beyond being an automation tool. It possesses the ability to learn from a designer's actions and preferences over time, enabling it to provide valuable suggestions that evolve alongside the designer.

Stable Diffusion

Stable Diffusion (Figure 2-11), an AI model developed by Stability AI, offers capabilities in the field of converting text into images. By using a diffusion mechanism, it can generate images based on prompts, add elements to existing images, and even make selective modifications to preexisting visuals.

Figure 2-11. *Stable Diffusion—DreamStudio*

However, it's important to acknowledge that Stable Diffusion does have its limitations. For instance, generated images are marked with a watermark that may be lost if the image undergoes resizing or rotation. Additionally, while the model can run on consumer-grade hardware commonly used by individuals like yourself, it does require an amount of RAM, which may pose accessibility limitations for some users.

Unity Muse, Unity Sentis, and Muse Chat

Unity (Figure 2-12) has an integration of generative and procedural tools called Unity Muse and Unity Sentis that could be accessed directly from the editor. Unity Muse is a tool focused on facilitating 3D content creation in real-time 3D applications from manual inputs like prompts or sketches. Unity Sentis is a system that enables developers or creators to integrate neural networks to supercharge real-time experiences. For those keen to learn about the use of these tools, Muse Chat is their new system that enhances the guidance search through their documentation tools.

Figure 2-12. *Unity Interface*

MusicLM (Google)

MusicLM (Figure 2-13) is a model generating high-fidelity music from text descriptions. MusicLM casts the process of conditional music generation as a hierarchical sequence-to-sequence modeling task, and it generates music at 24 kHz that remains consistent over several minutes.

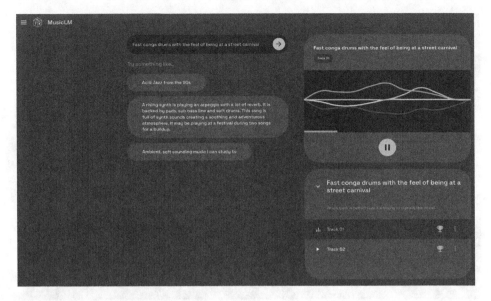

Figure 2-13. *MusicLM*

Keep in mind that with the advancement in GenAI platforms also come their share of challenges. To effectively utilize these platforms, one must possess knowledge about their underlying technology, be capable of interpreting their outputs, and possess the discernment necessary to apply them ethically and thoughtfully. Additionally, designers need to be aware of the strengths and weaknesses associated with platforms so that they can make informed decisions when selecting the most suitable one for their specific needs.

Case Study Concept Design with GenAI "Eunoia Centre"

Now that we are familiar with some of the platforms in the market, it's a good time to dive into a particular case study.

Since the current platforms in the market are constantly evolving and adding new features, there is more value in a particular example than in a general step by step that could get obsolete right away. Just keep in mind that adaptation is now our number one priority as designers of the future.

The purpose of this case study is not only to demonstrate the practical application of the ideas discussed in the book but also to provide insights into how these principles can be integrated seamlessly into real-world projects. The "Eunoia Centre" case was specifically chosen for its thematic resonance with our overarching idea of conscious design. "Eunoia," from Greek, embodies "beautiful thinking," a sentiment that echoes our intention to craft experiences that are not just aesthetically pleasing but also thoughtfully constructed.

In the following subsections, you will see this specific example of the process involved—from the spark of inspiration to the final realization of the concept. Suffice to say, this is also an example of the dynamic, iterative, and deeply collaborative nature of design in the age of AI.

Project Brief:

Title: Eunoia Centre

Objective: To produce a concept design for a wellness space that promotes relaxation and mental clarity.

Background: Euonia means "beautiful thinking" in Greek. The space will be designed in a spatial computing medium, specifically Vision Pro HMD, and will help therapists and wellness practitioners remotely to connect with their patients without travelling across cities to attend sessions.

Key Visual Design Elements: The space needs to align with therapeutic elements found in nature such as raw materials, like wood, rock, plants, water. The style of the space needs to be minimalist to enhance the sense of tranquility and clarity. The type of light is sunset, to promote feelings of happiness and balance. The acoustics are soft music using binaural audio to foster relaxation.

Target Audience: Therapists and wellness professionals along with their patients.

Technical Requirements:

Generative AI platform for the visual representation of the space

Generative AI platform for the acoustics and sound components

Photoshop AI for post-production (if required)

Project setup:

Project background research (including human profiles, style, and audio requirements)

Definition of GenAI platforms for the needs

Prompt iteration and feedback

Post-production

Final approval and deliverables

1. Project background research

   Since this project has a scope only, the generation of a concept design image, it starts by the further study of the requirements specified to make sure the overall intention is fully captured. This research involves diving into minimalism in therapeutic settings, benefits or disadvantages, art style, binaural sound and quality, as well as the use of physical components like light, color, texture, visual balance, layout, art and decor if required, natural elements, and any other feature pertaining to the design brief.

   Based on the brief and further considerations from the research, the space will feature neutral tones, clean lines, rounded shapes (as the 90 degree angles evoke rigidity), the incorporation of rock, water, wood, and natural plants (to produce a calming effect and promote connection), open space (to allow for free movement), minimal and modern furniture, and light that mimics the natural light spectrum (to enhance the sense of vitality and clarity).

2. Definition of GenAI platforms for the needs
    For this particular project, the best platforms upon research will be Midjourney, given its high photorealistic outputs, Photoshop AI for post-processing, and MusicLM (Google) as an initial test due to its beta stage for sound generation.

3. Midjourney setup

    3.1 Get a Discord account and create your own server (Figure 2-14).

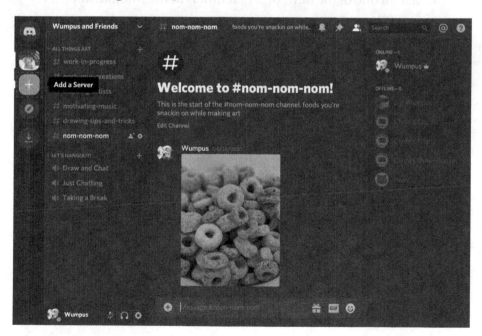

Figure 2-14. *Creating Your Own Server (Source: Discord)*

3.2 Join the Midjourney server (Figure 2-15).

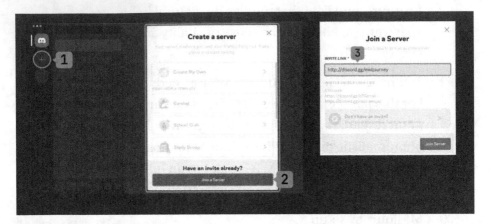

Figure 2-15. *Joining the Midjourney Server (Source: Midjourney)*

3.3 In one of the newcomer channels in the Midjourney server (Figure 2-16), type the command /Subscribe (complete subscription steps).

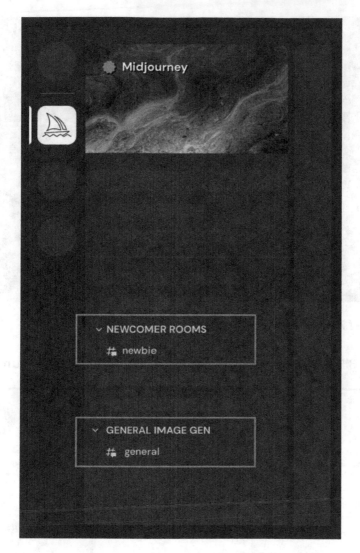

Figure 2-16. *Joining a Newcomer Room on Midjourney*

3.4 Select the Midjourney server (Figure 2-17) from the user
list and add server (so that you can work in your own
independent server, rather than in the public space of
Midjourney).

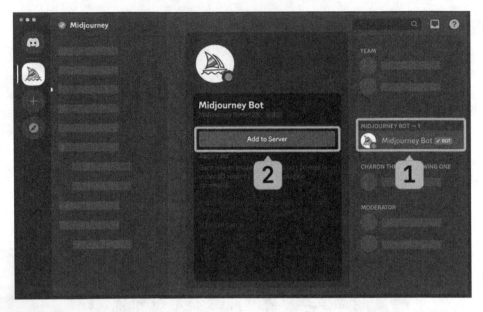

Figure 2-17. *Adding the Midjourney Bot*

3.5 Choose your own server and click "Authorize" (Figure 2-18).

Figure 2-18. *Authorizing the Midjourney Bot*

4. Prompt iteration and feedback

   Here, based on the project background research, we
   begin by recalling some good practices of prompting
   for Midjourney." Prompting means writing a series
   of words that describe the result we are looking
   for. As a side note, some early adopters of these
   platforms have made prompts a scarce asset, but the
   reality is that there is no need to create a market for
   it. The reason is that by understanding the general
   underlying principles of the model, anybody can
   generate any asset to produce good quality images.

   a. Shorter prompts facilitate the process because they are easier
      to control.

   b. The association of words matters, based on how close to
      each other in the general context they are located (assign the
      position of unwanted words away from each other, assign the
      position of relevant words closer together, assign a position of
      contrasting elements at extreme positions).

   c. If using images, all together they will have an influence of 25%
      in the general output.

Prompt general guideline:

Dominant Features + Subject Description + Visual Style and Secondary
Physical Features + MJ Parameters (--)

Let's prepare our first prompt:

[Relaxing natural mood space] + [neutral tones, daylight, rounded arcs,
modern sofa] + [Minimalist, clean lines, plants] + --ar 7:4

Input for Midjourney:

Relaxing natural mood space, neutral tones, daylight, rounded arcs,
modern sofa, minimalist clean lines, plants, --ar 7:4

Note   The --ar 7:4 means aspect ratio, and for this project, a 7:4 has been chosen as a good size for the final output for landscape detail purposes. More parameters like this one can be found at `https://docs.midjourney.com/docs/parameter-list`.

The next step is to head to Midjourney and type the command /imagine (Figure 2-19) and place the last prompt generated earlier.

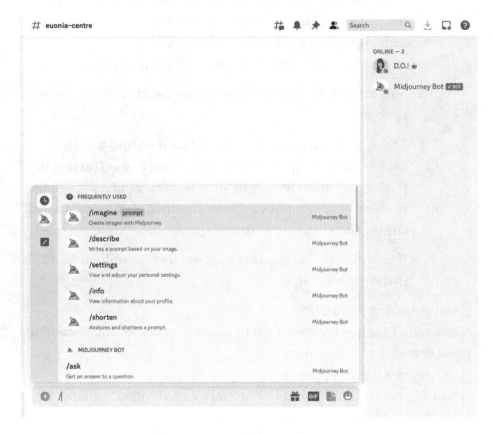

Figure 2-19. *Using the Command /imagine*

Then, insert the prompt (Figure 2-20) after the command /imagine is activated:

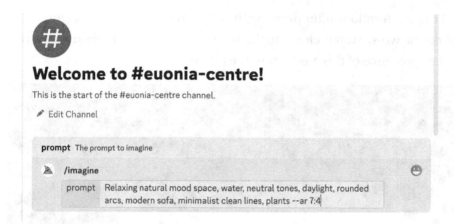

Welcome to #euonia-centre!

This is the start of the #euonia-centre channel.

✏ Edit Channel

prompt The prompt to imagine

/imagine

prompt Relaxing natural mood space, water, neutral tones, daylight, rounded arcs, modern sofa, minimalist clean lines, plants --ar 7:4

Figure 2-20. *Inserting Prompt in the Field*

The preliminary result is shown in Figure 2-21.

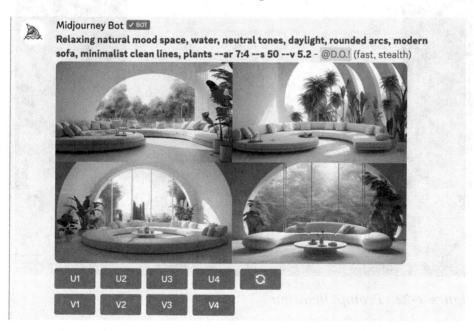

Figure 2-21. *Preliminary Results*

Further iterations after pressing the circle regenerate icon (Figure 2-22) moved the word 'water' closer to the start of the prompt to obtain a more evident presence of this element in the image.

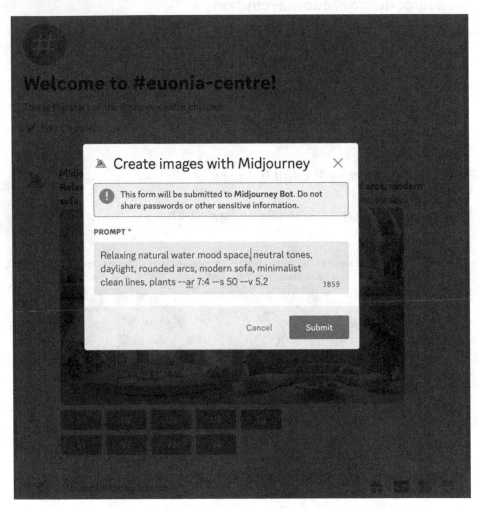

Figure 2-22. *Prompt Iteration*

After many more iterations changing the prompt and adding other elements from the brief like wood and rock, we are seeing a closer version in Figure 2-23.

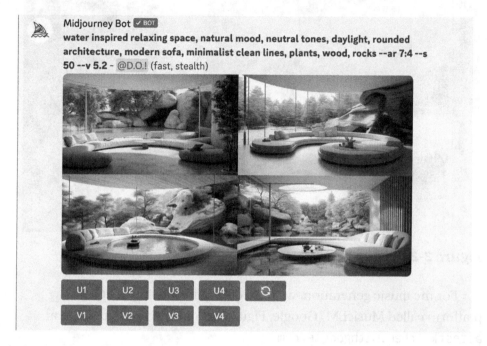

Figure 2-23. *Last Generations*

To generate the preferred image, use the command U (by clicking the letter U in the interface) corresponding to the grid number where the image is located counting clockwise. In this case, our image is the Number 2. Please note that if you were to create a variation of the Number 2 instead, you would click the letter V in the interface with the Number 2. From this, we can conclude that U is for upscaling the image (taking it out of the grid for individual use) and V is for variation, to create different versions of the same image.

The final output is shown in Figure 2-24.

Figure 2-24. *Final Result*

For the music generation, we have determined using the GenAI platform called MusicLM (Google, Figure 2-25), which can be found at aitestkitchen.withgoogle.com.

Figure 2-25. *MusicLM Interface*

Insert the prompt of the music you are looking for, in this case (Figure 2-26), we used binaural beats, therapeutical, calming, and soothing.

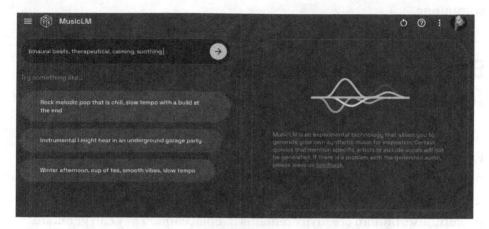

Figure 2-26. *MusicLM Prompt Input*

And we obtain the first results (Figure 2-27) which of course we also iterate on.

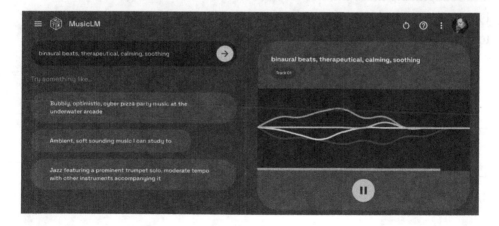

Figure 2-27. *MusicLM Final Result*

As a conclusion, for concept design we now have powerful AI tools that can cocreate with us, optimizing our process and allowing us to generate higher-quality renders for either real-life or digital mediums, like spatial computing.

Best Practices in Utilizing Generative AI for Design

Aligned with the principles outlined in the MSDF (Mindful Spatial Design Framework), GenAI platforms offer features that greatly enhance the design process. As we previously discussed, these platforms should be used as a tool not as a total replacement of our work, and while AI is a powerhouse, human creativity remains irreplaceable. They can generate designs and tasks seamlessly integrated with existing design tools, making them a valuable addition to any designer's toolkit. However, it's crucial to understand that like any tool they have both strengths and weaknesses and recognizing these nuances is necessary for harnessing their potential. Figure 2-28 introduces some of the topics related to best practices we need to consider.

Figure 2-28. *Best Practices Using AI for Design*

Goals and Data Quality

To start, we need to define clear goals and objectives based on the desired outcome for the specific experience to be designed, and it's of utmost importance to remember that GenAI is only as great as the quality of data that is trained on, so assessing pretrained models and the datasets is recommended.

Some companies have specific policies in place for the use of GenAI systems, and if we acknowledge them, we can avoid further repetition of work or, even worse, legal consequences. At the moment, we have access to platforms that have been trained on data from which the rights of the content are retained, such as Adobe Firefly for graphics generation, removing the risk of potential copyright infringement if at some point this were to become an issue.

Regularly testing and refining is a habitual practice that is necessary while working with GenAI to guarantee control, minimization of risks, and quality feedback.

Human Experience

As previously emphasized, prioritizing the human experience ensures that the designs are human-friendly and intuitive and that they serve the ultimate human needs and purposes. Therefore, it is important to integrate a standard practice of integrating humans in the concept development process facilitating and speeding up the final development stage. This is a practice that can be established by inviting a segment of the population that the experience would be for and deliver a session where the initial concept happens at the same time that the designer is generating concepts based on the wording used by the participant. For instance, you are creating a virtual space for historical buildings. While the participant describes exactly how the space ideally would look like, you could be using prompts into the GenAI platform to generate concepts in real time for them to take a look and assess, rather than the traditional process of subsequent meetings to try to find a concept where the participant is not seeing as they speak.

Ethics and Transparency

We are called to define our own principles, and providing transparent use of AI and communicating it to the human in contact with the experience is a practice that must be standardized.

When using GenAI, as previously mentioned, making sure about the policies around the final outcome and potential conflicts with AI-generated content is essential.

Security and Privacy

When utilizing AI platforms, on cloud-based systems, it's crucial to consider data privacy implications. It's important for designers to be familiar with how these platforms handle data so they can protect not only their designs and intellectual property but also human data obtained and in contact with the experience. Besides this, keeping the data and privacy of the participants in the design process before and after the experience under defined protocols of data management remains the priority. This is because during the design phase, any findings about vulnerabilities, psychological traits, emotional responses, and feelings could become evident and therefore used for manipulative purposes to exploit or expand features of the experience to increase the chances of "user engagement" and retention metrics that end up in a straight line profit model of experiences.

Mindful and Conscious Purpose

We need to aim to use GenAI platforms and related systems with a thoughtful and deliberate approach, making sure the data, designs, or any other kind of input or output has the intent to promote human well-being.

The conscious and mindful design principles along with the MSDF (Mindful Spatial Design Framework) can help to navigate the design work with a careful and protective approach toward the mental and physical balance of humans free of manipulation and addiction.

In summary, GenAI platforms can generate designs and tasks seamlessly integrated with existing design tools, making them a valuable addition to any designer's toolkit. However, it's crucial to understand that like any tool they have both strengths and weaknesses. Recognizing these nuances is essential for harnessing their potential. Despite their limitations, generative AI platforms represent progress in the field of design by opening up possibilities for creativity and innovation.

Summary

In this chapter, we discussed the foundations of generative AI (GenAI), studying different types of systems such as Generative Adversarial Networks (GANs), Variational Encoders, Autoregressive Models, Normalizing Flows, and Diffusion Models. Next, we talked about how generative AI is revolutionizing the design process by comparing the landscape of traditional design vs. AI-powered ones, marked by speed, efficiency, adaptability, and personalization.

We then touched on the differences between traditional and AI-driven designs, mostly validated by the type of tasks being executed by human designers and how the new AI-powered technologies would facilitate a transition of designers from creators to cocreators. Next, we studied some of the most relevant available generative AI platforms and how they are being used in the context of design, as well as best practices in utilizing these platforms, defining the goals and data quality and following ethical and transparency principles, among others.

CHAPTER 3

Principles of Conscious/Mindful Design

When it comes to design practices, consciousness goes beyond awareness. It involves understanding the interplay between intention, experience, and outcome. Every design choice and subtle detail has an impact on how people perceive, interact with, and emotionally connect to the world. As designers and technologists, we possess a tool that can reshape our perceptions and profoundly touch lives in ways we may not always fully appreciate.

So what exactly is "conscious design"? It's not about aesthetics or functionality or just focusing on the human. It's an art and science that integrates empathy, ethics, and a holistic view of the global impact of the design in society and in the individuals in touch with the experience from inside out and vice versa. It involves recognizing and respecting the experiences and backgrounds of every human in the design, as well as understanding the broader ethical implications of design decisions. It means considering not only isolated effects but also long-term ripple waves within the larger ecosystem.

© Diana Olynick 2024
D. Olynick, *Interfaceless*, Design Thinking, https://doi.org/10.1007/979-8-8688-0083-2_3

When we see around, technology is everywhere, and in this we can see how the stakes are higher than before. With interfaces becoming more ingrained in our lives—from our device screens to immersive augmented realities—the boundaries between experiences and tangible reality are blurring (consider Figure 3-1). This fusion presents opportunities as well as significant responsibilities, urging future designers and creators for a thoughtful and conscious approach to design.

Figure 3-1. *Reflection on Consciousness*

Why is conscious design crucial in the context of computing? Let's try a thoughtful experiment. Think back to your experience in a physical space—a tranquil garden, a bustling market street, or perhaps a cozy nook in your own home. What made it truly unforgettable? Probably it wasn't only about what you saw; it was about the sensations, sounds, scents, and above all else the emotions that were evoked. Now imagine recreating that experience capturing not only the visuals but also the essence and soul of that space. This is precisely what spatial computing has the potential to achieve. However, harnessing this potential requires an understanding of experiences and humans—an understanding that can only be achieved through conscious design.

In this chapter, we will explore the relationship between spatial computing and conscious design, the role of contextual awareness, and a foundation on how it is to design for the "interfaceless" future.

Principles of Conscious Design

These days, there has been a growing interest in utilizing AI to enhance the design process. This fusion of design and AI is evident in the new applications that every day we see coming to the market. For example, in fields like architecture and product design, we see now a wide and growing interest from companies and creators to generate design concepts leveraged by AI. They have found that contact with those tools expands the capabilities of creation, allowing them to explore other angles and uniqueness in the creative process while saving time in producing manual concepts.

When we combine the principles of design with the potential of AI, a new network of possibilities emerges. As touched previously, with the rise of AI comes the possibility to analyze datasets and identify patterns that can guide better design decisions. The keyword here is "better" design decisions, meaning so far we might have been working with the standard design thinking approach and implicitly fulfilling mostly the business goals rather than the actual human. Let's reflect on the impact that having in our hands such a sensitive technology can have with a biased approach. At having the possibility to understand in real time human behavior and discover triggers, there is a great risk implied here. In the wrong hands, this powerful technology could contribute to proliferating practices and business models only based on taking advantage of humans, uncovering their vulnerabilities as indicated by the data generated and using back the data to inform psychological manipulation.

This is the main reason why conscious design (the approach to design dedicated to respecting and preserving a positive impact on the environment and society through ethical principles), as well as mindful design (the approach to design focused on human empathetic practices, presence, and awareness), is absolutely relevant and imperative in the integration of design with artificial intelligence technologies.

To begin this process, a reflective assessment is offered to be used as a supportive tool in any of the experiences you design to make sure they are considerate of conscious and mindful design principles:

Human-Centered Focus

- Does this design truly serve humans and not just the technology or business side of things?

- Have I completely grasped the human's emotions, preferences, and needs?

Well-being

- How does the design impact the human's psychological, emotional, and physical well-being?

- Have I included features that foster healthy habits or behaviors, create joy, and reduce stress or anxiety? Does the design promote inclusivity and accessibility?

Sustainability

- What's the environmental impact of the design? Are there any steps to take to minimize this impact?

- Are there any energy optimization strategies or waste reduction or any kind possible?

Conscious Consumption

- How does the design prevent cognitive overload and encourage limiting screen time and breaks?

- Does this design encourage responsible and conscious consumption of digital content?

Just as it is important to assess the designs, it is as important to assess our nature as creators when we are engaged in the creation process itself. As previously discussed, ultimately all of our works are a direct reflection of who we are, our values, and our intentions. It is essential to self-assess our mental states before, during, and after our work, so that we also create from an open and focused mental condition. When we are distracted, we make so many mistakes, we don't process information in the same way, and we continue to feed those habits missing important details and rushing activities that need careful attention. The following are some questions to explore as a creator or designer to assess your disposition toward the designs you are creating.

Are you fostering and supporting a beginner's mind, opening up to new ideas, insights, and possibilities during the design process?

Does your design process uphold mindfulness principles, such as nonjudgment, acceptance, patience, presence, and the release of preconceived notions or attachments, for example, to certain ideas or design elements or willing to change direction based on human feedback or new insights?

Are you often aware of your nature as a creator, the implications of your work, and the harm or harmony that you could create in all humanity as the result of your work?

How are you cultivating mindfulness in your professional and personal life, practicing virtues such as resilience, compassion, presence, and empathy for yourself and nature that can help support your practice?

Are you adopting the iterative nature of the design process, practicing non-attachment to initial ideas and being willing to change direction based on user feedback or new insights?

A holistic approach to conscious design involves not only the common design considerations of the design itself but also its impact on the human, society, and the world, aiming to protect and enhance human experiences. It is beneficial for creators, designers, developers, tech enthusiasts or technologists, and anybody who wants to enter in the field to reflect on how we can create a better world by means of promoting good intentional use of technology, digital detox events, mindful communication, conscious consumption, compassionate AI, and digital interconnectedness.

Introducing the MSDF (Mindful Spatial Design Framework)

Design, by its nature, is a field that aims to create, improve, and enhance experiences. As we move into an era dominated by transformation, the interaction between humans and their surroundings becomes increasingly intricate. This calls for a perspective on design practices, which is proposed here in Figure 3-2 as the Mindful Spatial Design Framework (MSDF).

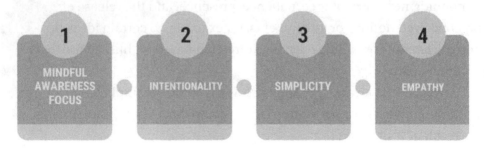

Figure 3-2. Mindful Spatial Design Framework (MSDF)

The MSDF offers an approach to design in the field of spatial computing. By integrating a holistic approach, mindfulness principles, inclusivity, and ethical considerations and advanced AI technologies like GenAI, this framework has the potential to revolutionize how we design experiences in spatial computing.

Let's discuss first the background and importance of guiding principles in traditional vs. mindful design.

When looking closely at the traditional design principles, we might realize that the approach is to separate the human into a factor in design that provides feedback to enhance the experience and output.

Mindful design, on the other hand, is an approach centered on creating experiences that support humans with awareness of their environment and presence, promoting a state of balance and self-control.

These are the key differences between traditional design and mindful design:

1. **Intent**

    Traditional design is centered in functional goals like aesthetics, convenience, and efficiency. In mindful design, the goal is to reduce stress and cultivate a sense of presence. The design elements in the experience are intentionally designed to facilitate attention and perception.

2. **Interaction**

    In this regard, traditional design focuses on prioritizing efficiency and speed, whereas mindful design encourages thoughtful interactions, allowing more freedom for the human to decide their next steps rather than anticipating the designer only paths to explore or interact with.

3. **Sensory Engagement**

   Traditional design usually is concerned with visuals, while mindful design is concerned with all the senses. It promotes awareness of the human's surroundings and senses. This might look like holistically considering sounds, smells, visuals, and textures.

4. **Emotional Design**

   In the traditional design approach, the emotional aspect is concerned with taking the "user" through a specific path of interaction and how to trigger certain behaviors or emotions to achieve certain specific results. For instance, ecommerce apps design the funnels and journey paths in a way that creates desire, releasing dopamine in the "user's" brain, using urgency to take the "user" to the final goal: buy the product. On the other hand, mindful design responsibly and deeply approaches the emotional impact of the human, aiming for the creation of positive and balanced emotional states and responses while eliminating negative ones, both striving to create positive emotional states and reduce negative ones. It acknowledges that different choices in the design can stimulate different emotional responses and utilizes this insight to encourage equilibrium and peace.

5. **Ethics and Sustainability**

   Traditional design has a marked tendency to prioritize business goals over global impact. Mindful design is essentially sustainable and ethical. It

considers the results of the choices used in the
design not only on the environment but also on
society at large.

6. **Simplicity and Minimalism**

   Since traditional design presents a more defined
   focus on business goals, products, and visual
   aesthetics, we often see a tendency to favor market
   behavior and trends from specific demographics.
   In contrast, simplicity and minimalism are key
   factors in mindful design. To support humans,
   it is understood that it is necessary to reduce
   unnecessary distractions and clutter, like the
   constant ones we are exposed to through
   advertisement, supporting humans to focus and
   maintain a clear and calm state.

Mindful design takes an all-encompassing approach, factoring not
only the end product but also the human, as its integral role in the design
process, including considering the impact of the complete experience
in the world. The key idea here is about creating intentional designs that
promote well-being for all of society.

Now that the key differences are laid out, let's now discuss why we
need "one more framework." During my experience teaching students
and being a student myself, I have come to realize two very important
breakthroughs. The first one, I call it "Passive Page Paralysis," or the
impairment to retain and apply information from a passive reading
approach. I was so suspicious of this phenomenon that upon further
investigation, I came to know that in neuroscience (study of the nervous
system), this is called the "retrieval effect," related to the fact that testing
information by yourself contributes to a higher retention ratio.

This first breakthrough, both personally observed and scientifically proposed, is that the framework proposed here is only a canvas, and you act on it as the artist. Of course, I wouldn't want you to waste your time reading this book; to make it completely effective, it is you that needs to create your own principles. I will formulate a couple of questions at the end of this section so that you can formulate your own set of principles and follow them sacredly knowing that they are completely your own.

The second breakthrough is that we have a tendency to blindly trust all the standards, methods, and blueprints that throughout history have been put forward and become popularized by famous proponents. I call it "The Validation Vortex." In full transparency, even this proposal needs to be doubted and put to test, but more than that, it is imperative to build your own and trust your instincts. Let's take a look at some of these dynamics to see the workings of "The Validation Vortex." First, from a neuroscience perspective, naturally the brain has a certain tendency toward "efficiency." Subconsciously, the brain prefers to maintain the frameworks already known and that we feel comfortable with. Second, the power of repetition and cognitive ease, which is a state in which without enough awareness, frequently we gravitate to what is already familiar to us, toward repetition. For example, we might not like a song that we listen to on the radio at first, but as this is repeated over and over, we might start to like the catchy music. On a conscious level, we also reveal feelings of fear of rejection and the unknown, so wanting to approve of all externally, already validated methods often comes as a more viable approach.

Another reason for "The Validation Vortex" is the societal condition that we have experienced from the time we were kids, including our family values and transfers or beliefs. Remember when we were told how to avoid coloring outside of the drawing lines? This is an example of the inhibition of creativity, and we come to trust that coloring inside is the only right way to color.

Finally and what I believe is the most important reason for mindful design is that confidently relying on your inner wisdom, which is a topic as many other practical ones we come to realize over the years, should be taught in every school, to every child. From the discovery of inner wisdom come confidence, reliability, security, and freedom. I truly believe that with a strong and calm mind, inner wisdom can be fully expressed in our work and all our creations. It just becomes a reflection of who you are and every single piece that you create, so with a pure and clear intention coming from a calm and balanced mind, we can create a set of principles and guidelines that follow our deep values of empathy and compassion with all humanity, therefore creating experiences that not only delight humans but also serve them as a tool for positive evolution.

Looking closely, you can see how much of our behavior is habitual rather than conscious. With that in mind, we can begin to see a sense of freedom and trust in ourselves and our values and, in that sense, acknowledge that with a good intention, we might be better positioned to undertake the role and responsibilities of the new conscious designer. This is the reason why the framework is proposed as a canvas, where you can create your own blueprint. I will guide you with key questions you can ask yourself, and you can build your own from there.

It's important to note that conventional design frameworks have served us well during the era of desktop computing and mobile devices. They provided guidelines that enabled us to create interfaces that were intuitive and visually pleasing. However, as we transition into the era of spatial computing, we discover that these traditional frameworks are ill suited to tackle the challenges presented by this emerging paradigm.

The Mindful Spatial Design Framework (MSDF) canvas presented here and that you will be creating, expanding, or adjusting to your own principles, in general, attempts to integrate elements of design and generative AI to leverage and augment creative potential that an independent designer could not fulfill alone. It also incorporates the interfaceless philosophy, achieved through spatial computing and mixed reality technologies, which are not common in traditional design. It also synthesizes the principles of conscious and mindful design related to balance, presence, awareness, and ethics which typically are not a priority in traditional design. The MSDF takes into consideration contextual awareness, studying the human surroundings and their mutual interplay, aiming to create designs that adapt to human needs. Finally, given the focus on using AI tools, spatial computing, and the interfaceless philosophy itself, the MSDF is future focused, aiming to prepare designers and creators for the future of experiences ruled by AI-driven systems—context-aware solutions that lack traditional interfaces.

The MSDF is guided by the following universal principles: mindful awareness focus, intentionality, simplicity, and empathy.

To illustrate these principles with a reflexive and proactive methodology, let's ponder the following questions:

Mindful Awareness Focus

- Have every element and feature in the design being studied to serve a valuable and clear purpose for the human?

- Have I assessed carefully if the features added are there just because they are possible rather than beneficial? Is the design respectful of human's time and attention accounting for distractions, multitasking, and different states of mind?

- Have I considered potential negative consequences of the design and how they can be addressed?

Intentionality

- Have I ensured that the design isn't just following trends or adding features for the sake of novelty? Is every feature rooted in genuine utility and enhancement of the user experience?

- Is every element of the design intentionally placed with a clear and beneficial purpose for the human? Are there any elements that lack a clear reason for their inclusion?

Empathy

- Is the design reflective of the real human's sentiments and the society's well-being at large?

- Have I considered the human's mental state while creating this design?

- Does the design involve clear ethical considerations that could impact society?

- Is there any encouragement in the design for value-added interactions and meaningful synergy rather than addictive, compulsive, or superficial engagement?

Simplicity

- Have I abstained from unneeded complexity that could frustrate or confuse humans?

- Is the design easy and intuitive to explore and navigate for the human? Are we incorporating natural interactions such as gaze, voice, gestures, and spatial navigation as it occurs in the real world intentionally?

In answering these questions during your design process, you are making sure that the process is considering the grounding foundations we previously discussed of empathy, presence, balance, and well-being. To create your own, we can begin by deepening your reflection with the help of the following reflection pointers:

Guiding Questions for Crafting Your Personal MSDF:

1. **Empathetic Approach**

    -   What considerations will you make to guarantee your understanding and give a diverse range of human experiences?

    -   How will you make sure that your designs encompass the psychological and emotional needs of humans?

2. **Understanding Humans**

    -   How would you describe the ideal human who would interact with your designs? What are their needs, challenges, preferences, and habits?

    -   How do you estimate your ideal human interacting with the spatial computing landscape?

3. **The Role of Mindfulness**

    -   How do you define mindfulness in the context of spatial computing design?

    -   In what ways do you foresee humans to be present and conscious at the interaction with your design?

4. **Feedback and Iteration**

    -   What processes will you follow for continuous iteration, adjustment, and reflection of your own framework?

    -   How will you obtain insight on your designs to the objective of making sure that it matches your MSDF principles?

5. **Personal Values**

- Which of the mentioned MSDF universal general principles resonate with you the most, and why?

- What values and beliefs are important to you regarding design for spatial computing?

6. **Future Vision**

- How are your designs facilitating the interactions for humans five years from now? What does it look like?

- How will the principles in your MSDF guide the preceding vision?

Let's take a look at an example of how this might look like:

Hypothetical Personal MSDF Creation

Based on the preceding questions for the development of a personal MSDF, Steve, a designer, might derive the following:

- *Value-Centric Design*: Steve believes strongly in human agency, transparency, and equality. With his designs, he allows humans to observe the background, the behind the scenes, so that an integral view of how data is used and processed is involved in the process.

- *Humans As Collaborators*: Steve doesn't approach humans as "users" or simply "consumers," but as collaborators. He appreciates offering flexibility, so in his designs, he makes sure that humans can customize and modify their spatial environments.

- *Active Mindfulness*: For Steve, active engagement is an element of mindfulness. He includes in his designs elements like invitations to pause and reconnect with themselves, to help humans to be engaged but present, transforming their interaction from passive viewers to conscious participants.

- *Fluid Evolution*: Steve creates designs that grow and evolve. The environments are not stagnant and aim to learn and adapt.

- *Emotion-First Approach*: Steve integrates tools as solutions to assess human emotional states, allowing the environment to adjust and offer support or comfort if needed.

- *Open Feedback Loop*: Experiences created by Steve feature a built-in feedback system, allowing humans to voice opinions to iterate for future improvements or updates.

Note   You can also leverage a checklist presented in Appendix D, to use as a guide to assess the principles of MSDF in a real-world design.

I like to compare the creation and use of the MSDF to the process of designing and creating a treehouse. Suppose you are going to build one. The MSDF is like a magic set of instructions that ensures it will be fun, safe, and enjoyable once it is built. When we build something mindfully, we are making sure that the person using it will feel completely good and safe in it; for example, the little kids that will play in it. You also ensure that instead of having switches and buttons, the house will know what the person in it wants, therefore facilitating their comfort while in it. If the kids want the lights brighter, the environment will know it and will provide a higher level of brightness without telling them. That's part of the magic of the interfaceless treehouse! Just as we don't want to hurt trees or the environment when building the treehouse, we make sure that through

conscious design, no other external factors, including other kids or
humans, get affected in the process or use.

By embracing these novel elements, the MSDF offers a fresh and
forward-thinking approach to design that is responsive to the rapidly
evolving technological landscape. It encourages designers to think beyond
the constraints of traditional interfaces and to envision a future where
design is less about crafting specific interfaces and more about curating
holistic, immersive, and responsive experiences.

The "Interfaceless" Approach in Spatial Computing

Starting to apply the MSDF, Figure 3-3 illustrates the philosophy of the
interfaceless design approach.

Figure 3-3. *The Interfaceless Approach*

What Is Spatial Computing?

In order to understand the "interfaceless" approach to design, we need to first understand what spatial computing is, its components, and how they serve interfaceless experiences.

Spatial computing in essence combines digital spaces to transform our surroundings, whether it's our homes, workplaces, or public areas, into playgrounds, blending them seamlessly. As this exciting evolution progresses, it raises a question: What role does the interface play in this situation?

The conventional interfaces that we are familiar with, such as keyboards and touchscreens, have limitations. These interfaces act as intermediaries for us to interact with our devices. However, spatial computing introduces real-time interactivity that necessitates a reimagining of these bridges. This is where the concept of an "interfaceless" approach becomes relevant.

The Natural Interface

The "interfaceless" approach doesn't completely eliminate interfaces. Instead, it shifts toward interfaces that are so intuitive and natural that they almost fade away from direct recognition. Consider the difference between typing commands on a computer and thinking or gesturing while the computer responds accordingly. The latter feels naturally seamless—like an extension of oneself.

Envision a future where designers don't rely on mice or styluses but can mold and shape designs using their hands in a three-dimensional space or a scenario where turning on lights doesn't require tapping a smartphone. In turn, you can simply make a gesture or just think about it. This concept is known as the "interfaceless" vision, for computing.

Have you ever found yourself frustrated while trying to use an app? It's so easy to press the buttons or get lost in menus. Now imagine a world where these limitations disappear and the environment itself becomes the interface.

Let's take a look at factors that we would need to consider for the interfaceless approach.

Holistic Experience

The essence of interfaceless design is to provide a holistic experience. This puts an important emphasis on interactions not just about tasks but the entire path of the human experience and emotions. When humans are the protagonists of the scene, the interactions become invisible, so the interfaces fade into the background, allowing the content and human freedom.

User respect and environmental harmony are ultimately behind the conscious motivation interfaceless design, as it involves prioritizing human mental well-being; avoiding any overwhelm, overload, and fatigue; and offering a supportive experience through smart systems that understand and blend into the physical environments without strain and digital obstructions (like ads).

Mindful Immersion

Although traditional UIs have been useful for the devices we have now, like regular desktops and, in some cases, even smartphones (you would be surprised to know that even with smartphones we could create apps with no traditional UI interfaces), they are not the norm in spatial computing. To facilitate the sense of presence in the spatial experience without distractions of physical controls or UIs, we need to define and establish the guidelines and purposely design for deep presence. At this point, it is very important to make a distinction between two types of presence that we often speak about in spatial computing applications. One type is the presence that is required to create immersion, which involves technical factors like high-quality graphics, low latency, consistent frame rate, spatial audio, haptic feedback, wide field of view (FOV), accurate motion tracking, seamless locomotion and interactivity, etc. In this type of "presence," the goal is that the human really feels in that space as if it were completely physical, like the regular spaces around us without any devices. Since the brain processes these experiences through the visual, auditory, and tactile senses, it comes to get tricked into the story, like believing it is totally inside the "movie" as when we are dreaming.

The other type of "presence" we discuss is the mindful presence, which is related to the state of the mind where it recognizes one's place at a specific point in time, grounding the self in the current reality without judgment. The title of this section presents an interesting discussion. How can we be immersed in the experience and at the same time present and aware of our own existence? This is a question that has defined a good part of writing this book, because if we can practice the awareness of our human presence in the real world, but cannot practice it in a simulated one, then this book would be pointless. As you can see, this also takes us to contemplate deeper reflections, like the ultimate nature of reality, the construct of this world as we perceive it. The technology that we are experimenting now is also a tool for this kind of exploration. Have you wondered if the solidity of the world as we know it is its real ground? What if this world is as imagined as the ones we explore in virtual reality? Of course, I am not suggesting that we are inside a binary simulation like the matrix, but maybe of another kind... In any case, the world keeps going in its own direction with us in it (or maybe the other way around), and everywhere we go, either apparent real or simulated places, as long as there is an idea of a self, there is always an opportunity to practice presence, and those are really good news! This means that we can be ourselves and come back again and again to this moment even if we are at a real beach in The Maldives, than if we are in a simulated one, because we always carry with us ourselves.

From one perspective, creators need to do a good job at creating experiences that facilitate immersion (presence) and also facilitate the mindful presence that humanity needs for its own evolution. In part, this depends on the experience itself (the simulated environment and its features), and in part, it depends on the type of practice every individual decides to undertake. Ultimately, conscious and mindful designs are the standards to protect and care for everyone, so independently of everyone's choice, we design under the standards that facilitate mindful awareness.

Adaptable and Empathetic Systems

Interfaceless designs aim to avoid overstimulation, using clutter-free approaches to ensure that the spatial environment doesn't contribute to human overwhelm with unnecessary information or graphics, making sure purposeful interactivity is at the forefront of the design.

The environments designed and built under conscious and interfaceless principles present interactions more customized and less generic, considering emotional resonance, adapting to human's emotional states, ensuring safety and comfort, and respecting the boundaries and personal space. In traditional designs, we are tied to draw specific journeys and constrained "user paths." In conscious and interfaceless designs, we provide humans with guidance or gentle cues rather than enforced actions to strict paths.

Conscious design in spatial computing acknowledges the importance of ethical implications in terms of data sensitivity, expressing care and responsibility with the data collected, ensuring its privacy, and avoiding manipulation of human behavior in their decision-making.

The future of conscious, interfaceless design continues to transform as human behavior and societal norms change; that is why now it's the perfect time to navigate the possibility of seamless integrations of technologies in a way that serves humanity, creating experiences that feel as an extension of ourselves, achieved through the understanding and proper implementation of conscious design principles.

Understanding Contextual Awareness in Design

Most of today's smartphones feature the ability to read environmental levels of light and adjust their displays based on the brightness required to perform optimally. In sunlight, the display increases the brightness level for better visibility, and in dim conditions, it might self-adjust to decrease the brightness, reducing eyestrain. I was pleasantly surprised when I went for a bike ride this summer and my smartwatch started to read without any command (as my hands were busy on the wheel) the distance, calories, heart rate, and other indicators. These are examples of what is meant by contextual awareness. It is the adaptation of the system to ambient conditions including human preferences and situational needs. As you notice, it is not just about adaptation in relation to the environment but, more importantly, to human's emotional states, time-based factors, and even cultural nuances.

Context awareness works as a support in interfaceless environments using conscious design principles (Figure 3-4). It aims to prioritize human needs and comfort levels while foreseeing potential hazards, for example, very useful for those with disabilities, supporting safety and accessibility, one of the main principles of conscious design.

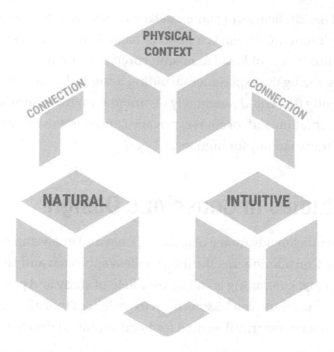

Figure 3-4. *Context Awareness in Design*

Levels of Context

Using context awareness, it is possible to identify when a human is in a group setting, public setting, or in an individual experience, and based on this, the interactions can adjust consequently. This is called a social context. We can also see gathering and analysis of data that can involve emotional states, physical environments, and temporal context, which would adjust depending on the surrounding conditions and influence design responses.

As we will see in Chapter 6, the process of gathering contextual data happens at the moment mainly through sensors and inputs, and the designer plays also a crucial role in being able to properly interpret this data for decision-making that comes from the human feedback as well to adjust any ethical and social considerations that the systems alone cannot adjust by themselves, facilitating the process of designing with context in mind.

Some of the challenges in contextual awareness systems include to be aware of the intent the system is trained or capable to avoid mistakenly reading context that could lead to misinterpretations or awkward adjustments during the experience, avoiding designs that change too often or inadvertently that could potentially disorient humans in the experience with over-adaptation and, of course, privacy concerns, ensuring control agency and transparency for humans.

Case Studies in Conscious Design

There is a significant advantage of learning from and analyzing real-world applications. Considering that the interfaceless approach and conscious design for spatial computing is still a novel field of study and practice, we can take some value-driven lessons from experiences that already exist, which were not necessarily designed for head-mounted devices (HMDs).

1. **Nest Thermostat**

    The Nest Thermostat from Google (Figure 3-5) is a device that connects and communicates with the home heating system to self-regulate the space temperature to save energy resources while providing human comfort without constant direct inputs.

Figure 3-5. *Nest Thermostat (Source: Google)*

It features a minimalist interface, since it is a device
that is focused on a single control, the rotating dial
with a display that activates only when needed.
This approach has made possible the removal of
unnecessary menus or buttons in the design, becoming
less apparent for the human to exert specific controls
for outputs.

In terms of contextual awareness, it learns from
periodic human behavior to self-adjust the temperature
levels, detecting the presence or absence of the space
occupants. When the person is approaching, it makes
apparent the display, getting ready to report the current
reading or settings. It also provides feedback on the
levels of energy efficiency through the leaf symbol,
signaling current potential savings.

When it comes to conscious and mindful design, we can see the principles of anticipatory design predicting and automating human needs based on their behavior, as well as a solution approach with sustainability and environmental consciousness, demonstrated in its design to preserve energy and reduce waste. Human well-being is considered, ensuring that the physical space remains comfortable eliminating frequent adjustments.

The challenges that this implementation could present include the balance between automation and human control and the trust from humans about the responsible use of their data.

2. **Apple's AirPods Pro (Figure 3-6) with Adaptive Audio**

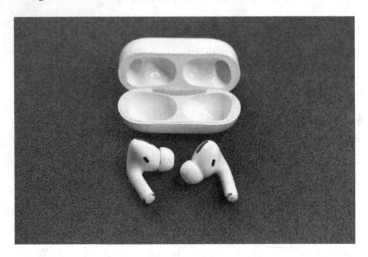

Figure 3-6. *Apple AirPods (Source: Apple)*

In its latest Worldwide Developers Conference (2023), Apple released its latest version of the AirPods Pro product, featuring adaptive audio, noise canceling, and conversation awareness.

Depending on the human environment, the device is capable of reading the type of mode best suited and self-adjusts. It reads the surroundings and tailors the listening mode. For example, if somebody approaches you to chat with you, it will understand the context and will reduce the volume to engage properly in the conversation without having to remove them or manually adjust them.

As feedback mechanisms, it uses simple tones to notify of low battery alerts, as well as using head tracking for a theater-like experience.

The capabilities of the AirPods Pro in using context awareness allow for an interfaceless interaction featuring the absence of buttons, controls, or external apps.

In its own design, we can see a human-centric design approach to adjust the experience to the user not only in the sound quality but also in the product comfort of the ear tips, optimizing each element to the individual while allowing them to maintain connection with the environment at any desired level. In terms of health integration, we can see an example here of the integration of features like ear health monitoring integrating human well-being in the round experience.

Current and Future Role of AI in Conscious Design

Currently, the influence of AI on design is quite evident. Conscious design, which inherently values human autonomy and well-being, is starting to reshape the narrative as well. In this context, AI serves a purpose beyond optimizing clicks and engagement; it now aims to promote healthier human behaviors (Figure 3-7).

For example, certain wellness apps now utilize AI to identify when a human is feeling stressed by observing usage patterns and other cues. Based on these insights, the apps suggest activities like meditation or taking a detox. These AI-powered features act as reminders for individuals to take breaks, breathe deeply, or even step away from their devices.

Figure 3-7. *AI in Conscious Design*

In the future, AI holds potential to revolutionize how we approach design in several significant ways:

1. *Proactive Support for Mental Health*: Imagine a world where our devices not only understand our routines but also recognize our mental states. Future AI could pick up on cues from our interactions, identify patterns that indicate stress or anxiety, and proactively offer suggestions or even adjust the device environment to create a more calming atmosphere. This wouldn't be invasive but would feel supportive.

2. *Genuine Personalization Without Exploitation*:
   Many current personalization algorithms aim to
   exploit vulnerabilities and keep users hooked.
   However, under the principles of conscious design,
   AI could provide empathetic personalization. For
   example, it could curate content that aligns with
   users' long-term goals, eliminating distractions or
   disruptive media and focusing only on what truly
   could support a human well-being.

3. *Ethical Decision-Making*: A conscious AI designer, in
   the future, would prioritize not human engagement
   but ethical considerations when making design
   decisions. This might involve suggesting more
   meaningful interactions even if it means reducing
   overall screen time.

4. *Self-Regulating AI Systems*: Future AI systems could
   include built-in limits to prevent distraction from
   the real world, essentially acting as an assistant
   that reminds us when it's time to take a break. This
   represents a shift from exploitation systems that
   prioritize maximizing "user" engagement to holistic
   systems that prioritize human evolution, freedom,
   security, and privacy.

As spatial computing becomes increasingly integrated into our lives,
AI can ensure that the digital elements in our environment are not only
informative but also introduced thoughtfully. The future of design in
AI is fascinating and full of potential. While we have made progress in
integrating AI into design, we are still on a journey to achieve ethical and
human-centric design priorities.

Our focus is not on technology for technology's sake; it's about utilizing AI's potential to create a more mindful, aware, and ultimately humane digital landscape.

This vision is not a fantasy. With the convergence of advancements in AI and an increasing recognition of the importance of design, we are at the verge of a revolution. In this new era, design goes beyond aesthetics and usability to enhance our encounters and support our humanity. Undoubtedly, AI systems will play a part in guiding us toward this vision.

Summary: Principles of Conscious Design

In this chapter, we discussed the foundation of conscious design and its role in the landscape of spatial computing. We studied the principles of conscious and mindful design, establishing a series of questions not only for the design itself but also for the designer.

We also presented the essence of interfaceless design as a holistic experience using invisible interactions, recognizing the conscious motivation behind this approach at establishing the focus on human respect, mental well-being, and privacy rights while aiming to create adaptable and empathetic systems by learning from humans and emphasizing emotional resonance.

To be able to create interfaceless designs that utilize the principles of conscious design, contextual awareness systems come as a handy tool for the work. We discussed the leverage from these processes to create interactions that adjust to the human needs in real time, providing more personalized and relevant interactions.

We studied some examples that showcase some conscious and contextual awareness principles like the Nest Thermostat and the latest Apple AirPods Pro devices, transitioning to a conclusion on the current and future use of AI in the context of conscious design and the potential outcomes and changes ahead.

Resources

You can refer to Appendix A, Table A-1, to study the Design Guide for Conscious and Mindful Design Experiences for Spatial Computing.

Additionally, although not specified, the preceding principles still apply to the Games field, and for extra support, you could check the Design Guide for Conscious and Mindful Design Experiences for Games in Appendix A, Table A-2.

CHAPTER 4

The Evolving Role of AI: Automation and Beyond

Automation is often perceived as a benefit associated with AI. It involves transferring tasks to machines in order to improve efficiency, reduce errors, and enable scalability. Nevertheless, when it comes to computing tasks, there is an art to automation.

We must ensure that when removing the interface we don't lose the touch in the experience. When we approach automation with a focus on design, it should not prioritize efficiency, aiming to enhance human immersion and overall experience (Figure 4-1).

D. Olynick, *Interfaceless*, Design Thinking, https://doi.org/10.1007/979-8-8688-0083-2_4

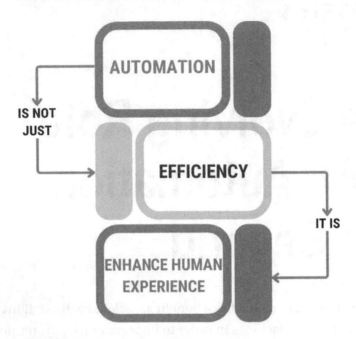

Figure 4-1. *The Evolving Role of AI*

While automation deals with tasks that are already understood and predictable, innovation is about exploring possibilities. It involves pushing boundaries, challenging conventions, and offering solutions that were previously unimaginable. In the fields of computing and design specifically, innovation means creating groundbreaking human experiences that adapt over time and set industry standards.

The Impact of Interfaces on Experience

In today's era, interfaces play a protagonist role in our technological interactions. They serve as the tactile connection between humans and the digital world. Like any bridge, the design and structure of an interface determine how smoothly and effectively we can navigate through it. It's worth questioning our reliance on interfaces, especially considering the design revolution we are witnessing in this digital era.

Let's take a moment to reflect on our three-dimensional world and its complexities. Our primary way of interacting with technology still remains rooted in two-dimensional concepts. This inherent disparity leads us to wonder if our current interfaces truly reflect how we perceive and desire to engage with spaces where the ultimate goal has been so far to create truly immersive and engaging experiences.

Think about a book, for example. When digital books were first introduced, they replicated the experience of turning pages. This choice wasn't based on necessity, but it was introduced because people were familiar with that interface. Now, after some iterations, some digital books still retain the page flipping animation, while others have evolved to a simple swipe gesture. This is for us to prove that we don't have to be bound by the standard conventions that are created when new mediums of experience are introduced.

Now, let's apply this perspective to digital interfaces. Our smartphones, computers, and tablets, with their app icons and rectangular screens, are essentially built upon the design principles that originated in the era of paper and ink. For example, icons were initially introduced to aid understanding in a way. However, as our technological literacy advances, we start to notice the redundancy of these symbols across applications.

This adherence to design is not purely driven by nostalgia; it also affects our capacity. Each unnecessary icon or incongruous animation demands a portion of our attention, which is already scarce due to the amount of information available. Two-dimensional interfaces confine us by forcing our multilayered experiences into a flat and limiting framework.

That's where the approach of conscious and interfaceless design in spatial computing comes in—a concept that enables computers to not only display content but also understand and respect spatial relationships. It goes beyond adding another dimension; it prompts us to reconsider how we interact with spaces (Figure 4-2).

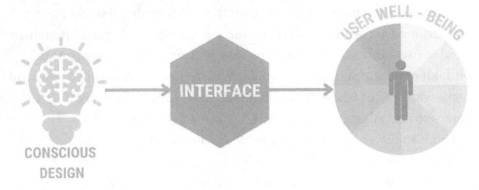

Figure 4-2. *Impact of Interfaces on Experience*

Spatial computing empowers us to leverage our abilities in comprehending, navigating, and manipulating 3D environments.

Imagine the contrast between observing a bird flying on a screen and actually having the bird gracefully flutter around your room interacting with the furniture and lights and maybe even acknowledging your presence.

Traditional design principles may suggest that a shopping app should display products in grids. However, in spatial computing, that same app could be transformed into a store. In this store, you can "walk" through aisles, "pick up" products to examine them closely or even "try them on." Instead of relying on taps and swipes, your own movements, voice, and even emotions become the interface.

In traditional interfaces, we see characteristics like buttons, sliders, and drop-downs. While those ones provided clear instructions for the time and medium used, it also created a significant cognitive load, at the point of abuse of human focus and attention. AI-driven interactions promise to facilitate traditional tasks through automation systems like predictive typing, gesture control, and voice recognition, being able to anticipate real, not fabricated, needs.

In this comparative parallel, we can identify how different interfaces can either disrupt or enhance human presence and immersion. AI can assist with the state of flow or being "in the zone," a concept introduced by Mihaly Csikszentmihalyi, referring to a time when we are completely absorbed in a task or activity, and the balance it requires to achieve it, between the line of neither too easy nor difficult. In this view, the flow is characterized by concentration on the complete task at hand, being moved by a sense of clarity knowing exactly what needs to be done.

Often, like when we are writing a book or composing a song, it is about feeling the reward in the activity itself rather than the external motivations or rewards, and experiencing a sense of control over one's actions. This approach invites reflection on how a human could display such a level of agency without having to draw every single journey or path for them to follow. If we design with the intent of freedom and the possibility for them to be "in the zone" or in the "optimal experience," the result is inevitable. By being able to flow and express our own humanity, we are better able to stay in balance with ourselves and the surroundings, appreciating more and anticipating our sense of comfort with ourselves and the experience. Specifically, AI systems can facilitate flow through personalization capabilities in the experience, feedback, and predictive analysis.

As we have seen over the years with gaming interfaces, for example, the shift has been toward intuitive control mechanisms, allowing the experience for more freedom and more decision-making in the storytelling and narrative. The interfaceless approach implies an ecosystem that is defined and supportive of continuous learning or adaptation. The historical context of gaming interfaces features fixed difficulty levels, limited adaptability, and rigid controls. Over time, we saw the use of adaptive difficulty settings and the introduction of AI algorithms adapting the difficulty in real time depending on player performance. Another example of this shift is in the use of coal commands, physical gestures, and predictive gameplay, adjusting game scenarios on the fly.

Now, you might wonder why this shift is so important. Well, beyond being novel and exciting, spatial computing has the potential to bring experiences closer to our instincts and interactions as humans. It reduces the effort required by aligning interactions with real-world ones. Additionally, by breaking free from screen limitations, we create more novel and supportive opportunities for design. Consider individuals who may face challenges with interfaces due to disabilities. Spatial computing can truly be revolutionary by providing personalized experiences tailored to individual abilities.

Embracing Automation in Spatial Computing

Spatial computing goes beyond being another interface—it represents a shift in our relationship with technology. In this context, automation becomes the driving force behind intuitive and human-centered experiences. The combination of computing and automation opens up possibilities (Figure 4-3) where design is not merely observed or interacted with but becomes a part of our lives.

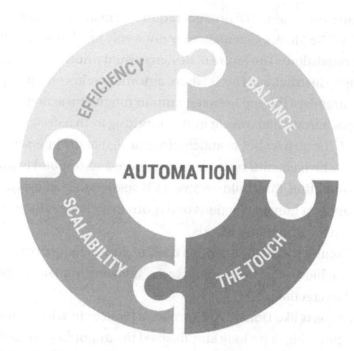

Figure 4-3. *Embracing Automation in Spatial Computing*

Amber Case, an anthropologist and author of *Calm Technology*, emphasizes that technology should not demand all of our attention but only when necessary. This sentiment holds significance in the era of spatial computing. Unlike 2D interfaces that often require focus and manual input, spatial computing enriched by automation promises to offer experiences that respect our primary focus while subtly and intelligently engaging when needed.

Consider the concept of a smart home as an example. In a setup, turning on the lights upon entering would involve locating a switch or issuing voice commands. However, within an automated home environment, the system would detect your presence and instinctively illuminate the room as you walk in. In this scenario, the space itself becomes the interface, while automation ensures that it responds to you effortlessly without commands.

Elon Musk once said, "If a product requires a manual to operate it, it's flawed." While Musk's statement may not apply to all products, it does contain some wisdom. The future of design should prioritize experiences that require no instruction. This is where automation in computing excels—it minimizes the gap between human intent and action.

How does automation truly fit into computing from a design perspective? The answer lies in anticipatory design at the intersection with automation, which enables systems to anticipate and respond to human needs. In computing, this could involve a VR session that adjusts its narrative based on human reactions or a room that changes its ambiance depending on the occupant's moods.

As we discussed earlier, conscious design aims to reduce overload. Automation achieves this by handling tasks, allowing humans to focus on meaningful interactions.

Design experts like Donald A. Norman, a pioneer in science and usability engineering, have long emphasized the importance of designing technology that caters to needs and capabilities. In the field of computing, automation plays a role by allowing systems to respond to natural human behaviors such as gestures, gaze, or voice commands. This reduces the reliance on learned interactions, making the experience more intuitive.

It's essential to acknowledge that there are challenges associated with the use of automation in spatial computing. Over-automation can sometimes lead humans to feel disempowered or out of control. An example of this is a recent interview published widely on social media about an MIT student who has been working on the development of a device that connects with Google to search for any type of information without any form of verbal loud communication. The device is placed close to his head and reads his thoughts. During the interview, there was a live demo and people made their immediate impression. By reading their comments, we can understand the risks of high automations when threatening human agency. Most of the comments were based on critique about the use of a system that does the same as we do and why that is needed if we already possess the capacity, which are all valid points. To address issues like this, designers must strike a balance between automating processes while ensuring that humans always feel in control. Humans should have the freedom to intervene or override automated decisions whenever they feel it is prudent to do so.

The integration of automation into computing has the potential to redefine how we interact with the world at its core. Kevin Kelly, cofounder of *Wired* magazine, aptly captured this sentiment when he said, "You'll be paid in the future, based on how you work with robots." Although he was primarily referring to job opportunities, his statement holds true for design as well.

To truly innovate in computing and deliver meaningful human experiences, embracing balanced and thoughtful automation is not merely a choice; it is an absolute necessity.

Successful Implementation of Automation: Case Studies

Part of the criteria for successful implementations include seamless and smooth transitions ensuring that the integration of automation is stable, without causing breaks in the experience. The human shouldn't need manuals or tutorials to understand the context, making the automation a background process rather than a forefront task to deal with. It should feel natural and comfortable. Context awareness, reliability, consistency, scalability, performance efficiency, flexibility, as well as ethics and practice constitute indicators to look for when a first audit implementation takes place.

Cubism VR

Cubism (Figure 4-4) is a puzzle experience created by Thomas Van Bouwel that features an intuitive design supported by a minimalist approach ensuring the experience itself supports human enjoyment and

101

relaxation. The absence of complicated settings or menus demonstrates the use of diegetic UIs at their direct integration with the experience. Interacting with the pieces is a task that leverages the medium and the use of natural interactions effectively and intuitively. The player picks up a piece and rotates it directly with their hands without the use of any additional commands or menus, just as we grab objects in the real world.

Figure 4-4. *Cubism Interface*

The experience is designed from the ground up to be distraction free, for which the emphasis is placed in the puzzle only, enhancing it with soft sound cues and a calming music piece that upon puzzle completion unveils a complete classical music composition.

In Cubism, spatial recognition is used effectively to allow the player to interact with the real world in a mixed reality experience, allowing the grounding and connection with the real world while enjoying the relaxing and calming music and the puzzle, feeling like a therapeutic activity.

In terms of ethics and privacy, in Cubism there is not a demand for excessive personal data, focusing only on the gameplay and diligently disclosing transparent permissions, such as spatial tracking. Since the game style is minimalist, it allows for optimized rendering and efficiency, preventing low latency interactions.

Tripp

This app (Figure 4-5) was initially launched for Oculus (Meta Quest) and then widely expanded to other platforms due to its features to support wellness and body health.

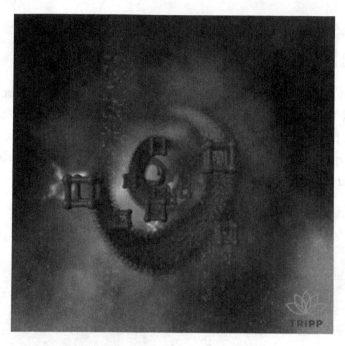

Figure 4-5. *Tripp Interface*

It aims to provide experiences that the human can customize based on their own preferences, making them the center of the design goals. Due to the nature of the app, it provides feedback on human's relaxation levels so that the very results of calm and stress release are the drivers for human engagement rather than other external gamified rewards. It provides dynamic visuals and synchronized audio that adjusts to the human needs, ensuring smooth rendering and transitions for an optimized experience.

Tripp features mood detection capabilities and adaptive feedback in some sessions, self-adjusting the experience according to the needs.

As the field of AI is progressing more into adaptive behavior, Tripp is one of the first experiences that looked to integrate its full capabilities to elevate the human experience and innovate in the area of mental health.

AI's Position in Fostering Innovation and Setting Industry Benchmarks

If we reflect on the course of modern advancements, the influence of AI in our daily lives stands out immediately. It has not only pushed forward innovation but also has contributed to new industry benchmarks, redefining quality experiences. Let's take a look at AI's role in guiding current and future technology developments (Figure 4-6).

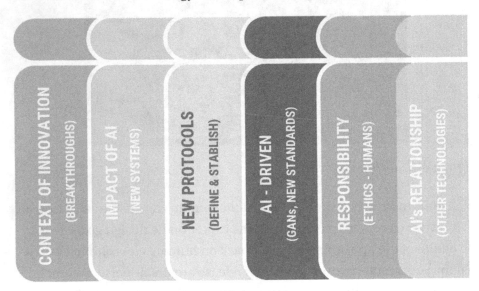

Figure 4-6. *AI's Position in Innovation*

The Historic Context of Innovation

Important technological breakthroughs over the last 100 years have taken place due to the convergence of several factors: the transistor, revolutionized the electronics industry; the laser, with useful applications in medicine; the Internet protocol, changed communications and entertainment; each of these markers having multiple ripples in their respective industries. Nonetheless, the current stage of technological advancement, mainly established by AI, is different. We are at the cusp of an era where a sole technological force begins a shift in the current standards, acting as both a catalyst and the outcome of innovation simultaneously.

The Impact of AI As a Multidimensional Force

Previously, in universities the most advanced research existed compartmentalized. Using algorithms, scientific researchers would use their own models and aim to achieve significant progress in their own fields. Today, the game has changed. With the use of neural networks, the unification of all systems of discovery can now feed from each other, making new AI systems more powerful than ever. This places a significant influence in sectors as diverse as finance, entertainment, healthcare, engineering, and the list goes on. These are some of the recent improvements in AI's capabilities:

- *Operational Efficiency*: Since the latest AI-driven tools have reformed industries by augmenting efficiency, decreasing operational costs, and setting benchmarks for performance metrics.

- *Behavior Analysis*: AI engine recommendation tools have transformed content consumption, setting new industry baselines for "user engagement." In social media, these algorithms are called "recommender systems" using content processing and content propagation methods.

105

- *Data Interpretation*: This is AI's ability to sort through vast datasets, reading patterns, trends, and anomalies. This has led to fundamental transformations, from personalized healthcare solutions to predictive analysis in finance.

AI and a New Age of Protocols

AI's intervention has accelerated the process of industry benchmark refinement. With machine learning models and the vast amounts of data processing, a need to define and establish new best practices and benchmarks in a fraction of the traditional time has become more evident:

- *Finance*: Trading algorithm models and their advanced analytics processing are defining new standards for areas like risk assessment, portfolio management, and market predictions.

- *Healthcare*: Having the possibility to analyze countless patient records to suggest treatment protocols has been a goal in this industry since the introduction of algorithms.

AI-Driven New Paradigms

Economist Joseph Schumpeter once introduced the theory of "creative destruction," where old models and methods give way to new, resulting in a more effective path for growth than only competition marked by price. The old benchmarks, no matter how established, are being incessantly questioned and, often, replaced by AI-driven paradigms. The advent of Generative Adversarial Networks (GANs) in art and design or AI-driven diagnostic tools in medicine exemplifies this "creative destruction" and the advantages it brings to the field. With new paradigms, new challenges arise, and it is up to us to lead the direction of the new standards safely for all.

The Ethical Dimension and Responsibility

With great power come great risks and responsibilities. New benchmarks in the AI landscape also bring with them an essential discourse on the ethical dimensions of the use and protection guidelines for humanity at large. AI benchmarks in facial recognition, for instance, raise questions about privacy and consent. It's pivotal for designers, creators, and tech professionals to reframe AI's role not just in the context of efficiency and innovation but also in terms of its broader socio-ethical implications.

The Road Ahead: AI's Relationship with Other Technologies

As discussed earlier, AI's current strength and influence lie in its synergy with other technologies. The combination of spatial computing, quantum computing, and blockchain, for instance, promises a future where benchmarks are not just met but reimagined.

In summary, as creators we are called to rethink the new benchmarks with the foundation of humanity at the center and establish those new principles as influence to the economic and social systems, aiming for a future where not only the business case and capitalism decide the direction of human experience, but humans powered by empathetic technology evolve more wise and kind than our present circumstances.

Reflections on AI's Future in Design

The imminent evolution of AI systems poses for creators and advocates an important reflection about the future. Do we envision an AI-dominated future? What is our role in the present and future of this technological landscape? As conscious designers, it's worth reflecting on the future that we foresee with human evolution at the forefront with or without AI. The essence of humanity has always been the same no matter the technological level of achievements. Today, more than ever, creators in this space are called to define the direction that this needs to take. Is it the one where machines are empowered by a humanity that is egocentric or a humanity that is empathetic and wise?

Figure 4-7 introduces some considerations for upcoming breakthroughs in design.

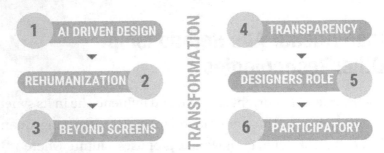

Figure 4-7. *AI's Future in Design*

1. **The Expansive Horizon of AI-Driven Design**

    The realization that deeply resonates with any designer deeply engaged with AI is the possibilities it brings forth. The traditional barriers to creativity are no longer confined by iterations. With AI, the design field becomes vast, dynamic, and constantly evolving. Generative designs that adapt to human needs in time or predictive human interfaces that anticipate actions before they even occur are just scratching the surface.

2. **A Future Beyond Screens**

As computing and AI blend, a new vision comes to life—a world where design surpasses the confines of 2D screens. Virtual and augmented realities infused with AI promise an environment where experiences become multidimensional, instinctive, and deeply personal. Here lies a space where the role of a "designer" transforms from being an artist into becoming a creator of worlds and architect of experiences.

3. **The Rehumanization of Design**

One of the thought-provoking aspects concerning the future of AI in design is the idea of "rehumanization." Surprisingly, AI has the potential to bring back a human-centered approach to design. In our pursuit of efficiency, many contemporary designs tend to overlook elements. However, with AI taking care of manual and administrative tasks, designers can now focus on creating experiences that deeply resonate with people's emotions. The focus shifts from "how can we make this functional?" to "how can we make this truly meaningful and authentic?"

4. **Transparency in Design Choices**

This upcoming design era will be marked by notable efforts to make AI decisions understandable to humans, especially in the context of the current "black box" paradigm we are facing. AI systems have showcased unexpected results that not even the most specialized researchers could predict, making this evidence of the uncontrolled nature that AI is taking.

Along with these efforts, there is a tendency of marrying artistic intuition with AI logic, reflected by the use of the systems in artistic fields like literature, music, and visual arts. A highlight of this trend is the "Edmond de Belamy" portrait, an algorithm-based art, auctioned and sold in the market for a significant sum.

5. **Anticipation of Potential Pitfalls**

Human oversight needs to be front and center of the design decisions, avoiding overreliance on AI, but using the tools as supportive makers of the creation. Due to human nature, unpredictable interactions in the interplay of spatial experience and human reaction might arise, making it essential to prepare AI systems for those kinds of challenges that could affect proper decision-making based on wrong interpretations. An example of this could be using AI models for the design of urban landscapes. Although AI can aid substantially with the city planning aspects of the design, it requires no replaceable human intuition to ensure livability and community essence to finalize other impactful decisions.

The Evolving Role of Designers: Guides, Ethicists, and Visionaries

As AI takes on a portion of the design process, designers will witness a transformation in their roles. They will become

> *Guides*: Leading AI tools to understand the core values and essence of a brand or experience, ensuring that automated designs evoke the desired emotions and reflect principles.
>
> *Ethicists*: Safeguarding the responsibility of taking care of humans. As AI brings forth self-developing capabilities, designers will serve as guides ensuring that design solutions maintain ethics and respect human autonomy.
>
> *Visionaries*: Liberated from getting caught up in every detail of design minutiae, designers can dream big, envision, and bring to life experiences that were once considered impossible.

The ethical dimension of this ecosystem is at the center of all upcoming creations. AI systems need to be trained and assessed at the values of respecting cultural nuances, human feelings, and moral values, promoting diversity of thought.

The Evolution Toward Participatory Design

In a future driven by enhanced human presence and AI tools, there is a potential for every individual to become an active creator and collaborator in the design process. As AI tools become more accessible, we may witness a shift toward design, where the once called "end users" play a role in shaping their own experiences. This inclusive approach to design has the potential to create solutions that are more diverse and impactful.

Reflection As an Action

As we ponder upon these potential future scenarios, it becomes imperative for every designer to take action. Contemplating AI's role in design should not be about mere reflection but active deliberations. Every decision made today, every interface carefully crafted, and every human experience meticulously mapped represent a step toward that envisioned future. By incorporating AI with a focus on conscious and mindful design principles, designers and creators are not only anticipating the future, they are actively shaping it.

Summary: The Evolving Role of AI—Automation and Beyond

In this chapter, we laid out the growing importance of AI and the vital role of interfaces, studying its impact on experience and immersion marked by personalization and human behavior in spatial computing. Barriers and limitations were discussed, arriving at a conclusion of the responsibility posed to creators leading this wave of progress. Automation in spatial computing was presented as part of one of the moving pieces by which conscious and interfaceless designs might take place, highlighting the aspects of efficiency, tailored experiences, consistency, and safety. The cases of Cubism and Tripp were presented to take a look at some elements already leveraging context and automation and opening up the potential for further customizations. A reflection on innovation and a look at new industry benchmarks arising from the latest AI advancements lead the path toward deeper understanding and transformation from old paradigms to new ones, involving not only designers or creators but all humanity at large.

CHAPTER 5

Complexity, Simplicity, and True Minimalism

In the world of design, there is a saying that often reflects the core principles of creators: "Less is more." This phrase, credited to architect Ludwig Mies van der Rohe, encapsulates the appeal of minimalism—the art of simplicity distilling something to its elements. However, simplicity holds a hidden depth. Beneath its clean lines in design, simplicity can sometimes conceal a level of complexity that can augment further challenges and complications.

Historically speaking, there has been a debate in design around simplicity versus complexity as drivers for different creations, from early art movements like the arts and crafts in the late 19th century; Bauhaus, De Stijl, Modernism, and Postmodernism in the late 20th century. The latter, bringing forth iconic figures representing simplicity in design, like Dieter Rams, who quoted "less, but better" and "indifference towards people and the reality in which they live, is actually the one and only cardinal sin in design", touching these initial ideas in his ten principle for good design. Drawing from the principles of minimalism in traditional architecture and design, we can learn important lessons and breakthroughs.

The visual aesthetics of this design often catch our attention, leaving a lasting impression. As designers and developers, it's crucial to recognize that the visual elegance of an interface or product merely scratches the surface. There is much more beneath it. Hidden in this composed exterior,

© Diana Olynick 2024
D. Olynick, *Interfaceless*, Design Thinking, https://doi.org/10.1007/979-8-8688-0083-2_5

there might be a world of confusion for humans with missing required guidance or unintentional obstacles. What may seem like a design on the surface can sometimes become a maze for humans to navigate. The problem doesn't lie with minimalism itself, but rather with how we interpret and implement it (Figure 5-1).

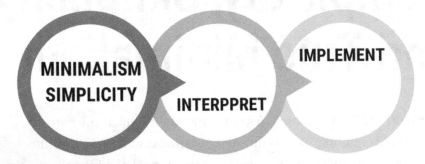

Figure 5-1. *Minimalism in Design*

Have you ever come across a product that appeared simple, yet ended up spending an amount of time trying to figure it out? Maybe you have encountered a modern website that left you frustrated because you couldn't find the specific information you needed? These examples illustrate that minimalism goes beyond reducing elements; it's about achieving clarity and purpose. This book focuses on the idea of "conscious design." True minimalism aligns perfectly with this philosophy—it's not about doing less. It's about doing what's right.

The ongoing debate between form and function has been around for ages. It revolves around finding the balance between beauty and practical usefulness. As we progress in this direction, we introduce another partner into this dance: consciousness. A genuine minimalist design is fully aware of human needs, its impact, and its consequences. It doesn't hide behind its beauty; instead, it leverages aesthetics as a tool to enhance utility and provide a joyful and meaningful experience.

You might be wondering why we are here in this chapter discussing minimalism anyway. What does it have to do with spatial computing? To aid with this understanding, let's set the stage by borrowing an explanation from the field of neuroscience. Our brain, a complex and remarkable organ, is constantly handling and analyzing a vast amount of information. Research in this field indicates that in visually intricate scenarios, the brain has to work harder to deduce and interpret information. The design approach to minimalism aims to decrease cognitive load, allowing for quicker decision-making and promoting a more relaxed mental state. This isn't just design—it's neuroscience-backed design. This is one of the reasons why a company like Apple, not only in physical products but also in operative systems and apps, uses this approach as a statement of their creations. Since we are aiming for experiences that are considerate of human's health and well-being, it is only natural to bring this design approach into consideration for the purpose of intentional experiences that support human wellness. Moreover, suffice to say, not all experiences could implement this particular design approach, but if you ever need to use it, you would know through this study its benefits and limitations.

As we explore the core of this chapter, I invite you to see minimalism from a distinct perspective. Let's examine it not as a design style, but as a philosophy—a thoughtful decision-making process and a dedication to enhancing human experience.

This chapter aims to challenge our beliefs and initiate a conversation about the essence of minimalism in design. By combining it with the power of AI and spatial computing, we can create designs that are not only visually captivating but also intuitively functional.

Together, let's join a conversation about the balance and the lines between complexity and simplicity as we unravel the mystery of true minimalism. May we discover new insights and perspectives that potentially might have previously escaped our consideration.

The Nuances of Minimalist Designs

In the field of design, minimalism has greatly influenced designers to create interfaces that are clean, streamlined, and free from elements. However, as we delve deeper into the world of computing, it becomes necessary for us to reassess our understanding of minimalism. In this era of interaction design, simplicity goes beyond reducing components. Contrary to common belief, minimalist designs are far from being simplistic.

Designing for minimalism in computing extends beyond aesthetics. It requires consideration of how virtual elements are positioned, sized, and moved in relation to the physical world. It involves creating interactions that feel natural and intuitive while taking into account the capabilities and limitations of our bodies. Additionally, it encompasses leveraging AI to customize interfaces based on human needs, preferences, and behaviors— that level of personalization, sometimes absent with traditional interfaces.

Oversimplifying design by trying to hide or downplay complexity is an important issue worth studying. Designers might reflect on this and acknowledge and embrace these intricacies, aiming to effectively manage complexity while still delivering exceptional human experiences. To strike the balance, it's important to find a ground between simplifying things too much which can confuse and frustrate humans and keeping certain complexities that can actually improve the human experience and presence.

Looking ahead, it's crucial to grasp this equilibrium when creating computing experiences that are both impactful and captivating.

Minimalism has roots that cross various fields, from literature to arts, from architecture to design. It has always been portrayed as a standard of elegance, projecting a sense of clutter-free, focused experiences or products. Studying some of the nuances (Figure 5-2) in minimalist design assists us in understanding not only its visual appeal but also its philosophical underpinnings, its relationship with efficiency, and potential challenges when applied out of a conscious perspective.

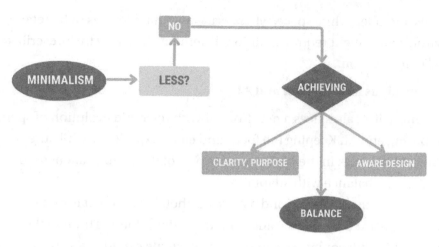

Figure 5-2. *The Nuances of Minimalist Design*

Here are some of those subtleties:

Minimalism As Presence of the Essential

What are your first thoughts when you think about minimalism? Commonly, this design style has been confused sometimes with boring, clinical spaces and lack of life in a few tonalities. True minimalism is about intentionally bringing front the elements that really matter, harnessing each design element to the point where nothing extra needs to be in the experience: every pixel, every interface, every space, every shadow, presenting their own intent and reason.

The Emotional Spectrum of Minimalism

Designing with unnecessary elements doesn't mean designing without life or interest. In fact, minimalist experiences can evoke deep emotions. A balanced and well-crafted story could make use of the right ambiance, typography, space, and color, invoking feelings from excitement to serenity.

Context Is Determinant

In a setting where a design might work fine, in another one, it might fall short. As an example, a website showcasing art, an online art gallery, can make use of a minimalist form and function approach using large

117

visuals and open white space, whereas a game that requires rich, detailed environments might require additional elements to satisfy the prescribed level of immersion.

Conscious Minimalism and AI

Minimalism also faces a new frontier with the rapid evolution of spatial computing and AI. Keeping the focus and clean experience while the AI algorithms work in the background is part of the main challenges to maintain the balance with adaptation.

True minimalism is beyond a mere aesthetic decision; it is rich in subtleties, backed by science and rooted in mindfulness. Through the study of this philosophy, we can potentially create experiences that are both visually delightful and deeply resonant, functional and considerate of human's wellness.

Overcoming the Traps of False Simplicity: Case Studies

In the evolving world of design, we often hear the advice to "keep it simple." However, there are challenges associated with this principle. One such challenge is what is called "false simplicity." I first heard this concept from Golden Krishna in one of his live speaking events in Stockholm. To understand the nuances of this roadblock and learn how to overcome it, we need to know its limitations and implications.

Understanding False Simplicity

False simplicity refers to the nature of a design that appears straightforward and user-friendly but may actually be oversimplified to the point where it becomes counterproductive. While designers may have noble intentions when aiming for modern applications or interfaces, they can unintentionally create confusion for humans, by omitting essential functionality or introducing hidden layers and menus. In reality, what seems simple at first glance might introduce more complexity.

Another example to reflect on is the use of skeuomorphism, which is the representation of an object or element through another one of real life. With the first computers, we saw the folder icon to be useful as it really offered the right cue to resemble the real-life action of storing documents. Over time, platforms began to use skeuomorphism more often, and it led to great breakthroughs. Not all assumptions were correct, and instead of offering quicker ways for humans to interact with apps, it actually did the opposite.

Now, let's explore a few real-world case studies that exemplify this concept and demonstrate how designers successfully navigated through the challenges posed by simplicity.

Case Study: Apple iOS 7

In line with our preceding discussion about skeuomorphism, up until 2013, Apple had made a leap in the redesign of the mobile interface. Moving away from skeuomorphism, due to the fact that, by then, people were more familiar with the use of the device and where to find most of the actions needed, a more minimalist approach was introduced. As per the feedback received, there was still confusion on where to find things, and some even found it too confusing despite the efforts to make the design simpler. Apple since has iterated the interface and icons continuing to integrate direct feedback and gaining a more balanced approach between human interaction and the minimalist approach that characterized them.

Case Study: Microsoft Windows 8

One year before Apple released its Apple iOS 7 in 2013, Microsoft released its Windows 8 version, featuring a new tile-based interface named "Metro." Early feedback showed the frustration coming from a start departure with a start button and traditional desktop buttons. The new design was more minimalist and clean, but for some, it was a case of prioritization of form over function.

As a result, Microsoft had to adjust the features and, based on feedback, reintroduce the start button by the release of Windows 8.1, implementing a more practical balance between minimalist and clean design and function.

In summary, in these practical cases, we can see how there is a fine line where minimalist and clean design can help experiences and humans interact more easily with systems, and even if in the near future some traditional UIs continue to be used, deeper reflections on potential outcomes can be realized early on.

Revisiting the Traditional Design Process

When oversimplification occurs, it is often a sign that a consideration aspect in the design might have been overlooked. Here, we take a look at the traditional design process (Figure 5-3) and how it is reimagined in light of the challenges posed by simplified designs for spatial computing.

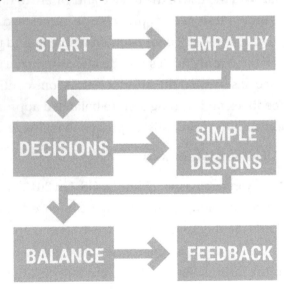

Figure 5-3. *Revisiting the Traditional Design Process*

A Brief Overview of the Traditional Design Process

Traditional design has been notoriously rooted in tangibility, designing and experimenting with the physical in mind, like textures or materials. An example of this is the fields of engineering and architecture, where the first outcomes of designs were produced in architectural blueprints, print layouts, and detailed design drawings. Stable environments have been part of this evolution, where designs have been created for unchanging environments. We can see this with the stagnant nature of print media, billboards, and even the early web pages. With the introduction of the Bauhaus principle in the 1920s, the application of design that is double fold: functional and appealing, was prioritized, with an emphasis on purpose. For instance, the classic chair designs of the era began to introduce more importance to human ergonomics trying to achieve a balance. During those times, early feedback occurred only post production, and it was incorporated back into future designs only after customer letters and reviews were submitted, processed, analyzed, and incorporated. The immediate, sometimes real-time, feedback that we have in this era was not common by then. The use of tools often also relied on a physical medium and manual performance, like pen, paper, and ruler, and over time we saw the presence of computer-aided tools for design software, such as Adobe Suite.

The inherent challenges of the traditional methods we have carried over the years are that the digital platforms of today and the spatial computing grounds are not static, but highly fluid and continuously evolving. The user interactivity also poses an interesting case for study, because unlike a chair or a print ad, human interactivity is different and many times unexpected in digital mediums.

These sets of complexities continue to change in our current times with data-driven designs that need to leverage information to become more responsive and adaptive while also being flexible and fast to iterate on.

The Hard Lessons from "False Simplicity"

Being aware of the potential conflict of oversimplification is part of accepting that cleaner, aesthetic designs do not necessarily equate to human-friendly or more intuitive interactions. Every design movement from art to architecture has undertaken the complexity of balancing the required function with a dynamic form. In architecture, for instance, we can remember the backlash caused by the introduction of the Brutalist style, with its raw simplicity and its consequent mirrored effects in the tech industry.

Some of the most important lessons learned not only by big companies but also by small ones, following suit, of this approach to design, are the avoidance of decisions favoring aesthetics at the expense of human experience and the high relevance of early feedback while navigating the lines between simple designs and functional products. With that understanding and the awareness gained through the mistakes of other companies, we can gather some good practices for spatial computing and establish principles that aim to protect and empathize with humans on deeper levels.

Some of the transfer of the regular design methods can include an in-depth study of what traditional design has called "user journey mapping" that for spatial computing can be approached from a more holistic view. This is similar to the comparison between the role of the individual when watching a movie and when entering the movie stage in a VR headset. When an individual is watching the movie, there is a passive role of not participating in any of the scenes or affecting the story in any way, for what the typical "user journey" had some application, but when entering the movie environment in a VR headset, there is no absolute control anymore of the direction that the human might consider or how to engage with it. For this reason, this human journey needs to be approached integrally and multidimensionally, not linearly.

Beyond the visual interface elements, the entire experience with response times, sounds, haptic feedback, etc., also needs to be assessed against the "false simplicity" test, balancing innovation with familiarity.

Design Funnel Reimagined

Immersive Requirement Gathering

In a traditional design model, design has a requirement gathering in the format of regular stakeholder meetings, surveys and interviews, preliminary research, and market analysis, all with its own reason and purpose for the medium. For spatial computing, we see a potential for immersive requirement gathering, using methods such as participatory design meetings performed in 3D, for example, in a virtual design studio. Since there is an option now to experience real-world context in the simulated environment, it is possible to capture the subtleties of an app developed for spatial computing. To some extent, the equivalent of the same actions spans participatory design sessions in simulated environments to define requirements collaboratively, using real-world context to be able to capture the nuances of the environment in which the solution will operate, as well as using emotion mapping to study the emotional responses that the immersive setting triggers, aiding in getting a deeper understanding of the human needs.

Multidimensional Conceptualization

The activities of brainstorming, sketching, wireframing, and mood boards are performed using a variety of 2D tools. In 3D design, some of these tools have begun their own evolution toward creating plug-ins and 3D capabilities. For spatial computing, these tasks become multidimensional, with ideation processes performed in 3D, making use of XR tools to iterate on concepts in real time, generating spatial storyboards, considering the movements and interactions in space, along with using collaborative virtual methods to bring together cross-functional teams to brainstorm and iterate.

Conscious Design

At this point in the traditional design process, typically the activities span the creation of mock-ups, prototypes, and design reviews. In this stage for spatial computing, the application of a core aspect of conscious design comes into play as this is where decisions for human comfort, safety, ergonomics, and intuitive interactions take place. With a human centricity approach, inclusion and accessibility are also determined here to ensure everyone can navigate and interact safely, using feedback loops and incorporating mechanisms within the design to access continuous data. Since all of these processes ideally should not be created and tested in a flat screen, it is consequent that the prototypes and design reviews created here happen in the simulated immersive setting for the intended design. For this purpose, one of the most widely used apps available is ShapesXR (Figure 5-4), a simulation 3D platform where teams can meet and create prototypes ready to be transferred for further development.

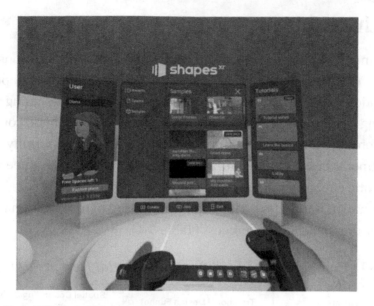

Figure 5-4. *ShapesXR Interface*

Immersive Testing

Activities such as usability testing or A/B testing together with feedback iteration from the traditional standards could get translated for spatial computing as immersive simulations, testing designs not on 2D screens, but in the real space where the experience would take place. Human experience (HX) playtests, where individuals can interact with the design while obtaining nonquantitative and preliminary feedback, are another aspect to incorporate in this conceptualization phase for spatial computing, along with physiological measurements, such as the use of biometric sensors to capture real-time data on the emotional and physiological responses during the test. Apps like ShapesXR mentioned earlier have recently indicated new capabilities to test gestures like gaze and pinch, indicating that the direction of the full design process for XR more and more goes in the direction of full immersion.

Adaptive Implementation

Development, quality assurance, and deployment of 2D applications are processes that, in spatial computing, would look like: real-time adaptive modifications, integrations with other digital ecosystems, designing and producing elements that adjust based on human's environment, context, and preferences. For spatial computing, in this stage, the continuity of adjustments based on ongoing feedback is essential to guarantee a relevant and effective design functionality.

To summarize, let's take a look at a comparison of the traditional design vs. the spatial design process (Table 5-1).

Table 5-1. *Comparison of Traditional vs. Spatial Design Funnels*

Phases	Traditional Design Funnel	Spatial Computing Design Funnel
Requirement Gathering	- Stakeholder Meeting - Human Surveys and Interviews - Market Analysis	- Immersive Workshops using VR/AR - Human Experience Journeys in 3D environments - Gathering spatial interactions and feedback
Conceptualization	- Brainstorming - Sketching and Wireframing - Mood Boards	- Ideation in VR/AR spaces - 3D Prototyping - Layered Experiences Drafting
Design	- Mockups - Prototyping - Design Reviews	- Mindful 3D Model Creation - Interface-less Design - Integration of Real and Virtual Elements
Testing	- Usability Testing - A/B Testing - Feedback Iteration	- Human Testing in Immersive Environments - Real-time Feedback Collection in VR/AR - Iterative Design based on Spatial Feedback
Implementation	- Development - Quality Assurance (QA) - Deployment	- Deployment in VR/AR Platforms - Real-time Adaptive Modifications - Integration with Other Digital Ecosystems

The Power of AI in Elevating Minimalist Experiences

At its core, minimalism involves distilling design down to its essential elements, eliminating excesses and allowing function to drive form. With its capabilities, AI is custom made for enhancing this principle. Given the processing of vast amounts of data to identify patterns and behaviors, AI empowers designs to comprehend human context in time. This enables interfaces to remain visually streamlined while dynamically catering to the individual's needs.

AI has the potential to improve human experiences by anticipating their actions and providing guidance through minimal interfaces and processes. This ensures a seamless journey without overwhelming the interface.

One of the criticisms often raised against minimalism is its lack of customization. However, with AI we can introduce minimalist designs that adapt to human's preferences and habits. The result is an interface that is specifically tailored to each individual achieving a blend between universal aesthetics and personalized functionality.

The advancements of AI have greatly influenced the evolution of minimalism. In the exploration of the conflict between reduction and function, we now discover a concept called dynamic minimalism. This approach goes beyond simplicity and embraces designs that can adapt and change based on human needs and contexts (Figure 5-5).

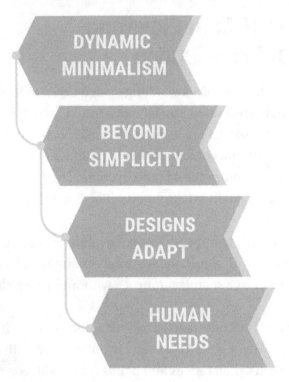

Figure 5-5. *The Power of AI in Minimalist Experiences*

To illustrate this, let's consider a music streaming app. A traditional minimalist design would typically offer an interface with buttons like play, pause, and next. Conversely, with an AI-driven dynamic minimalist design, the app would intelligently adjust its interface based on how humans interact with it. For instance, if a user frequently shuffles songs or creates playlists, these options could be prominently displayed during times like Friday evenings. This optimization enhances both functionality and aesthetics.

In Appendix A, you can find a tool to help you begin an assessment of your experience against the minimalist principles.

The Road Ahead

Currently, we find ourselves at a juncture where the worlds of AI and design principles are converging, leading us into a new era. This era transcends appeal and delves deep into human-centric intuition, taking minimalism to new heights.

Let's reflect on this. Is it not the true essence of minimalism in design not in reducing what we see but in amplifying what we experience?

As we blend the power of AI with our insights, we discover that the answer to this question lies in designs that truly grasp our essence, evolve alongside us, and infuse every interaction with meaning. As designers and technologists, our challenge and opportunity is to embrace this amalgamation to create experiences that appear simple on the surface but hold depth within.

AI is no longer an addition to the design narrative; it is becoming its foundation. By integrating AI's predictive, adaptive, and analytical capabilities with the elegance and functionality of minimalism, we hold the potential to redefine human experiences. In doing so, we will establish standards for designs that transcend what can be seen or touched—they will be truly felt at a profound level.

Summary: Complexity, Simplicity, and True Minimalism

In this chapter, we touched on the equilibrium between aesthetics and functionality using a minimalist design approach, emphasizing the potential consequences of oversimplifications. Going over the nuances of minimalist designs, we discussed the historical context, underlying philosophies, and the spatial computing unique stance at the transition from 2D screens to 2D spatial environments in the context of clean designs. We also studied some case studies as examples of the traps of false simplicity and how companies adjust to new interactions based on feedback, presenting a rather preventative approach. Finally, we made a comparison between traditional design and spatial computing design to understand how these processes can be equated and best practices for every stage.

Resources

You can refer to Appendix A, Table A-3, to study the Design Checklist for Minimalist Experiences.

CHAPTER 6

A Deep Dive into Interfaceless Environments

In this chapter, we discuss interfaceless environments and how they can potentially get from conception to establishment, discussing the requirements for it. As humans shift from using their daily devices, like smartphones, tablets, and laptops, to spatial computing, we begin to see how the human experience transforms from traditional interfaces to no interfaces.

This shift implies a transformation in the evolution of interaction that began with punch cards to input commands through devices and has evolved to voice commands and gestures, representing the next frontier of human-computer interactions. With AI as the underpinning force, especially deep learning, interfaceless experiences are getting closer to a complete frictionless execution.

As we move from a fundamental basis for design using conscious principles and clean approaches without oversimplifications, we begin to dig deeper into the symbiosis of AI and spatial computing, setting the stage for new ways to communicate with machines, using new devices, sensors, and evolved hardware that extend our digital experience into our physical world.

D. Olynick, *Interfaceless*, Design Thinking, https://doi.org/10.1007/979-8-8688-0083-2_6

Ambient intelligence is presented as the pinnacle of the new approach to immersive creations, using devices that understand and respond to human presence without the traditional human input, making a revolution in the paradigm shift we have had so far: humans don't adapt to technology, but technology adapts to humans (Figure 6-1).

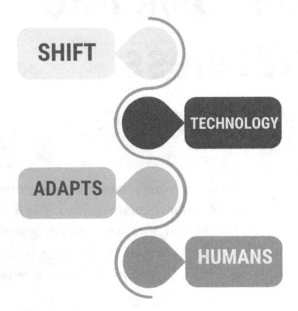

Figure 6-1. *Interfaceless Environments*

The Holistic Ecosystem: AI, ML, DL, and Physical Devices

When we talk about an "ecosystem," we are referring to a network where the collective impact is more significant than the individual components. In the technological field, especially as we move toward interfaces that don't require any interaction, the way artificial intelligence (AI), machine learning (ML), deep learning (DL), and tangible devices interact is changing our approach. What really defines this ecosystem as a whole? Why is it important for our advancement in computing?

To truly grasp the concept of interface design, it's crucial to have an understanding of its fundamental elements: artificial intelligence (AI), machine learning (ML), deep learning (DL), and physical computing. Let's start by drawing a parallel. In layman's terms, AI is the universe, ML is a galaxy within, and DL is a star system in that galaxy. These technologies work together (Figure 6-2) harmoniously intertwining to create an environment where intuitive and innovative interactions can thrive.

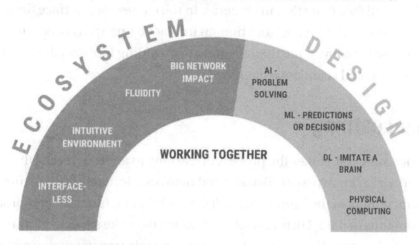

Figure 6-2. Ecosystem Design

Artificial Intelligence

Artificial intelligence (AI) serves as the overarching concept that encompasses machines or computers capable of emulating functions akin to the mind. This includes problem solving, learning, and adapting. Examples of this include rule-based systems, decision trees, and expert systems. In the context of interface design, AI plays an important role in enabling systems to interpret complex data, learn from it, and make informed decisions. This ultimately leads to interactions that rely less on traditional interfaces.

Machine Learning

Within the field of AI lies machine learning (ML), which is a branch of AI that empowers systems to learn from data and enhance their performance without programming. ML models are trained using datasets, allowing them to make predictions or decisions without being programmed for each task at hand. Examples of this include voice recognition in smart speakers and face detection in cameras. In the context of interface design, ML allows systems to learn from human interaction patterns over time. As a result, they can fine-tune their responses, providing individuals with a personalized and seamless experience.

Deep Learning

Deep learning (DL) takes the process of learning to another level. DL networks, also known as artificial neural networks, imitate the structure and functioning of the human brain. This enables machines to learn from vast amounts of data. DL is crucial in handling data like speech, gestures, and even thoughts. Examples of this are image style transfer where a photo is rendered in that particular style. In spatial computing, these capabilities can be translated as semantic scene understanding, real-time object recognition, and the generation of better overlays. These capabilities are becoming increasingly important as we move toward intuitive ways of interacting through interface design.

Physical Computing

Physical computing is another component in this ecosystem. It involves hardware that captures, processes, and delivers spatial experiences, capable of responding to their surroundings. These systems use cameras, accelerometers, gyroscopes, LiDAR for environment scanning, specialized chips for AI operations, and output devices like mixed reality headsets or holographic displays. Physical computing works with interface design by bridging the gap between the digital world of AI, ML, and DL and our physical reality.

As in any system or ecosystem, a feedback loop is present. It analyzes how sensors provide data, then ML/DL processes it, and the physical devices display the experience as a result of the interaction of these systems. Here, there is a compelling significance of real-time processing capabilities due to the requirement for instant data management to guarantee a seamless experience. An example of this is gesture control using hand tracking, where a camera captures hand movements, the neural network processes and analyzes the gesture, and the system consequently reacts based on the inputs and surrounding conditions.

As you might estimate, some of the challenges of this architecture involve the handling and storing of massive amounts of data that require more advanced computing systems and hardware capable of handling the loads and processing, as well as cloud services that effectively support these types of tasks.

When we consider these technologies together, they create an ecosystem that enables interface experiences to exist. AI, ML, and DL provide cognition and learning capabilities, while physical computing translates these cognitions into real-world actions. This completes the loop of interaction without relying on interfaces.

This ecosystem is characterized by its fluidity and dynamism where each technology complements and enhances the others.

As progress continues in all these domains, we can anticipate a strengthening of this connection, which will further improve the abilities and expansiveness of interface-free design.

Moving Beyond Traditional Computing

The significance of this interconnected ecosystem is not solely reliant on algorithms or advanced gadgets; it lies in the experiences they provide. In the past, computing was mainly reactive. You would input a command and the system would respond accordingly. However, today's approach is predictive and proactive. Devices no longer wait for instructions; they anticipate our needs, understand contexts, and offer solutions even before we realize we need them.

Democratizing Knowledge Through AI

An overlooked but crucial aspect of the AI, ML, and DL device ecosystem is its potential to make expertise available to all. For example, DL models can now analyze images with precision that rivals or surpasses trained radiologists. When integrated into handheld devices or specialized equipment, these models offer expert insights to nonspecialists as well. This bridges knowledge gaps and ensures that this expertise becomes universally available.

The Exciting Possibilities and Unexplored Frontiers

While the current advancements are already remarkable, we're only scratching the surface of what's possible. With quantum computing making progress, we'll be able to process larger datasets in real time and amplify the capabilities of AI, ML, and DL exponentially. Moreover, physical devices are continually becoming smaller and more efficient—so much so that they will seamlessly blend into our surroundings and make it nearly impossible to distinguish between physical surroundings.

Emerging Challenges and Ethical Considerations

Nevertheless, this journey is not without its challenges. As machines gain autonomy in decision-making processes, issues regarding privacy protection and security measures for data handling become ethical concerns that need addressing.

Who should be held accountable if an AI-powered medical device gives a diagnosis? How can we make sure that the algorithms behind our experiences are fair and unbiased? These questions go beyond consideration.

The Role of Sensors and Hardware in Spatial Computing

Sensors and hardware are the elements that allow us to engage with the world around us (Figure 6-3). As we navigate through our lives, sensors integrated into our devices and environment continuously collect information about both our surroundings and ourselves. This data is then analyzed by intelligence systems seamlessly utilizing it to provide us with a user experience that feels effortless and organic.

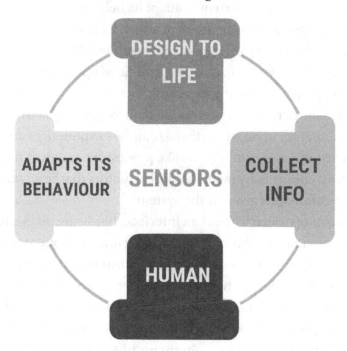

Figure 6-3. *The Role of Sensors and Hardware in Spatial Computing*

Sensors actively contribute to bringing interface design to life. From touch sensors in smartphones to LiDAR sensors in vehicles, these components capture data points. Subsequently, this data is processed by AI algorithms empowering the system to comprehend user needs and effectively adapt to changes and facilitate interactions.

Voice assistants, like Alexa from Amazon and Google Home, rely on microphones which are a type of sensor to capture the commands we give using our voices. On the other hand, smartwatches and fitness trackers use sensors to keep track of our physical activities and health data. For instance, gesture recognition systems used in virtual reality (VR) or augmented reality (AR) applications rely on motion or optical sensors to interpret how we move. In each of these cases AI, ML, or DL is used to process the data collected by the sensors and turn it into actions.

Additionally, sensors can provide information about the human's surroundings, allowing the system to adapt its behavior accordingly. For example, light sensors can help a system adjust its display brightness based on how bright or dark it is in the environment. Similarly, proximity sensors can enable a system to change its mode of operation depending on whether there is an object or a user nearby.

While sensors play a role in gathering data for these systems, hardware forms the foundation upon which these seamless experiences are built. Hardware encompasses components like processors, memory modules, power sources, connectivity modules, and actuators that respond physically to commands given by the system.

In the realm of design without an interface, hardware plays a role as the foundation that enables the functioning and implementation of AI, ML, and DL algorithms. As these algorithms become intricate, the requirement for effective hardware has soared. This necessity has prompted the creation of hardware, such as Graphics Processing Units (GPUs), Tensor Processing Units (TPUs), and Field Programmable Gate Arrays (FPGAs), to handle the requirements of AI tasks.

Understanding Sensors and Input Devices
Depth Cameras

In the most basic sense, depth cameras are devices that capture images and detect the distance that exists between the camera itself and the subject/object.

The system that allows these devices to measure depth is analogous to the echolocation system used by bats, emitting a series of high pitch sounds. Once the sound hits an object, it produces an echo, making their detection abilities to calculate the time it takes between emitting the sound and receiving back the echo, determining like this the actual distance to the object. Even beyond just distance, bats can also perceive the frequency, intensity, and quality of the echo, determining the shape, size, and even the texture of objects in proximity.

The depth cameras leverage a similar system sending out light signals (often in the infrared spectrum), reflecting off from objects in the path, reading the returning light signals, and calculating the distance to objects to be able to create an accurate depth map of the scene. This is called the Time-of-Flight (ToF) principle, under which these types of ToF cameras work.

Depth cameras need an infrared projector to work, which is a component that emits light patterns or signals. It also needs an infrared camera that captures the reflected light, helping with the depth calculations, as well as an RGB camera, which is the standard camera module used to produce regular images, which often works together with infrared systems.

Firstly, we can find depth cameras in AR apps that need to understand real-world surfaces so that digital objects are accurately placed in the virtual-real world. Secondly, we will see these cameras working for gesture recognition, allowing devices to read and interpret human gestures, replacing regular interface commands, and, finally, for 3D scanning purposes to create digital 3D models of real-world objects.

The reason why devices use these types of cameras is because of their precision level, featuring high accuracy in measuring distances (highly important for spatial computing), as well as safety, since the infrared light is invisible to the human eye, unlike other scanning systems.

It's of importance to note that depending on their sensors, to read accurately, depth cameras need to have decent lighting conditions and be at the range of distance minimums and maximums to work properly. This is why some of the latest head-mounted devices (HMDs) in the market advise wearing them in good lighting conditions to ensure safety and for the sensors to read properly the digital objects or scenes.

As technology evolves, depth cameras are becoming smaller in size and greater in depth resolution, facilitating the integration in mobile devices and wearables.

LiDAR (Light Detection and Ranging)

The general mechanism under which LiDAR systems work is very similar to the depth cameras explained earlier. They work by means of pulsed laser light to measure distances. In LiDAR systems, we can also find the Continuous Wave (CW) LiDAR, which uses a continuous beam of light to gauge distances based on beam shifts of the reflected light.

The key components of a LiDAR system are a laser, which emits the light pulse; a scanner, which moves the laser beam in different directions to capture the surrounding space; photodetectors, which receive the reflected light pulse; and GPS (Global Positioning System) and IMU (Inertial Measurement Units), which help in positioning and orienting the LiDAR system as a whole, especially in systems that require airborne LiDAR.

We can see some technologies applying LiDAR systems, such as in environmental mapping for flood modeling, coastline management, and forestry studies, among others, as well as in autonomous vehicles, reading navigation, lane marking, and object detection. Specifically, spatial computing uses LiDAR systems to enhance the immersion experience by accurately understanding and mapping real-time world surroundings.

When comparing LiDAR systems with traditional cameras, we can see that LiDAR scanners present higher precision at mapping out more intricate details, relevant for driverless vehicles and geospatial studies, as an example. Also, LiDAR systems are advantageous at working more effectively in more challenging conditions like darkness, rain, or fog.

IMUs (Inertial Measurement Units)

Using gyroscopes, accelerometers, and even sometimes magnetometers, IMUs are used to determine the body's specific angular rates and forces. Let's take a closer look at those components.

Gyroscopes measure the rate of rotation around specific axes in a time frame, while magnetometers, which are not always integrated in all IMUs, measure the direction and strength of the magnetic field. Since the main function of IMUs is to measure the movements of an object, accelerometers in these devices are integrated to measure the changes in velocity along specific axes.

IMUs are used in spatial computing to determine the orientation and movement of the devices. For example, their readings can determine if the device is rotated, tilted, or moving in a specific direction. They also help in stabilization, which, as you might presume, is essential in spatial computing applications, helping balance or stabilize the visual experience, making sure the head movements smoothly correspond to what is seen or rendered. Spatial computing also utilizes tracking systems that are essential in understanding when an object or body is moving and determining through predictive models its accurate location.

Eye Tracking Systems

Eye tracking systems use sensors to gather data related to the direction of gaze, reading the pupil's position. It measures the movements of the eyes and their blink patterns.

These systems use infrared lights and cameras to record eye movements. Think of the infrared lights as a sort of flashlight that emits a special light on your eyes and the camera as if someone was trying to observe where you are looking, by means of observing the light's reflection.

Eye tracking systems use software that adjusts the eye tracker to the individual to make sure it is accurate and uses advanced data processing algorithms that interpret the raw data from the cameras.

As evident, these systems are used in spatial computing, especially the latest HMDs in the market, to create interactive experiences where the content can change in relation to the direction and angle to where the individual is looking. These systems, in particular, serve as an interaction alternative for individuals with disabilities, facilitating virtual navigation with their eyes.

Designers or creators might find advantages in the data generated by eye tracking systems, to understand what virtual spaces are more enjoyable and to iterate designs based on these evaluations, as well as combined with AI capabilities, enabling models to predict what is an individual's intention to do next in a spatial environment.

Understanding Rendering and Displays

OLED (Organic Light-Emitting Diodes)

As per their name, OLEDs are devices using emissive electroluminescent layers of an organic compound (organic molecules or polymers), and they emit light when electricity is applied. The other component of these systems is electrodes (usually two, an anode and a cathode), which are responsible for conducting the current into the organic layers. Often made of glass, foil, or clear plastic, OLEDs use a substrate as their support mechanism.

OLEDs are capable of delivering high contrast ratios producing pure blacks, making them essential for immersive spatial computing applications. They are used for reduction of motion blur in rapid movements/scenes and are often found in the most modern HMDs due to their flexibility (for foldable displays), transparency (in mixed reality applications where the digital and physical blend), and thinness, to reduce weight for wearables.

MicroLED (Micro Light-Emitting Diodes)

MicroLEDs are usually less than 100 micrometers while capable of higher resolutions. They don't require backlights, producing their own light and utilizing an array or grid collection that forms a full display. In spatial computing, MicroLEDs are used to achieve higher levels of brightness while reducing power consumption, which in turn allows for longer runtime experiences.

Recent advancements of these displays have allowed for more integrated circuits, producing brighter, smarter, and more compact displays.

Waveguide Optics

Directing light through a material in a controlled fashion, waveguide optics allow mixed reality devices to overlay digital images onto the real world without obstructing the individual's view. They work under the principles of total internal reflection and gratings or diffractive elements. The operational system is based on tiny structures which have the function of redirecting the trapped light out of the waveguide into the individual's eyes, guiding the light through a reduced medium, reflecting off the boundaries.

In spatial computing, we often see the use of waveguide optics in experiences using holographic displays. They often integrate with other systems like sensors to create dynamic, responsive experiences, detecting the individual's surroundings and adjusting the overlays respectively, as well as displays like LEDs or lasers.

Recent advancements in this field have allowed the use of nanotechnology, leveraging nanostructures, especially to improve light extraction while reducing unwanted artifacts.

The most relevant advantage in HMDs is the reduction of weight, which makes them look and feel sleek and light, as with the recent Vision Pro spatial computing device announced by Apple.

Projection-Based Displays

Suggested by their name, these displays' function is to project images or videos onto surfaces like transparent screens, walls, or even in the air. They work using a light source like an LED or laser, making the light modulated to create the rendered images on the surface. Other components of them are DLP (Digital Light Processing), which uses small mirrors that move catching the light and displaying colors and images, and LCOS (Liquid Crystal on Silicon), working somewhat as a liquid crystal display but reflecting light rather than passing it through.

It is important to note that some HMDs use projection-based methods to beam images directly into the individual's eyes, and we often see them on walls or tables that react at the direct interaction with our touch. They usually are integrated with depth cameras and sensors to read where a person or object is, facilitating surfaces for "touch-sensitive" applications.

Other Infrastructure and Platforms

The following is a preliminary, non-exhaustive list of components for the interfaceless ecosystem.

AI Algorithm Stack

- Sensory perception algorithms for computer vision such as Convolutional Neural Networks (CNN) and Generative Adversarial Networks (GANs)

- Auditory processing for voice and sound recognition including text-to-speech and speech-to-text algorithms

- Natural Language Processing (NLP) to understand written or spoken language, with algorithms such as transformer architectures GPT and BERT

- Environmental context understanding with sensor fusion algorithms to combine data from sensors like cameras, microphones, and gyroscopes, localization, and mapping used in Simultaneous Localization and Mapping (SLAM), for example, used in augmented reality applications

- Kinematic and gesture recognition with motion tracking to predict human motion and pose estimation to detect gestures and body posture in real time

- Behavioral and predictive analysis with modules of reinforcement learning that allows the system to learn sequences of actions adapting to human needs and human behavior prediction with Recurrent Neural Networks (RNNs) or Long Short-Term Memory (LSTM)

- Dynamic content generation with adaptive rendering using AI-powered rendering techniques for optimization and procedural generation algorithms to create content in real time

- Feedback systems with auditory capabilities to offer real-time cues or responses and haptic feedback algorithms to provide tactile responses based on human interactions

- Cognitive and emotional analysis with systems that understand where human attention lies in the spatial context as well as the sensorial data that interprets human emotions from text, visual, and auditory inputs

- Memory and knowledge graphs using knowledge representation with frameworks and algorithms to recall, store, and use knowledge and semantic networks that mimic human semantic memory

- Optimization and efficiency for pruning and quantization (techniques to optimize AI model size without compromising its performance) and Neural Architecture Search (NAS) to automate the design of machine learning algorithms

- Privacy and security mechanisms with encryption and secure computation for sensitive data in spatial computing and differential privacy to ensure data security

Processing Units

- Graphics Processing Unit (GPU) for rendering graphics in real time

- Central Processing Unit (CPU) for the task management processes

Display Systems

- Head-mounted displays for mixed reality experiences that blend the physical and virtual spaces

Tracking Systems

- Magnetic tracking to detect changes in the magnetic field for orientation and position

- Optical tracking using cameras to track markers or natural environment features

- Inertial Measurement Units (IMUs) to track orientation through gyroscopes and accelerometers

Software

- Computer vision to interpret and make decisions based on data

- Physics engines like Unity or Unreal for simulations of physics

- Mapping and location to create and update the environment and human's localization in space

Connectivity

- Bluetooth, Wi-Fi, and 5G for cloud processing and near-field communication (NFC) for close-range interactions

Storage

- RAM and Solid-State Drives (SSD) for software, maps, and other data, cloud services, and computing

Case Study: Apple's Vision Pro (Figure 6-4) and Spatial Computing

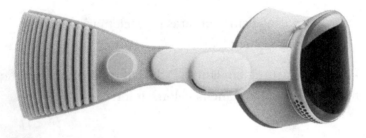

Figure 6-4. *Apple Vision Pro (Source: Apple)*

In summer 2023, during its WWDC (Worldwide Developers Conference), Apple released its own head-mounted device for spatial computing: Vision Pro.

The Vision Pro envisions a future where our surroundings transform into canvases creating an immersive multiscreen ecosystem. This innovative system provides users with a groundbreaking experience, allowing them to freely adjust, move, and resize elements in their environments. It's like UI design practices we're already familiar with but taken to the next level. The Vision Pro environment offers a progressive approach to design by seamlessly integrating digital information with our physical space blurring the lines between the two.

As part of its technical innovations, the device harnesses cutting-edge technologies, making use of AI, sensors, high-definition displays, contextual awareness, gesture recognition, voice commands, and gaze tracking. One of the special aspects of this device is the no use of hand controllers as typically happened in the past with other head-mounted devices. This gives us a hint to the type of experiences a company like Apple is envisioning to create—experiences that are as real and authentic to our daily lives as possible.

One of the standout features is the "meeting mode" in Apple Vision Pro. It facilitates remote collaborations, shared content, chat, and note taking—each designed specifically for their intended purpose to minimize distractions.

Additionally, individuals have the flexibility to create and save custom templates according to their needs. This human-centric approach demonstrates how spatial computing emphasizes adaptability and personalization.

Vision Pro's dynamic workspaces also showcase the fluidity and customization that can be achieved within this ecosystem. By combining interactions that behave responsively and intelligently, adapting to human interactions, it empowers individuals to truly make these virtual environments their own.

With its interaction between natural interactions and our physical space, Vision Pro enters the world of spatial computing by seamlessly blending digital elements into our real-world surroundings.

Designing for Vision Pro: A Blend of Old and New

One of the reflection factors that one might wonder is why Apple would design a device with strong capabilities for interfaceless design but focus a good part of their effort in the interactions with the traditional 2D content screens. One reason for this might be the natural transition that humans need to go through once adopted to other methods of interaction. It is expected that due to its capabilities, the experiences to be created for it will increasingly leverage the possibilities toward interfaceless experiences.

The dilemma of choosing between designing within the Vision Pro ecosystem and sticking to Android systems is quite common within new designers and aspiring developers. Looking ahead, it seems that a combination of both approaches will be the way to go, as different studios creating world-class experiences would aim to bring their content to different audiences from different platforms. This approach mirrors how mobile and smartwatch designs are currently refined through contextual processes. It's likely that Vision Pro designs will undergo a similar evolution.

AI and Predictive Behaviors

After exploring the captivating world of computing through Apple's Vision Pro, it becomes clear that interfaceless environments are not about getting rid of screens but rather about completely redefining how we interact. As we dive into this frontier, artificial intelligence acts as our guiding compass, predicting and facilitating our every move. The combination of computing and AI leads to predictive behaviors—AI's ability to foresee things that enhance our spatial experience (Figure 6-5).

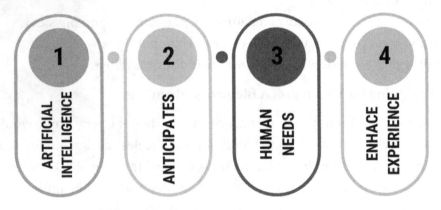

Figure 6-5. *AI and Predictive Behaviors*

Let's imagine stepping into an augmented space. As you glance around, the environment responds not reactively but proactively to your gaze. For example, if you find yourself in a mixed reality workspace and your gaze lingers on a spot, AI might predict that you want to add something and offer relevant tools or suggestions. In this scenario, AI goes beyond reaction; it anticipates your needs.

This anticipation is built upon the wealth of data that AI processes. Every gesture captured by Vision Pro, every prolonged gaze, or quick dismissal—it all contributes to AI learning from these interactions and tailoring the computing experience to become more intuitive with each session.

Unlike user interfaces where actions are primarily reactive (clicking an icon opens an application), the leap into predictive interfaces changes the game entirely.

When using Vision Pro and spatial computing, the level of interactivity is improved by incorporating layers of predictability. Imagine being in a meeting and needing to find a tool or function. Of having to search through menus, the AI, based on your actions, anticipates the tool you're probably looking for. This saves time and makes the overall experience more seamless.

Computational Methods in Spatial Computing
Scene Understanding

In mixed reality uses, we can see the application of what is called SLAM (Simultaneous Localization and Mapping) system. For the device to be able to update a map of an unknown surrounding while simultaneously tracking the subject's location within it, a computational model is used to aid with this construction (Figure 6-6). The basic principles for this to work are localization, mapping, landmarks, and features, and each ultimately aims to create an accurate representation of the environment using points of reference. Besides HMDs, we can see SLAM models in robotic navigation, for example, ground robots or drones. They are usually integrated with depth cameras, LiDAR, and IMUs, providing additional data about the environment, increasing accuracy.

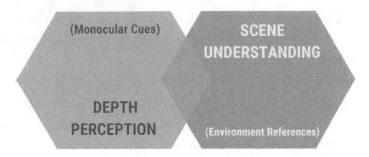

Figure 6-6. *Scene Understanding Relationship with Depth Perception*

Recent advancements of these systems are linked to the utilization of deep learning models, such as neural networks specifically trained for SLAM, to increase precision and accuracy while reducing computational intensity.

Depth Perception and Occlusion

Depth perception refers to the ability to gauge spatial relationships and distances between bodies or objects, reading and understanding how far everything is located. Occlusion is related to the visual blocking that one object can present in relation to the other, rendering them in front or behind each other.

The basic principles for depth perception and occlusion are monocular cues, binocular cues, and occlusion. Think of a drawing, for example, if you see train tracks getting closer together as they move further away, this would produce the visual effect of a longer distance. These are called monocular cues or depth cues available from the image in one eye like shading and perspective. Now, let's do a more dynamic exercise to understand binocular cues. Hold your index finger in front of your nose and close one of your eyes. Now, close that eye and look at the finger through the other eye. In this exercise, the finger seems to be moving because each eye is looking at it from a different angle. This is why these cues are called "binocular" as they use both eyes.

Integrated with depth cameras, LiDAR, and eye tracking systems, depth perception can be improved, and data can be used to determine object or body depth and positioning.

As with SLAM systems, using neural networks can be leveraged for predicting depth maps which can also decrease the use of multiple sensors.

Interaction Paradigms in Spatial Computing

Figure 6-7 illustrates three interaction paradigms we'll be exploring in spatial computing.

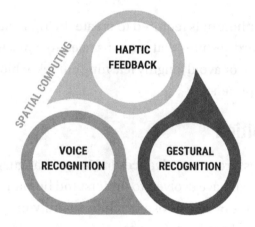

Figure 6-7. *Interaction Paradigms in Spatial Computing*

Gestural Recognition

In the latest HMDs, we see more often the use of gestures, thanks to the capabilities of computerized systems to read and interpret them. Whether identifying face movements or hand signs, today's advanced spatial computing devices are able to read those inputs as commands and translate them into data outputs to trigger other consecutive tasks.

The basic components of gesture recognition include skeletal tracking, which uses depth cameras to identify in real time the human skeleton; fingertip recognition, which tracks the fingers reading detailed hand interactions; and neural network–based gesture classifiers, as you might suspect, using AI to learn and recognize different movements and gestures. They integrate with infrared sensors and depth cameras to map the movement and shape of the hands and fingers.

Gestural recognition is one of the central aspects of interfaceless designs, as they offer a more natural way to perform movements or gestures than clicking buttons or using controllers, eliminating their use altogether, emulating more closely the interactions as they happen in our everyday life.

On a particular note, it is required to create the right balance on the universal or standard gestures that humans need to typically be familiar with, so as to reduce or avoid lengthy learning curves, which can hinder the individual's experience.

Voice Recognition

Voice recognition is a result of advances in Natural Language Processing (NLP) systems, which have evolved to understand human speech in this natural form. It works by means of a machine identifying, processing, and responding to natural spoken language.

They feature keyword spotting techniques and speech-to-text conversion, detecting specific words or phrases and understanding and turning them into written text. In spatial computing, they allow selecting, navigating, and controlling digital spaces without physical inputs or touch. A clear example of this system is the rise of virtual assistants, powered with AI holding a simulated human conversation using natural speech.

Interfaceless designs leverage the ability of the most advanced voice recognition models to introduce a hands-free experience, fostering more inclusivity in supporting individuals with dexterity limitations or with

154

mobility issues and facilitating the concept of universal interfaces, using voice as a common medium, reducing literacy issues, and mirroring the fluidity of real human-to-human speech.

Haptic Feedback

Used to simulate the sensation of touch, haptic feedback technology uses vibrations, forces, or motions, increasing the sense of immersion in the experience.

Force feedback is one of its components and uses a resistive vector to simulate the feeling of simply holding or touching objects, feeling a pushback, as an example when trying to lift an object. Vibration-based feedback sends a series of motions to alert or indicate an event, and ultrasonic haptics, instead, uses sound waves without any direct contact on the skin, aiming to create realistic sensations. They are used in object interactions to emulate their texture, weight, and shapes, as well as in navigation cues.

In terms of inclusivity, haptic feedback works well to support individuals with auditory or visual impairment, allowing them to interpret the experience with additional enhanced sensory options.

In mixed reality devices like Vision Pro, haptic feedback could be achieved, for example, by using external gadgets as haptic feedback gloves or even finger hardware, where contextual awareness and gesture control seemingly would work together to make the experience even more real through touch simulations.

From 3D Interfaces to Interfaceless

3D Interface (UI) Design

Since there are many books already discussing the traditional UI interfaces, let's begin by discussing the rise of 3D interfaces. With the notable improvements from wearable devices, the traditional interfaces started to be rethought by some designers in the 1960s, particularly with Morton Heilig's works with the Sensorama simulator featuring a virtual environment. At this time, 3D UIs began to be explored as interface elements that we can interact with, in a three-dimensional space, through which we can establish a communication with the machine.

The basic principles of 3D UIs (Figure 6-8) displayed the importance of intuitiveness, implying the need for humans to instinctively know how to interact without further training. It also called for ergonomics, ensuring that the interactions were more natural and comfortable, as well as clarity or simplicity, trying to eliminate unnecessary elements.

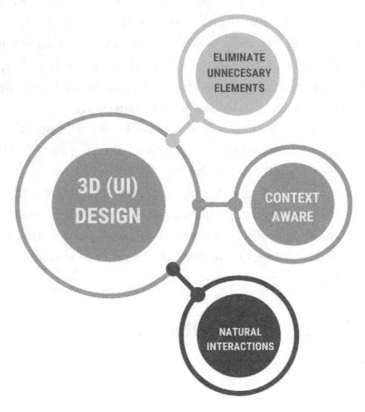

Figure 6-8. *From 3D Interfaces to Interfaceless*

The early challenges of this type of interface included ensuring that elements wouldn't overlap essential information, ensuring humans could judge the right distances to the UIs, and avoiding fatigue and strain overuse time.

With this in mind, we can see another iteration of the 3D UIs: even more natural ways to communicate with computers as they get more sophisticated. The role of the interfaceless design approach is to encourage more natural and fluid interactions, reducing the reliance on traditional slides, buttons, etc., while using voice, gestures, and context-aware responses as the inputs for the experience.

Although the switch from traditional interfaces to 3D interfaces has considered more intuitive and natural interactions, it is still based on a framework of widgets rather than on a completely natural and unobtrusive interaction.

The basic principles of interfaceless design account for natural interactions, voice and emphasizing gestures, and as we see the AI technology evolving, even thought-controlled inputs and context awareness; combining systems that understand and behave based on human and environmental conditions. Moving beyond visible interfaces involves the use of ambient feedback systems where using, as an example, haptic feedback or sound replaces the use of only visual cues. A clear example of interfaceless design could be a voice-activated AR experience that doesn't rely on any button or menu for interaction, fading the boundary between the human and the technology.

Furthermore, interfaceless designs aim to minimize any learning curve that might require humans to learn different functions of 3D virtual navigation menus, command-based buttons, sliders, dials, or widgets, by making the interactions as close to the natural human behavior as possible.

Optimization and Performance Considerations

Figure 6-9 leads us through this process beginning from real-time rendering.

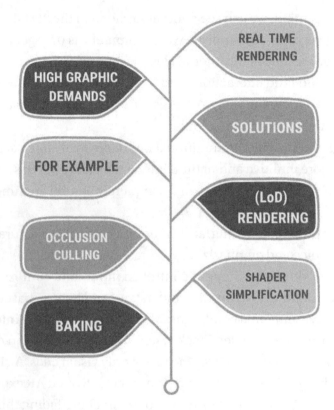

Figure 6-9. *Optimization and Performance*

Real-Time Rendering

Imagine trying to draw an image of a landscape super fast, repeatedly, with the purpose of making it look like the elements are moving. That is what computers do when they render in real time. Technically, but in simple words, real-time rendering is the process of creating and displaying those images with high frame rates to ensure the movement is smooth.

Real-time rendering is essential for interfaceless designs in spatial computing because it aims to provide a seamless experience, and to make it feel natural, the virtual elements must react instantly to the human interaction inputs without delays; otherwise, it runs the risk of breaking immersion.

Challenges and Solutions

Due to the fact that detailed virtual environments require heavy computational loads, high graphic demands are to be considered. This is also linked to the use of realistic features such as dynamic lighting, which needs to emulate how real light behaves, changing constantly, plus the interactivity from humans requiring instant outputs. It is key to consider the type of devices used for this type of demand.

To overcome some overload challenges, optimization techniques are presented as a reliever:

Level of Detail (LoD) rendering, which is like drawing a far away tree as a simple blob rather than attempting to display all the details of the leaves at once. As someone looks closer, the details start to be more evident. Similarly, when we are working with a photo in an editor like Photoshop and when we zoom in enough, we start to see the details of every pixel.

Occlusion culling is another technique often used, which in simple terms is not rendering objects that are hidden by other objects in the human's line of sight.

Shader simplification, as the name indicates, consists of minimizing the complexity of shaders for less evident or relevant objects, like the ones in the distance, to reduce the computational loads.

Finally, baking is often used as well, which is a process where certain lighting and shading elements that don't need as many changes can be stored and precomputed, reducing the need for real-time calculations.

The Future of Rendering

With advanced use of algorithms, it is possible to use predictive models that help determine user movements to render ahead potential scenarios as well as which scenes or objects need the highest level of detail at any given time.

For ultrarealistic experiences, ray tracing is also evolving in its capabilities, allowing high-level detail for the interactions of light with objects for realistic reflections, refractions, and shadows. These capabilities combined with future neural rendering processes (using AI models) to generate lifelike images would revolutionize the level of realism in a variety of experiences.

Load Balancing and Distribution

Maximizing throughput, minimizing response time, and ensuring optimal resource utilization are goals for load balancing, which can be tackled by distributing tasks across multiple servers or systems. This is another item to consider in the design of interfaceless experiences, as the aim is to avoid overloads or interrupted interactions due to efficiency issues. Using local and cloud resources helps with this optimization process.

When it comes to load balancing and the efficient distribution of computational tasks, transmitting sensitive information across networks and having dynamic workloads and latency issues when transferring data between local and cloud servers are some of the main first issues we can check to make sure risks are prevented. To mitigate some of these issues, using dynamic load distribution (algorithms that monitor and redistribute tasks) as well as edge computing (processing data on local sources) can be explored in combination with Content Delivery Networks (CDNs) as local servers to reduce speed and latency.

As we have discussed so far, using predictive algorithms is now being used to forecast system demands. AI models are now being used in real-time changing conditions or needs for distribution and to determine the fastest and most efficient routes or paths for data transfers. With quantum computing, these tasks tend to become more radical in parallel processing as well as the use of blockchain technologies for distributed task management and security.

Security and Privacy in Spatial Computing

Figure 6-10 illustrates how encryption systems play a key role in security and privacy issues in spatial computing.

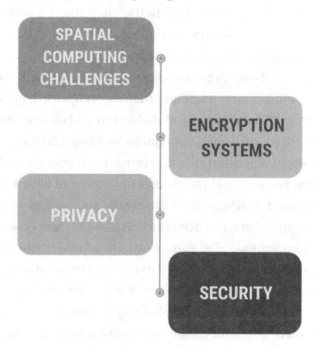

Figure 6-10. *Security and Privacy in Spatial Computing*

Data Encryption

Since interfaceless designs would involve more reliance on human data, data encryption is fundamental to assure the privacy and security of it. Data encryption is the process of transforming data into a secret code to prevent unauthorized access. This is crucial for spatial computing, for example, with the processing of personal data, involving collecting detailed and sensitive information such as movements, facial expressions, interactions, and most likely even thoughts in a not so distant future. If any of this data was to be exposed, it could be a dangerous threat in the wrong hands with potential misuse for manipulation and control.

In encryption, we find symmetric encryption and asymmetric encryption. In the symmetric category, one key is used to encrypt and decrypt the data, whereas in the asymmetric encryption, a pair of keys is used, including a public one to perform the action of encryption and a private one to perform the action of decryption.

Encrypting spatial data presents some challenges as well; due to the complexity of the environment and many systems working together simultaneously, spatial data can be multifaceted and diverse, which involves the use of sophisticated encryption techniques. In spatial computing, efficient algorithms are also required to encrypt and decrypt data in real time, keeping encryption keys updated and with high levels of security, for example, making sure that only the sender and recipient can access the decryption keys, not even the services provider is essential.

Encryption systems are also another area where AI is entering to optimize the processes. AI can be used to develop more robust and safe encryption techniques as well as in the identification of potential vulnerabilities and security breaches, helping to take more immediate action. As the use of quantum computing systems increases, new quantum-resistant encryption methods will also be required, and systems like homomorphic encryption allowing processes or computations on encrypted data without directly decrypting it come as a potential good use for cloud-based spatial computing experiences.

Anonymous Data Collection in Spatial Computing

We can think of anonymous data collection as if we were collecting puzzle pieces without the picture; we might get useful information without necessarily revealing the complete image, gathering the data without associating it back to an individual or device.

This is imperative for spatial computing due to the intimate nature of the data at hand, such as how the human moves, where they look at, their preferences, and their interactions.

To anonymize data, various techniques can be used, like data masking, data perturbation, data aggregation, and differential privacy. Let's take a look:

- *Data Masking*: It involves transforming private data with prefabricated, yet similar in structure, information or data.

- *Data Perturbation*: This is the process of adding "noise" to the data to impede the access to the original source.

- *Data Aggregation*: In this technique, the goal is to make the individual data points indistinguishable by grouping data in a way that cannot be deciphered.

- *Differential Privacy*: It makes use of advanced algorithms that protect the data when the individual's data is part of larger databases.

It's important to note that as part of best practices of anonymous data collection for spatial computing, a minimum data collection principle should be followed, only gathering data that is undoubtedly necessary. Also, it is vital to perform periodic reviews and tests of data and systems, obtaining informed consent from humans before collecting and anonymizing data and informing them of how it is used, regardless of it being anonymized.

AI and Machine Learning for Behavior Analysis

Real-Time Scene Segmentation in Spatial Computing

Scene segmentation is a system for categorizing and separating each distinct object or element in a digital scene. This process contributes to spatial computing to enhance human interaction, enabling the system to adapt to changes in real-world scenes. Neural networks place their role here, trained on various databases to be able to independently recognize elements in a scene. Convolutional Neural Networks (CNNs) are also used in image and scene understanding for their ability to establish pattern differences and categorize objects.

When working with real-time processing data for segmentations, it is important to remember that faster processing might result in less accurate segmentations and the other way around. Due to higher computational demands, analysis and segmentation operations for a scene in real time require significant computing load and power, which is important to establish a balance between quality, accuracy, and speed.

Predictive Human Behavior Analysis in Spatial Computing

As touched upon previously, in the near future we will be able to see the use of predictive models more often in every experience. Imagine if your favorite game could predict what will be your next move and adjust itself to either present more challenges or to provide more support or help. This is the function for predictive analysis, and it is not limited to games.

Utilizing data analysis and AI models, predictive behavior helps to foresee human needs (Figure 6-11) or actions based on past patterns and anticipate proper responses. This is one of the approaches to the reduction of cognitive load, as the automation of certain actions facilitates human's capacity to focus on more complex tasks. This predictive user behavior analysis could include biometrics, like brainwaves, heart rate, and eye movement, and as emphasized previously, this sensitive information must be kept protected and respected. Since predictions are always created on the basis of the most probable event, they may not always be totally accurate. Some automation systems are supportive of the processes required to provide environments that closely simulate human behaviors, but we need to remember that there is a fine line between helping users and taking away their own sense of presence and self-control.

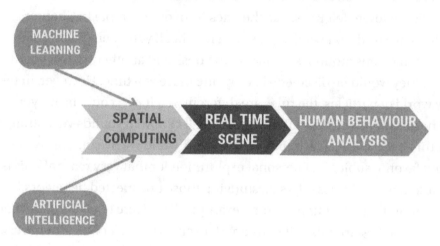

Figure 6-11. *AI and Machine Learning for Behavior Analysis*

Due to the evolution and use of more advanced predictive user behavior analysis systems, we will be able to create training or educational applications or experiences that self-adapt in real time to the learner's style and pace. Would that not be very useful? I have sat in many trainings feeling how off it was from my own learning style!

Quantum Computing and Spatial Experiences

To understand the field of quantum computing, we need to first study a brief background in quantum physics, specifically quantum mechanics. In simple terms, while quantum physics is focused on the general study of the smallest particles in the universe and their behavior, quantum mechanics focuses on the rules and mathematical frameworks to try to describe and predict those particles. It is like the "manual guide" for how particles play the game.

Let's take a look at a fun example to get started. Imagine you have a box with different felt pens, like the ones from our example in Chapter 2. In the real world, you would agree with me that if you open the box and place some pens around, say, one on the desk and another one on your left hand, they would be discreetly in only one place at a time. However, in the tiny world of particles, the rules are different. A felt pen could be on your left hand and on the desk at the same time!!! I know, it sounds very strange, but this is the magical, extremely mysterious world we live in. This is one of my favorite subjects of personal exploration for that very reason! This is what quantum physics refers to, studying those unexpected behaviors.

Continuing with our preceding example, if we were to take a couple of the magical best friends, felt pens apart, even if you took one of them very far away from the other one, it would still know what their other friend is doing and vice versa. What an amazing ability, eh? It sounds very magical and yet it is part of our current universal structure.

The example described earlier with the felt pen on the hand and the desk at the same time is called "superposition," or the ability of a quantum system to be in multiple states simultaneously, whereas our second example, of the felt pens and their inseparable friends, both connected and depending on each other even at larger distances, is a similar behavior that particles present at a very small scale. This is referred to as "entanglement."

The word "quantum" derives from the Latin "how much," expressing the powerful energy contained in every particle the smaller it gets. Quantum computing derives its origins from the principles of quantum mechanics, aiming to enable exponential speeds to accelerate processing for various computing tasks.

Entanglement in quantum mechanics is related to quantum computing based on the systematic binary traditional operational systems. Unlike regular computers, quantum computers don't use bits in 0 or 1, but another system called qubits, which exist in superposed states, meaning 0 and 1. When these qubits become entangled, their states are reciprocal; one affects the other and vice versa. This is one of the factors that allow quantum computers to work with massive data and possibilities instantaneously and simultaneously. These types of computations are fundamental for the advancements of different fields of studies, like cryptography, material science and chemistry, financial modeling, climate modeling, supply chain and logistics, nuclear fusion, agriculture, drug discovery, and of course artificial and machine learning.

As it begins to appear evident, quantum computing matters for spatial computing (Figure 6-12) as it potentially allows for handling complex spatial data with exponential speed, leveraging the superposition or parallelism ability to process multiple options or possibilities simultaneously, facilitating real-time simulations. This would be reflected in the simulations of ecosystems or entire cities in real time, as an example.

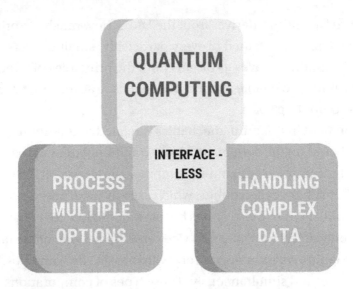

Figure 6-12. *Quantum Computing in Spatial Experiences*

Interfaceless designs also leverage this type of computational advantage to obtain immediate responses to human actions, reducing any potential or perceptible lag.

It is to be observed though that quantum computing is an evolving field like advancements in artificial intelligence, so it is not available mainstream yet. Companies like IBM have made great advances and have many operating quantum computers around the world, for example, serving other companies like Mercedes-Benz in their quest to transform their complete fleet of vehicles to electric sources, relying on advanced studies to prolong the life of sustainable batteries.

Neural Interfaces: Bridging the Gap Between Brain and Machine

Neural interfaces are devices that connect directly with the brain to understand, interpret, and process electrical signals.

The capture of electrical signals works by means of devices installed as headbands or helmets outside the skull (other devices are invasive, installed as microchips tracking neural activity), reading and processing those brainwaves as responses.

Applications in spatial computing span the direct thought command approach, where elements from the virtual space can be manipulated directly by means of thought. Personalized environments also change based on mood or preferences and adjust to provide balancing experiences. In education, it can be used to provide guidance and training based on the individual's cognitive patterns.

Beyond spatial computing, these types of interfaces have potential wider applications in medical fields, like neurodegenerative diseases, paralysis, and other neurological conditions.

Although these types of upcoming implementations and advancements are exciting for many fields of study, they also come with very high risks for humanity. We make a discussion about this type of application in Chapter 8.

The New Era of Virtual Assistants

Virtual assistants have played a role in the evolving landscape of technology. From voice-activated search tools, they have transformed into AI-driven entities. However, as we navigate deeper into computing and conscious design, the role and capabilities of assistants are once again being redefined. They are no longer utilities; they now serve as companions, guides, and guardians in the physical space.

Conscious design has brought about an era of personalization that goes beyond human preferences. In the past, virtual assistants were customized based on what humans liked—playing their music, turning on lights at times, or reminding them of appointments. In spatial computing, personalization takes on a more profound meaning. Virtual assistants now have the ability to understand humans' emotional states, their surroundings, and their intentions, within a specific context (Figure 6-13).

Figure 6-13. *The New Era of Virtual Assistants*

Imagine having an assistant that not only listens to your words but also detects the stress in your voice or notices the lighting conditions in your room. It can suggest a meditation exercise to help you relax or adjust the lighting to create an ambiance. In this context, personalization goes beyond functionality; it becomes about promoting well-being.

The Envoys of Interface Experiences

In a world shaped by computing, where the boundaries between the physical and digital realms blend together, virtual assistants serve as the seamless connection. Gone are the days of relying on typing or speaking commands for every interaction. A simple gesture, a glance, or even a subtle change in posture becomes a means of communication.

For example, while using Apple's Vision Pro, a slight narrowing of the eyes could prompt the assistant to adjust the brightness or clarity of the display. A repeated motion of rubbing one's temples might trigger the assistant to suggest taking a break or engaging in a different activity.

Guardians of Ethical Boundaries

With their integration into our lives, the new generation of virtual assistants takes on a greater responsibility. They become the guardians of ethical spatial computing. As these assistants gather and process incredible amounts of data, their design and functionality must prioritize human privacy and consent. They should have the ability to periodically remind humans about the data they share, provide choices for opting in or out, and maintain transparency regarding data usage.

Collaborative Companions of Cognition

Moving beyond being tool assistants in spatial computing, they have the potential to transform into cognitive companions. Drawing inspiration from design principles, they would work collaboratively with humans, understanding not only commands but also intentions, aspirations, and even fears.

For a designer deeply engaged in a project, the assistant could offer insights on design practices, share nature-inspired insights (following design principles), or even remind the designer about the significance of inclusive design—all tailored to fit within the context of the project.

Toward a Harmonious Symbiosis

The future path for assistants does not revolve around adding features or refining voice modulation; it revolves around achieving a harmonious symbiosis. It is about finding a blend where humans and digital entities coexist and enhance each other's experiences.

Gone are the days when virtual assistants were simply used for reminders and playing music. Now they have a role to play in our daily lives within spatial computing. Do you recall a scene from *Iron Man* (2008) where Tony Stark cocreates with his sophisticated assistant J.A.R.V.I.S (Just a Rather Very Intelligent System). J.A.R.V.I.S manages and takes care of all the internal systems including advanced building security systems and real-time construction and modifications of assets. The future will be marked by these types of capabilities, allowing us to focus on our own visions and passions.

As spatial computing continues to expand our possibilities, virtual assistants are on the brink of redefining their purpose. No longer limited to screens or devices, they are becoming our partners in the physical environment, guided by conscious design principles. They will cater to our needs, understand our emotions, protect our privacy, and enhance our experiences in ways that we are only just beginning to comprehend.

In this emerging technological world, technology's true power lies not only in its ability to innovate but also in its capacity for empathy. At the core of this empathy is a generation of assistants—a revolutionary chapter in technological advancement that is both mindful and compassionate.

Understanding Voice User Interfaces (VUIs)

The key element of the assistant experience centers around the "voice user interface (VUI)." VUIs are a type of human interface that relies on speech recognition technology enabling humans to interact with a system using their voice. Unlike graphical user interfaces (GUIs), VUIs don't require attention, making them ideal for situations where multitasking is needed or for individuals with impairments.

VUIs primarily function by acknowledging human inputs in the form of voice commands and producing responses based on these inputs.

Interacting with a Virtual Assistant

When you interact with an assistant, there are steps involved that usually happen within a few seconds. Here's a typical breakdown:

1. *Wake Word Detection*: The virtual assistant listens for a word or phrase to activate itself. For example, with Alexa the wake word is usually "Alexa." Once the virtual assistant recognizes this wake word, it begins recording what you say next.

2. *Speech Recognition*: The recorded speech is then transformed into written text using Automatic Speech Recognition (ASR) technology.

3. *Natural Language Understanding*: The converted text is analyzed by the Natural Language Understanding (NLU) system, which determines the intention and details of your command. For instance, if you say, "Alexa, play 'Imagine' by John Lennon," the NLU system identifies that your intention is to "play" something and recognizes "Imagine" as the song and "John Lennon" as the artist.

4. *Action Execution*: Based on the identified intention and details of your command, the virtual assistant carries out the requested action. This might include tasks such as retrieving information from a database, operating a connected device, or producing a response.

5. *Speech Synthesis*: In case the task involves generating spoken responses, the text is transformed into speech using text-to-speech (TTS) technology, then communicated to the individual.

6.   *Gathering Feedback*: During the conversation,
the virtual assistant gathers feedback to enhance
interactions based on human satisfaction.

Challenges and Innovations

When it comes to interacting with an assistant, there are some challenges
that differ from traditional graphical user interfaces (GUIs). One of these
challenges is dealing with the forms of ambiguity that exist in language
such as words that sound the same but have different meanings, different
accents, and contextual interpretations. Virtual assistants also need to
handle environments, interruptions, and situations where multiple people
are speaking at once.

To overcome these challenges, virtual assistants rely on machine
learning algorithms and large sets of data to improve their accuracy
and ability to handle scenarios. They also take advantage of context,
individual history, and personalized features to tailor their responses for
each human.

Additionally, virtual assistants incorporate modal inputs whenever
possible. This means they can use touchscreens or gestures in addition
to voice commands to provide an interactive experience. For instance,
when using Google Assistant on a smartphone, the screen can display
information or options alongside the voice-based interaction.

Steps Toward Inclusive and Accessible
Interfaceless Designs

As we find ourselves at the intersection of computing, design, and
interfaceless environments, a great responsibility emerges: ensuring
inclusivity and accessibility (Figure 6-14). In this realm where technology
seamlessly blends our digital lives, it's essential that everyone can fully

participate without encountering barriers. How can we ensure that interfaceless designs embrace everyone?

Figure 6-14. *Inclusive and Accessible Interfaceless Design*

Understanding the Context

In general, inclusivity plays a role in design by making products, services, or environments accessible and usable for as many people as possible irrespective of their age, abilities, or backgrounds. Within the scope of interface design, inclusivity becomes paramount. With methods of interaction, such as voice commands, gestures, touch-based interactions, and more, emerging in this field, designers must consider an array of human needs and capabilities to create truly inclusive experiences.

Universal Design Principles

Universal design principles serve as a foundation for promoting inclusivity in interface design. These principles advocate for designing products and environments that can be used by all individuals to the extent without requiring adaptations or specialized designs.

The principles of design have relevance within the context of interfaceless environments. It involves anticipating human scenarios and capabilities, ensuring that the interfaceless system can adjust accordingly. For example, a voice-controlled system, such as Alexa, needs to be adaptable enough to comprehend accents and speech patterns in order to be truly inclusive.

Personalization and Adaptability

Another crucial aspect of inclusivity in interface design is the focus on personalization and adaptability. It is important for the system to have the ability to learn from and adjust to each human's needs and preferences.

As an example, a voice user interface (VUI) can gradually comprehend an individual's speech patterns over time, thereby enhancing its accuracy in responding to commands. Similarly, a gesture-based system can learn the gestures preferred by an individual and adapt its recognition algorithms accordingly. This emphasis on personalization and adaptability not only enhances the human experience but also ensures that the system accommodates various abilities and preferences.

In summary, integrating inclusivity into interface design involves recognizing and respecting human abilities, needs, and cultures. By adhering to design principles prioritizing accessibility, demonstrating sensitivity, and promoting personalization and adaptability, designers can create truly inclusive interfaceless experiences that cater to everyone.

Practical Pointers Toward Inclusivity

1. **Redefining Inclusion in the Digital Age**

   When it comes to computing, inclusion goes beyond designing for different abilities. It's about recognizing that these abilities can change and evolve over time. An inclusive design without interfaces adapts to situational or permanent accessibility needs. Whether someone has an injury in an environment or has permanent hearing loss, the design should effortlessly cater to everyone.

2. **Embracing Multiple Modes of Interaction**

   In this era of design, virtual environments need to engage senses and modes of interaction. We shouldn't limit ourselves to auditory cues alone. Incorporating feedback, environmental clues, and even scents can create a range of interactive experiences. By diversifying our approach, we not only enhance the experience but also ensure that if one mode is inaccessible, another one can compensate.

3. **Continuous Learning and Adaptation**

   Spatial computing empowered by AI provides a relevant advantage: the ability to learn and adapt over time. Interfaceless designs should constantly learn from human interactions and understand requirements so they can adjust the experience, in real time. This way, the system becomes personalized for each human's needs.

4. **Designing Together with Diverse Groups**

   To truly achieve inclusivity, it is mandatory to involve a range of people in the design process. By including individuals with abilities, backgrounds, and experiences, we can gain insights that might otherwise be overlooked. Collaborating in this way ensures that the resulting environment is not for everyone but created by everyone.

5. **Balancing Personalization and Privacy**

   While personalization has the potential to greatly improve accessibility, we must also be mindful of the privacy implications it brings. It is important to approach design with a focus on upholding the standards of data privacy and ethical use, while systems learn and adapt.

6. **Education and Advocacy**

   Promoting an environment without interfaces is a responsibility shared by not just designers but all parties involved. Organizations, developers, and even individuals need to be educated about the significance and methods of inclusivity. Advocacy plays a role in ensuring that inclusivity is not an afterthought but a fundamental principle.

7. **Real-World Testing Scenarios**

   While laboratory testing is important, it may not capture the challenges of real-world situations. Designs without interfaces must undergo testing in diverse real-life scenarios, considering factors such as different lighting conditions, sound environments, and human contexts to ensure strong accessibility.

8. **Embracing Feedback Loops**

   Feedback serves as the lifeblood of design. Establishing feedback mechanisms allows humans to share their experiences, difficulties encountered,

and suggestions for improvement. This ensures
that the design remains adaptable and constantly
evolving.

9. **Understanding Cultural Contexts**

   Spatial computing transcends boundaries
   emphasizing the role of cultural contexts in design.
   Inclusivity also involves comprehending and
   respecting nuances to ensure that the technology is
   universally respectful and intuitive.

10. **Transparent Design Narratives**

    Humans should always have an understanding of
    how an interfaceless system operates, particularly
    when it comes to accessibility features.

This allows humans to make informed choices, fully utilize all features, and have confidence in the system.

As we delve deeper into interfaceless environments, it is necessary to remember that technology at its core serves humanity. Its success is not measured by its innovation and its ability to be accessible to all, providing equal opportunities for everyone to thrive.

By incorporating design principles into the fabric of computing, we champion a future that is not only technologically advanced but also compassionate, inclusive, and truly beneficial for everyone. While the path toward this future may present challenges, it is imperative for a world that embraces diversity in all its forms.

Summary: A Deep Dive into Interfaceless Environments

This chapter was marked by understanding the intricate but beneficial aspect of interfaceless designs and the holistic ecosystem that works behind the scenes to support its strength. We presented the ecosystem that powers interfaceless for spatial computing such as artificial intelligence, machine learning, deep learning, and physical devices to understand the complete scenario where interfaceless becomes effective. Paired with these systems, we also discussed the role and utility of sensors and hardware available and how this shapes the landscape of interaction design in the future.

Taking a look at the case of Apple Vision Pro, we discovered how companies like Apple are working toward this goal of bringing human-centric experiences using spatial computing and artificial intelligence. To complete our study of interfaces, we also bought the case of virtual assistants and how they will continue to shape the direction of interaction, aiding in our day-to-day tasks. Finally, we brought principles of universal design to reflect on how to create inclusive and accessible interfaceless designs.

CHAPTER 7

Toward Interfaceless Experiences: Leveraging AI and Spatial Computing

In this chapter, we set a goal to bridge the gap between understanding the traditional design stages to interfaceless practices for spatial computing. Examining the current landscape and the experiences created so far for XR (extended reality) mediums, we take a look at the prevalent practices and draw parallels identifying gaps that beckon a shift to the interfaceless design approach.

As with other fields of study, examining the evolution of disciplines aids in comprehending the bigger picture, clarifying why today we experience the current limitations and what we can do about it. We trace the journey from early human experience definitions when there was not a formal term for it, along with the transformation of expectations and perceptions of humans over time, contributing to constant changes in design.

© Diana Olynick 2024
D. Olynick, *Interfaceless*, Design Thinking, https://doi.org/10.1007/979-8-8688-0083-2_7

To open this discussion with more specificity into what it means and the fundamental impact of creating interfaceless experiences, I share another example. During one of the regular interviews I have with creators and XR leaders, I met Robert, an engineer and the founder of Thrive Pavilion, who eventually decided to create his own work and profession around the demographic segment of senior adults. Inspired by the possibility of bringing an opportunity to senior individuals who often suffer from loneliness and depression in the later stages of their lives, he embarked himself on a mission toward building a simulation environment where they could connect and enjoy activities together. The space was built and more members joined, finding a place for comfort and support. There was something particular about this experience though: it was intentionally built so that members could immerse themselves using a Meta Quest device. When I asked him why it was built that way considering we would assume that for seniors it would probably be more challenging to deal with the technology learning curve, his response was that actually for seniors it was more challenging to navigate 2D screens through mobile phones and that the learning curve was far more complex, rather than in an immersive media, and with the complete absence of interfaces, seniors feel a less steep learning curve, given that the interactions in this digital media naturally get transferred from the physical world without much obstruction. This was another lesson for me about one of the great benefits of interfaceless design.

And finally, since most of the practices established for XR design are still relevant for interfaceless experiences, in this chapter we take a look at these practices that pave the way for seamless, intuitive, and human-centric designs for spatial computing. This led us to study a set of good practices to begin early designs for interfaceless experiences, coupled with examples and potential roadblocks and approaches to overcome them.

The Parallel Between XR Practices and the Interfaceless Approach

Let's examine how this connection between traditional UX for 2D interfaces, XR, and the interfaceless approach came to be.

Part of the traditional methods for 2D screens involves a focus on visual hierarchy, where the design guides the human's eyes in a specific order and direction, applying consistency with elements like links and buttons for navigating; ensuring responsiveness and adaptability to different screen sizes and resolutions. This traditional method features a limited interactivity due to the medium, often restricted to clicks, scrolls, and keyboard commands or inputs.

When it comes to XR (extended reality), we integrate a new layer, which is the 3D space, as a canvas. As a result, the designs involve immersiveness, where humans now feel part of the simulated environment, considering the function and how objects and elements appear in the 3D space. In terms of interaction, new factors are added, like gestures, locomotion, and haptic feedback. Therefore, comfort comes as a determinant factor in the experience, avoiding motion sickness and other consequences of poor design. Spatial audio is also a new layer that needs to be accounted for, directly affecting the immersive experience.

Interfaceless experiences, in turn, feature more natural experiences, simulating real-world actions, without the need for hand controllers. Using contextual awareness, the infrastructure itself becomes aware of the human's environment and accordingly adapts to the real-time needs presented. In the absence of traditional screens, feedback can come in the form of haptic responses, visual indicators, and audio cues in the individual's environment. Without explicit commands, the system predicts and recognizes human intent, and with more sensors and data collection, understanding human needs is both beneficial and risky, due to privacy and safety.

183

In summary, traditional 2D design focuses on consistency and visual hierarchy on flat screens with limited human natural interactivity; XR design emphasizes immersion in a 3D space with multimodal interactions and user comfort, and interfaceless design for spatial computing prioritizes real human interactions, context awareness, and the understanding of human intent without the use of traditional interfaces.

With this background in mind, we can now proceed to dive deeper into the special considerations for traditional XR practices and then move on to more tailored practices for interfaceless environments, keeping in mind that, at times, both types of practices can be intertwined and leveraged against each other.

The Background of UX and XR

Now, let's dive into why UX in XR, the UX transformation, and how to delight humans.

One of the top barriers to adoption along with the devices for XR (virtual reality, augmented reality, mixed reality) is poor design, poor UX design. Because of this, it makes all the sense that we need to study and deepen our knowledge and experience in how we can produce a design that has attended to the nuances of function and engagement.

In regular design, we speak about "User Interaction" and "User Experience." In "User Interaction," typically we are speaking about the 2D interfaces, the screens, the visual elements, and the graphics that the human interacts with, whereas in "User Experience," the scope broadens because it involves everything that is around the individual and how they perceive that experience in relation to the environment.

Let's take a closer look at some early uses of UX throughout history (Figure 7-1). From ancient cultures, humans have had a different sense of interaction and the need for physical elements for their survival. Since the resources were limited, they evolved in their practices the idea that the less, the better. So Feng Shui, for example, makes its appearance around 4000 BC, showing the selective approach to the interaction with the world around using some minimalism practices and arranging elements and objects in a particular manner to promote well-being.

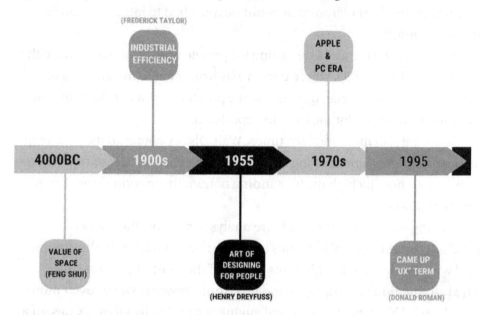

Figure 7-1. *UX History*

Then we see the next leap in this evolution with the ancient Greeks and ergonomics (500 B), becoming a fundamental aspect of study and promotion of health and safety. In simple terms, ergonomics is the study of how the positions of the body are in relation to the environment and how we can prevent movements that could lead to injuries or discomfort. In engineering, we take ergonomics as a very indispensable aspect of the design and a determinant factor for potential well-being disruption.

Toward the end of the Industrial Revolution, Frederick Winslow Taylor, a mechanical engineer, initiated a quest for workplace efficiency (1900) consisting of a set of principles to introduce speed in production, which gave birth to the discipline of Industrial Engineering. While this

was not a human-centric approach, but a business-centric approach, his
study evoked a first look at the relationships between humans and the
interactions that happen with their tools. This industrial era also led to
Toyota inquiring about the value of human input and performing analysis
of how the tasks or environment could be modified to introduce more
human comfort.

The first time the art of designing for people was introduced was with
Henry Dreyfuss in 1955, where design was brought into the analysis of
the products, considering humans, since previously it was prioritized for
function rather than for the human experience.

Entering into more modern times, Walt Disney comes to the next leap
as the first UX designer, having a profound effect on the design that we see
nowadays, showing high understanding of human emotion throughout
their creations.

During this period, there is more analysis into how the user can
produce certain types of activities and how they interact with the computer
and with the devices, marking this as one of the most important shifts.
The introduction of computers and electronic devices evolves even more
with Donald Norman, an electrical engineer who finally gives UX design a
name, introducing cognitive science to interaction. In his book *The Design
of Everyday Things*, he discussed human-centered design and elements,
like affordances and signifiers, what they mean, and how we can integrate
them in a way that is very relevant, proposing the design from a complete
human perspective, which means an emotional perspective.

How to Delight Humans

If we are going to design any type of app or any type of game, these are what
have to be at the front of this design: What are their emotions? What are
they looking to get? What are their very deep feelings and how is it that they
want to discover and explore this experience? What would be the end result
for them? As the next level of UX, designing for humans is at the center of

the new XR design scenery. This is why this book focuses more specifically on humans vs. users, so we understand that although in the tech field the term "users" has always been used, coming from the function; whereas, humans is coming from the emotional and psychological spectrum. When we use the word humans, then there comes the shift, and the perspective is different. It comes from a place of embracing immersion, opportunities, discovery, authenticity, evolution, and openness.

Factors to Consider for XR and Spatial Computing Design

Traditionally and even in XR, we have on one side the art aspect of design, which is the typical interface, and UX, which is somewhat related to the function but also the overall experience as I have mentioned. So what's the personal experience with the total system? The idea here is to look at the complete experience, but from a holistic system perspective—how the interaction happens with the whole environment and what the synergy is. Sometimes, when we access experiences in VR, for example, there are many elements around and we get overwhelmed; we don't know what they mean or what their purpose is. At this point, there are a considerable number of platforms where anybody can create without any major technical restriction. Platforms, such as VR Chat, Mozilla Hubs, Rec Room, Horizon, Neos VR, and Spatial, allow creators to upload their own worlds, some of them to be experienced on any device and some of them in headsets only. The question that comes here is this: If anybody can upload content that is not vetted with all the technical aspects required to guarantee a human-centric approach that stems from good design practices, what type of experience are we offering to the millions of individuals that join on a daily basis to discover and explore those spaces? This is a hot topic since the companies are there to make an income as any business, but from a human perspective, we know there is more than can be done.

This encompasses of course a broader study in design, graphics, the interface, the physical interaction, ergonomics, and the contemplation of all of these areas. And on the other side, we have this fundamental factor which is the emotional approach, and that's where the secret to delighting humans lies. The emotional approach is the psychology that is behind that design, at which point the design wouldn't be just about the interface, the graphics, the connection of elements, the colors, and the font, but about the emotional and feeling background behind all of this.

Visual Grammar

When studying UX for XR, we have some typical elements that have been working together very well for the medium so far, which are visual grammar. Visual grammar is not just about letters, it's about graphical elements, meaning what is the role of every single element in the whole experience. This starts from designing at a very basic foundation where there is a mindful use for the dots, the lines, the planes, and how they interact with humans at a deeper level.

Language and Typography

Typically, in interior design when you are developing a concept, you get presented with a mood board or a concept board where you can see the possibilities or a general idea of the environment, how it could look combined with different elements. In human interaction, human experience is the same type of approach we should aim to have in terms of language.

So for that, we need to create what is called "Word Boards," which is similar to a mood board, but it's made of words. It's like a dictionary of words that we know that deeper in the human psychology of that potential person would really resonate with their own language. So it is different to

design, for example, a cyberpunk type of experience or environment and
to place there some wording that resonates more with a formal type of
meeting or conference.

So in regular design work, to help with the understanding of the
experience from a psychological ground, we need to begin with emotions.

And on the other side, we also have what is called typefaces. Here, we
can see the use of different fonts, which is not just related to the colors
and the sizes but also the type of typography that could resonate with
that person. Again, in our example of the cyberpunk type of environment,
maybe there are certain fonts that could look boring even in the
environment or even not look totally realistic in the actual context.

Narrative Design

Beside the graphical elements, we also have the narrative design
storytelling aspect of design. In this factor, similar elements are going to
still apply for extended reality mediums, but the difference is that now we
are dealing with a three-dimensional space where it's parallel as if we were
going to be participating in a movie as it is being recorded. That's why the
filming industry is one of the best ones that we can use in order to learn
more about how to actually nail down storytelling techniques.

In narrative design, we need to study how people move through the
story and how it's paced because it's not the same as if you begin the story
with a very fast pace and try to continue with the same pace during most of
the story, it will be overwhelming. Conversely, if the experience starts too
slowly, then the individual is not going to have that feeling of excitement or
the mysterious factor of what we want to experience, the feeling of "what
is going on?" that leads to excitement. So this is where we can use the
storyboarding tool commonly used in cinematography, using the inverted
pyramid method which is related to the hierarchy of information or how
information is delivered.

In movies, for example, we would have this opening moment where we are in awe and we are engaged right away in the story, so much so that we forget that we are the person who is watching the movie. In classical experience design, this is the ultimate goal. However, since we are working with conscious and mindful design, we know there must exist a balance. We are actually believing that we are the actor there, the main character, but at the same time, we are encouraged to be aware of our existence as a human. Therefore, we can begin the story with unknowns but also with the elements of excitement and in context.

The inverted pyramid, as a tool to inform the storyboarding process, is about delivering critical info at the very beginning so the person has a context of what is going on. This is important in XR for storytelling. Then, it moves into delivering the background and contents and ultimately the nice-to-have elements in a story. For example, we can see in the movie *Spectre* (2015, *James Bond* series) a well-done sparking of curiosity in an opening scene. They did a good job at maintaining an interesting pace and at the same time managing the expectations in a way that sparks our curiosity, giving us an approximate idea about the context of the movie. This is the level of quality we need to bring to spatial computing experiences in order to make sure that humans are delighted, they are not confused, and they have whatever they need in order to understand their place in the environment and how to interact with it in a very easy and fun way.

Special Considerations for XR Design and Spatial Computing Design

Bodystorming and Acting

In bodystorming, instead of coming up with good ideas for a product as it is in brainstorming, we use our own body. The idea here is to create the scenes exactly as in the final product experience, simulating the human who would interact with the elements inside the experience.

The core of this technique is supposed to leverage first the direct access
we have in a real environment to our everyday objects. In a way, this is
like when we were children and we enjoyed playing with a sofa pillow and
simulating a spaceship in the living room, emulating the final experience
and potential risks to watch out for. Bodystorming is a very good practice
technique in order for us to make sure that what we are trying to design
is understood from a real body and kinetic perspective, clarifying aspects
such as the situations that the human could be facing, what they would be
wondering about, what could be confusing, what sense of space they have,
and what type of behaviors they might express.

Proprioception

Continuing with these types of special considerations, there are some that
are particular for XR, for example, the proprioception. Proprioception is
the sense of movement in an environment and how you perceive your
body: the sense of the length of your arms, the sense of your hands, your
head, when you move, every part of the body in relation to space. In
designing for XR, this is very fundamental because now, as living entities,
we are performing in a three-dimensional space, for example, if we place
two screens too close to each other or even the action of typing boards
inside a virtual reality experience.

Affordances and Signifiers

Affordances have been confused with the actual signals that let us know
what we can do with an element, but these involve more the relationship
and potentiality of seeing an object and getting a clue of how it could
be used.

Signifiers on the other hand are the actual fact of recognizing the object
and knowing what can be done with it. So affordance is the relationship,
while signifiers are the signal that tells us what the chair is for, to sit on it.

191

We need to be careful and use a thoughtful approach for affordances and signifiers to make sure that the human has a barrier-free experience.

Poses and Gestures

Introducing pose and gesture in new experiences supposes a great risk. This stems from the potential that the individual might not understand at the first try how the gesture is supposed to work. This is a factor to avoid when possible, especially in highly interactive experiences. Creating potential learning curves for humans is a technique that needs a lot of consideration to avoid frustration if the system is not immediately responsive. You might also think: What if the gestures are natural, such as pointing or grabbing? It is risky to create artificial arbitrary gestures, but natural ones are really good ways of interacting with the digital world in the context of spatial computing.

Grid Behaviors

If we are designing experiences where the human is expected to interact a lot with many elements, then these grid behaviors have to be designed in a way that makes the object and the hand fit together just as it happens in a real-world environment. Here, we have the application of mappings, feedback, guidance, and instruction.

When an individual accesses the experience, they are going to know exactly how to navigate and how to properly interact with all the surroundings. It's always recommended to offer introductions and to provide feedback that could be represented, for instance, in the form of sound, reinforcing the correct use of the experience.

Best Practices for Spatial Computing

Since the current technology available continues to evolve toward higher
quality and faster processing, we still face some technical challenges
due to rendering capacity and devices available. Despite this challenge,
there are good practices that we can implement to alleviate some of the
limitations posed by the technology stage.

Let's observe some important factors first.

Field of View

Field of view or FOV in simple terms is the width of an area that we
can see without moving the head or the eyes. For example, if we look
through a small window in a large room, we can only see part of the
room, but not all at once. To put it in perspective, some XR devices, like
Meta Quest Pro, have a reported field of view of 106 degrees horizontal
and 96 degrees vertical. With the new Vision Pro device from Apple, it is
described by early testers to have around 110 degrees and the monocular,
horizontal human eye field of view is about 135 degrees, 180 vertical,
with a binocular approximation of 114 degrees horizontally. This factor
is important because some devices have a narrow FOV, which implies
careful considerations in design where the human is not required to turn
their head to see or approach any object out of the natural FOV, in addition
to the restrictions posed by head-mounted devices. To properly address
comfort zones, as a general guideline with the current capabilities of
commercial headsets, the most essential objects can be placed at the range
of 94 degress horizontal and 32 degrees vertical, with a maximum head
turn of 204 degrees and comfortable range of 154 degrees.

Frame Rate

Frames per second (FPS) are how many frames (or pictures) are rendered every second of a video. For instance, if we were to use a flipbook and flip it slowly, the movement won't look as real or natural, whereas if it is continuous, it will show as a movie. In XR applications, if the FPS is too low, the movements won't render as smooth, therefore breaking immersion and the sense of a real experience. This is another essential component of the design experience as this mismatch can produce visual-vestibular negative effects, leading to motion sickness due to the motion experience being seen but not felt.

Degrees of Simulation

It refers to how real the simulation feels, for example, playing with toy bubbles vs. playing with real bubbles. The toy bubbles don't feel as touching as real bubbles with the action of soap and water. In XR, sometimes we might see the experience not completely matching real expressions, and to some extent, this is part of the technology evolution.

Latency

This is the syndrome of the delay. It involves a mismatch in time when we do something and the time it actually appears or renders in the simulated scene. Imagine clapping your hands and listening to the sound seconds later. It would be weird. In XR, if there is too much latency, the processes appear out of sync. It's opportune to note that motion-to-photon latency, or variances in rendering, is another cause of visual-vestibular mismatches, causing as a consequence motion sickness.

Optics

Dispersion and chromatic aberration are other parameters to check for precision. In dispersion, or the result of refraction of light, we can think of a prism where it turns a beam of light into a rainbow, causing an unintended spread of colors in objects. On the other hand, in chromatic aberration, we see a distortion of colors where they don't match accurately, causing a "fringed" look around the objects. As we can see, errors in these parameters can degrade the visual quality of the experience. Potential ways to address these factors are using high-quality optics for headsets and allowing humans to manually adjust settings as these levels appear different for every individual.

Health and Ergonomics

For most of the commercial headsets out there, special recommendations must be followed for individuals sensitive to conditions such as PTSD and epilepsy seizures and females, more than males, vulnerable to vision disorders like mismatches between interpupillary distance (IPD) and the device's lens distance causing headaches or eyestrain. To avoid fatigue, a clear way to exit the experience needs to be incorporated, allowing them to continue the experience saving progress. The considerations about the field of view, degrees of simulation, and frames per second also contribute to ergonomics since any wanted movement to try to reach objects out of the range of view can cause muscle strains or other ergonomic issues.

Locomotion

This factor refers to the methods to navigate throughout the environment. In XR, when designing for virtual reality mediums, some of those methods include teleportation, or pointing toward a specific place with a controller button input for motion; walking in place; simulating walking through leg movements, allowing the simulated walking experience; physical walking, which involves real motion in the real world that matches in the 3D world; and other types such as slide/glide movements, treadmills, motion platforms, swinging or flying, flying or levitating, grabbing and pulling, vehicle simulation, and redirected walking. When it comes to spatial computing, especially using devices that don't use controllers, we can see that when designing for devices such as Vision Pro or Meta Quest Pro, there is no need for simulating movement since the experience blends with the surroundings in the real world and requires the real motion to interact with the objects or surroundings. Because of this, the recommendation remains to be aware of the limits of the digital with the physical world to prevent injuries or elements that could cause confusion of movement.

A Framework for "Interfaceless" Design

Interfaceless designs are still a novelty. Although there are current advanced tools and resources available, the journey is long in accepting that while traditional design principles are foundational, they may not directly apply in spatial computing environments. This new paradigm progresses in the direction of the generation of new tools, strategies, and methods that are particular for interfaceless scenarios.

To ensure accessibility, consistency, and functionality in the absence of traditional interfaces, we foresee the need for a set of guidelines that can help shed light on upcoming design challenges. This guiding tool (Figure 7-2) is not intended to be a rulebook, but a living blueprint that can be tested, adjusted, modified, and iterated, allowing for flexibility and creativity. This is an initial step, and you, as a creator, can carry over the next extensions of this work.

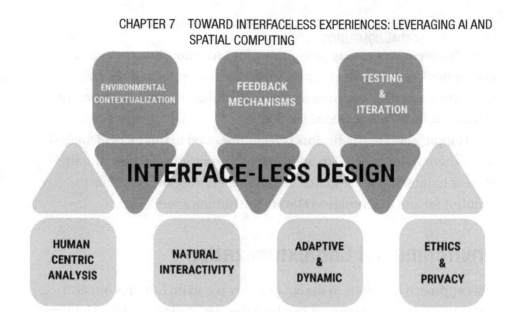

Figure 7-2. *Interfaceless Design*

Human-Centric Analysis

In traditional design, we might have heard about the definition of "user personas" as a base to understand preferences and potential behaviors and needs. As it turns out, in spatial computing this concept is transformed based on a different approach to understanding humans in spatial and context-aware ecosystems.

In spatial computing, we come to the acknowledgment that classical personas, based mostly on web-based behavioral data, fall short for the new medium. Since the predominant space places a major influence on human behaviors, guiding how actions can change based on the surrounding environment, human state, and immediate context, the classical personas based only on demographics cannot sufficiently serve as predictive input for design. Reinventing human personas is our next step in our new set of guidelines for spatial computing. We could call them "conscious personas" accounting for individual human habits and preferences, considering new variables like digital and real-world distractions, human's movement dynamics, and physical environment as a starting point for other spatial factors.

Mapping intuitive behaviors is recommended in this layer of analysis, as it is here where we can identify actions and responses that naturally appear to humans in the spatial landscape, offering key elements to account for and to leverage to elevate the human experience.

Environmental Contextualization

This approach invites us to design not only based on humans but also the surrounding environment in which the application will live. Here, we analyze factors like real-world influences, available space, and ambient conditions.

Looking back in history, we can see how for mobile phones the environment influenced its own UX paradigms. A symbiotic relationship exists between humans and nature, which is inevitable; one depends on the other, and to draw a parallel, this is a similar case. In the landscape of physical vs. digital realities, spatial computing often resides in the overlap, with the influence from both affecting the human experience. This is similar to the relationship of the architect designing based on both the site's environment and the intended human to live in the property. For the purposes of the human-environmental dual factor, considerations need to be placed in lighting, sound, temperature (of the real-world space), and spatial dynamics such as available physical space, human movement and boundaries, safety concerns, as well as potential physical interruptions and digital overlaps that might occur during the experience.

Natural Interactivity

When we talk about interfaceless design, simultaneously we talk about natural interactions. From tactile interfaces like touchscreens to regular behaviors from day to day in the real world, natural interactivity is the base for the leap required to eliminate the abstractions that the 2D screens in devices like smartphones brought to us.

Gesture-based interactions, leveraging hand and body signs as command inputs, have now become part of the decision-making we need to consider to ensure they are intuitive and not easily misinterpreted. As discussed in the previous chapter, with the rise and refinement of voice assistants entering spatial computing, we aim to balance voice commands with ambient noise and privacy considerations, maintaining an ecosystem that comprehends tone, context, and emotions.

As seen in recent head-mounted devices in the market, the benefits of eye tracking span accessibility improvements, enhanced immersion, and faster interactions. This comes with avoiding some potential challenges, like the "Midas touch" that refers to the issue of not knowing exactly when the human is only intending to look at something (passive gaze) or to actually execute a command (active gaze). This requires the design of eye tracking interfaces that can discern intent, incorporating methods such as blink-based selections, dwell times (time a person holds the gaze), or a combination of gaze and gesture modalities for confirmation.

While naturalness is an aim that would eventually facilitate human interactions, there is still a need to keep some balance between familiarity and naturalness, to help humans in the transition, so individuals don't experience feelings of overwhelm.

Feedback Mechanisms

The role of feedback is directly linked to the way humans are guided and provided reassurance during the experience. In interfaceless scenarios, the goal is to create subtle yet clear feedback mechanisms, reducing the reliance on traditional interfaces or visuals. This is achievable by making use of nontraditional feedback mechanisms like spatial audio cues and haptic feedback. Just as there are important challenges in eye tracking implementations, in feedback, a balance needs to be considered to avoid being overwhelmed with a repetitive number of unwanted sensations— what is called "haptic noise." When using spatial audio cues, it is recommended to check the science behind traditional stereo sound and spatial audio, which can also help in guiding individuals using directional sound cues and volume modulation, taking care of audio quality while avoiding auditory fatigue. Since conscious designs for interfaceless environments hold a strong attention for inclusivity, it is necessary to make sure humans with disabilities can still enjoy the experience.

Adaptive and Dynamic Designs

So far, we have mostly seen in most commercial devices, including smartphones, static designs. In spatial computing, the principles shift to fluid, adaptive systems, creating a need for reactive environments. As studied in the last chapter, the use of sensors and scanners is essential for capturing real-time spatial information, exerting in immediate context changes an influence for design adaptability. Thanks to specialized algorithms for adaptive environments, it will be not only to predict human preferences but also to provide interactive modulation, dynamic content placement, and response timings based on AI-driven data analysis. Part of the challenges to watch out here involves the computational demand of continuously adaptive systems that can be tackled with optimization strategies, ensuring fluid and smooth human experiences, reducing the overload in the system's capacity.

Testing and Iteration

When working in spatial environments, the traditional A/B tests to assess metrics like conversions and engagement are rather complex. This is because a human inside a 3D simulated space can choose options not from a set path or "user journey," but from an exponentially vast potential course of actions. Typical tests measure clicks or screen views, and in spatial computing with multisensory feedback, it doesn't capture the full scope of human feedback. Another layer of the common tests for 2D screens is the real-world variables that influence human focus like external distractions, due to the fact that they cannot be dually split between A and B groups. Because of this, there is a need for ethical and conscious multidimensional testing, using inputs such as depth and space movement, gesture, voice, and in general human behaviors that could affect the enjoyment or comfort level of the experience, as emphasized often, in an ethical and responsible way, meaning not utilizing the testing or data itself for exclusive manipulative purposes, respecting legal, perceived, and expected human rights.

Ethical Considerations and Privacy

This is perhaps the most sensitive area of the framework for interfaceless design. As we have witnessed ourselves, technology advances so fast and in so many unexpected directions that it is even difficult to catch up with it. Ultimately, having technologies more evolved to produce better and better experiences is not the real problem, since we know we are getting there anyway. Here, we can see two important issues with this paradigm: first, we never become happy at the level everything is and want more and more; second, the speed at which technology evolves is way ahead of our level of comprehension of it and our human evolution as species that have overcome the deep desire for power and capital.

As designers, creators, developers, technologists, enthusiasts, and anyone in general, we are at the cusp of great responsibilities coming up. To successfully implement interfaceless environments, the ones that respectfully and transparently consider our preferences to offer us great experiences, there is so much more to it than creating more and more advanced technologies.

In creating interfaceless and conscious spatial computing experiences, we are faced with ethical dilemmas such as the definition of intrusive design; pyschological impacts of the overreliance on technology; the protection of our most regarded private place, our mind; involving human rights and privacy; data security; the new standards of transparency in design with empathy; the legal implications of the whole emerging paradigm; and many more that might begin to arise as the machines take on more human activities. The invitation here is to proceed with caution, considering the weight and impact of the creations we are bringing to the world, and continue to educate ourselves, aiming to evolve in positive ways, out of scarcity models of human exploitation and capitalist systems that deter our own self-discovery and evolution as a collective and holistic ecosystem.

We will expand on this discussion in the next chapter, diving deeper into the nuances and considerations that designers and creators need to be aware of to contribute to a healthier society.

Potential Use Cases and Case Study

In the same way we can establish supportive methods to avoid the misuse of these evolving technologies, we can also celebrate the best potential use cases that could effectively aid humanity in its own well-being experience of life (Figure 7-3). This section intends to showcase some of those examples that, although are not completely adopters of conscious design and interfaceless methods, can potentially evolve quickly toward this vision. Let's take a look at some useful examples.

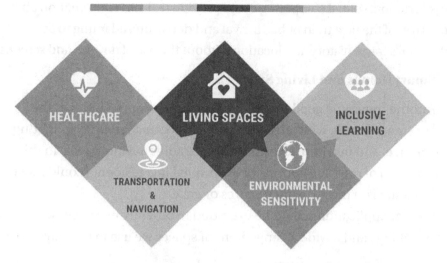

Figure 7-3. *Potential Use Cases*

Healthcare Innovations

In the field of surgery, we see the continuous use of algorithms in research to find less risky methods of performance and allow access to procedures to broader demographic segments.

Remote surgeries are a field where specialists could execute procedures from a distance, using spatial computing tools that would adapt following the specialist surgeon's movements as well as the patient's anatomy without having to recur to traditional interfaces, just as it happens in real life. As for rehabilitation purposes, simulated environments can help patients in the recovery process from physical injuries, providing progress in real time and generating functional feedback for other specialists to provide more accurate post-recovery procedures.

Transportation and Navigation

Considering safety standards and procedures, vehicles could use smart windshields displaying navigational data in real time that would self-adapt to traffic conditions, driving habits, and external factors, allowing drivers to talk to the system to provide further guidance or directions. In public

transportation, spatial computing could provide real-time information about
the arrival of the next train or bus arrival and departure, adapting to the
individual's travel history and location without the use of devices and screens.

Smart Homes and Living Spaces

Another potential good use of the interfaceless approach is in the
field of smart homes, with adaptive rooms that can change their lighting,
appearance, and furniture layouts without traditional interfaces. In this
case, instead of pressing buttons or even speaking, residents could make
modifications on the go using gestures or gaze.

Similar applications could be extended to other living spaces like
urban settings and a wide arrangement of spaces we use in our day to day.

Environmental Sensitivity

In continuation with the urban setting, spatial computing experiences
that offer opportunities for easy navigation in city exploration can
provide a rich context background in cultural education, such as history,
navigational information, and tourist attractions, based on the person's
direction of exploration or navigation. On the same line of action, walking
in nature could be enjoyable at learning more about local flora and fauna,
adapting to the walker's interests, location, and pace.

Inclusive Learning

One problem that I have seen trouble my students very often is the
fact that when faced with creating a project to showcase the technical
skills gained, there is a wall that usually appears in the creation process:
not having the clarity of what to build and the reasons behind it. I feel
that this book should aim to provide support to anybody already in the
industry or for anybody starting to explore the field, and this stage is quite
important. As mentioned previously, we are in the age where anybody
can create anything, being one of the reasons why designers and creators
would tend to get more specialized, considering that nowadays, without
any background or foundational technical standards, anything can be built

in an open platform. Because of the observance of this phenomenon, it is
my responsibility to try to help with a new awareness of the responsibility
we all have in this journey. When faced with doubt, my shared thought
process is to come inside and respond to the following questions:

- What type of experience can I build to delight humans
  through purpose- and value-driven solutions?

- How can this creation promote a balance between
  the digital and physical fields, without creating strong
  dependencies?

- How can this experience improve the quality of life
  for humans?

Starting here, we can already gain many interesting insights on what
a safe direction our potential creations could take and what our role as
protectors come to be.

Practical Case Study: "Imagined Realities"

"Imagined Realities" (Figure 7-4) is a particular, practical project that
harnesses the capabilities of AI for concept design and artwork. It consists
of a series of spaces in the art style of architectural dreamscape and
minimalism. The function of these dreamscapes is to offer the visitor
an experience to discover the level of creativity and rendering abilities
presented by generative AI tools in combination with human direction,
as well as serving as inspiration and relaxing places for mindfulness
purposes. The intention behind the dreamscapes is to serve as spaces that
can support therapeutic purposes in hospitals for patients undergoing
stress or unbalance. They are to be built using spatial computing mediums
to be accessed in 3D dimensions. Although this project is ongoing, it
begins to offer an early example of the leveraging of interfaceless principles
with conscious design foundations for spatial computing.

Figure 7-4. Imagined Realities Book

Project Background

"Imagined Realities" began as a traditional artistic work published
through a curated collection of artworks compiled in a standard
hardcover physical book. This collection of works is accompanied by
reflections around self-discovery and invites the reader to contemplate the
dreamscapes and its abstract qualities, to stimulate a sense of relaxation
and calm. Research was used to understand the effects of light, color,
elements, placement of objects, and visual harmony in general to generate
these effects. As an extension of dreamscape capabilities and to serve its
purpose of working with health practitioners, the use of regular interfaces
has been eliminated. This project is part of a macro endeavor to bring the
relaxation experience to people in treatments as a charity contribution.

To be able to showcase the first steps of this project, a gallery with
some of the book artworks has been created to illustrate not only the
technological side but also the cross section with mindful practices, using
AI. Later, you will find early iterations of this project represented in the
gallery as a case study for the implementation of some of the principles
presented in the conscious design, Chapter 3, and the interfaceless,
Chapter 4.

Key Features

- *Dynamic Environment Generation*: Adaptation of
  dreamscapes upon every different visit.

- *Adaptive Storytelling*: A different narrative is featured
  in each dreamscape, unfolding based on its visual
  characteristics.

- *Guided Exploration and Feedback Loops*: Subtle
  audio cues help visitors with a sense of presence and
  guidance.

- *AI-Augmented Artworks*: Although the 3D spaces are
  manually crafted (due to the fact that generative AI
  capabilities are not mainstream yet), they are enhanced
  by AI-generated artworks and sound.

- *Gesture Integration*: The visitors interact with the
  environment through gaze and direct touch (gaze
  triggering the size of artworks, for example).

- *Dynamic Soundscapes*: A combination of AI-generated
  sound for the gallery showcase is featured as well
  as handcrafted music to stimulate brain waves for
  relaxation.

Design Milestones

1. *Discovery and Research*: Visitor profile (empathetic profile), hardware research (Vision Pro specs, capabilities, and limitations), competitive analysis (analyze potential pitfalls, risk assessment, and contingency plan)

2. *Holistic Conceptualization*: Immersive ideation, storyboarding, bodystorming and acting, art conceptualization (using Midjourney for artwork generation and 3D environment conceptualization), interaction mode definition

3. *Design Development*: Environment design, AI integration planning, interaction prototyping (using Unity for gesture, gaze, and facial recognition), audio design

4. *Technical Development*: Vision Pro SDK Integration for gesture, gaze, and facial recognition, AI element generation (not yet available, but it is set to be trained for generating art, dreamscapes based on mood, and ambient sounds), feedback system implementation mechanisms for interaction (visual cues, sound guidance), error handling (for unrecognized gestures or other issues like maintaining immersion)

5. *Mindful Testing*: Alpha testing to fix glaring bugs; beta testing to gather visitor feedback on function, immersion, mental health impact, and technical issues; iterative refinement

6. *Release and Launch*: Performance optimization for Vision Pro's specs, visitor documentation and guidance, graphic materials for release

7. *Postlaunch*: Visitor feedback loops and reviews, updates, and maintenance

Design Domains and Outcomes
Spatial Sensitivity

- Key Factors: Ambient awareness, human comfort, visual boundaries

- Desired Outcomes: Environments that resonate with human spatial understanding and comfort

Engagement Dynamics

- Key Factors: Human focus, immersive depth, interaction fluidity

- Desired Outcomes: Seamless immersive experiences that captivate and maintain human attention

Information Architecture

- Key Factors: Contextual relevance, spatial data, human orientation

- Desired Outcomes: Clear, intuitive information structure that aids spatial understanding and decision-making

Human Autonomy

- Key Factors: Spatial choices, interaction freedom, intuitive controls

- Desired Outcomes: Empowering humans to navigate and interact with agency and in the spatial environment

Community Cohesion

- Key Factors: Collaborative spaces, shared experiences, group dynamics

- Desired Outcomes: Foster collaborative and harmonious group interactions within the spatial environment

Spatial Social Interactions

- Key Factors: Authentic avatars, relationship dynamics, social presence

- Desired Outcomes: Genuine, meaningful social interactions that respect and enhance human relationships in the spatial context

Metrics

Human well-being and satisfaction

- Metrics: Surveys and feedback focusing on emotional well-being , longitudinal studies in long-term impact

Ease of Interaction

- Metrics: Task completion rate, error rate

Depth of Engagement

- Metrics: Time spent in meaningful engagement, mindfulness metrics from surveys

Inclusivity and Accessibility

- Metrics: Diverse human testing, feedback from various demographics

Environmental and Ethical Impact

- Metrics: Carbon footprint measurement, regular ethical reviews and ethical audits

Cultural Sensitivity and Respect

- Metrics: Feedback from different cultural groups, cultural impact assessments

Holistic Safety

- Metrics: Incident reports, safety surveys

Genuine Value and Meaning

- Metrics: Testimonials and depth interviews

Community and Social Impact

- Metrics: Community feedback, social impact assessments

Development Phase

This phase has been organized using ClickUp (a platform for project management to track milestones), which we use for that purpose as well as bug tracking and to set the development sprints.

The following setup activities are an example of the implementation that you could find in your projects as well. However, it is important to highlight that this is part of the activities that a developer would execute on, so if you are not a developer, you can use it to get familiar with the process, and if you are a creator, potentially you would come across a similar framework where not only the aspects of design but also the development would have to be defined for the completion of your project. As with any project, there are always changes, especially in this case where the PolySpatial for Vision OS is being released slowly, and most developers don't have access at the time of writing this book, so changes would be important to make once it is fully released.

211

This is how the procedure looks like:

Unity and Vision OS SDK Integration:

1. Setting Up Unity with Vision OS SDK:

1.1. Install Unity:

- **1.1.1.** From the official Unity website, download the Unity Hub.

- **1.1.2.** Install Unity Hub on the computer.

- **1.1.3.** Open Unity Hub and sign in with your Unity ID.

- **1.1.4.** Click the "Installs" tab on the left sidebar.

- **1.1.5.** Click the "Add" button and select Unity version 2022.3.5f1 or later. Ensure you select the appropriate modules for the development, such as "Windows Build Support" or "Mac Build Support," depending on your target platform.

- **1.1.6.** Wait for the installation to complete.

1.2. Add the Vision OS Module:

- **1.2.1.** In Unity Hub, under the "Installs" tab, find the version you installed (2022.3.5f1 or later).

- **1.2.2.** Click the three vertical dots next to the version number.

- **1.2.3.** Select "Add Modules."

- **1.2.4.** From the list of available modules, find and select "Vision OS Module."

- **1.2.5.** Click "Done" and wait for the module to install.

1.3. Install Unity PolySpatial Packages:

(Note: The Unity PolySpatial packages for Vision OS are in closed beta at the time of writing this book, but you could apply to get access through their website.)

- **1.3.1.** Apply for the Unity PolySpatial closed beta program (or through the link provided in the official documentation).

- **1.3.2.** Once you receive access, open your Unity project.

- **1.3.3.** Navigate to "Window" ➤ "Package Manager."

- **1.3.4.** In the Package Manager, click the "+" button and select "Add package from git URL."

- **1.3.5.** Enter the URL or package details provided by Unity for the PolySpatial packages.

- **1.3.6.** Wait for the package to be imported into your project.

1.4. Setting Up Your First Vision OS Project:

- **1.4.1.** In Unity Hub, click the "Projects" tab.

- **1.4.2.** Click "New" to create a new project.

- **1.4.3.** Select the Unity version with the Vision OS module (2022.3.5f1 or later).

- **1.4.4.** Name your project and choose a location to save it.

- **1.4.5.** Ensure the Vision OS settings and PolySpatial packages are enabled for this project.

- **1.4.6.** Click "Create" to initialize your new Vision OS project.

2. Creating an Immersive Interfaceless App for Vision OS:

2.1. Setting Up the Immersive App:

- **2.1.1.** Open Unity Hub and create a new Unity project.

- **2.1.2.** In the Unity Asset Store or Package Manager, search for and import the Vision OS SDK, which includes PolySpatial as its XR solution.

- **2.1.3.** Once the Vision OS SDK is imported, navigate to "Edit" ➤ "Project Settings" ➤ "Player." Under the XR Settings or XR Plugin Management (depending on your Unity version), ensure that PolySpatial is selected as the XR SDK for Vision OS.

2.2. Configuring the Immersive Mode:

- **2.2.1.** In the Project panel, right-click and create a new scene named "ImmersiveApp."

- **2.2.2.** Open the "ImmersiveApp" scene.

- **2.2.3.** Navigate to the Vision OS SDK settings or tools within Unity. Look for an option or setting related to "App Mode" or "Display Mode."

- **2.2.4.** Select "Immersive" as the mode, ensuring that the application will run in full-screen, interfaceless mode on the Vision Pro device.

2.3. Setting Up the Environment:

- **2.3.1.** In the "ImmersiveApp" scene, set up your 3D environment. This could be a room, landscape, or any other 3D space where the human will interact.

- **2.3.2.** Ensure there are no UI elements like buttons, panels, or windows, as the goal is to create an interfaceless experience.

2.4. Integrating Vision OS SDK Features:

- **2.4.1.** Using the Vision OS SDK, integrate any necessary features or tools that will aid in creating an immersive experience. This could include spatial audio (this feature might come available later on, as right now it is not being supported yet), haptic feedback, or other sensory enhancements.

- **2.4.2.** Ensure that any SDK features used are compatible with the immersive mode.

2.5. Preparing for Gaze Interaction:

- **2.5.1.** Before transitioning to gaze interaction, set up placeholders or markers in the environment where gaze-based interactions will occur. These could be objects that the human will focus on or areas where gaze will trigger an event.

- **2.5.2.** Ensure these placeholders are easily distinguishable and are placed logically within the environment.

2.6. Finalizing the Immersive App Setup:

- **2.6.1.** Save the "ImmersiveApp" scene.

- **2.6.2.** Test the scene in Unity's editor to ensure everything is set up correctly and that the environment provides a seamless, interfaceless experience.

- **2.6.3.** Make any necessary adjustments based on the test run.

3. Implementing Gaze Interaction with Vision OS SDK in Unity:

3.1. Setting Up the Camera for Gaze Detection:

- **3.1.1.** Open the Unity project tailored for Vision OS development.

- **3.1.2.** Select the Main Camera in the hierarchy panel, representing the human's viewpoint.

- **3.1.3.** Reset the camera's position for centering. Right-click the transform component and select "Reset."

- **3.1.4.** Adjust the camera's field of view (FOV) to match the human's natural field of vision in Vision OS.

3.2. Leveraging Vision OS's Gaze Detection:

- **3.2.1.** Access the Vision OS SDK's gaze functions or components provided by the SDK to be attached to the Main Camera or other relevant objects.

- **3.2.2.** Configure any settings or parameters related to gaze detection, such as sensitivity, duration, or feedback.

3.3. Highlighting Gazed Objects:

- **3.3.1.** Ensure any built-in visual feedback is enabled and configured as needed.

- **3.3.2.** If it's not, manually implement visual feedback by changing the appearance of gazed objects, such as changing their color when gazed upon.

3.4. Triggering Events with Gaze:

- **3.4.1.** Use the Vision OS SDK's functions or events related to gaze to trigger specific actions or events.

- **3.4.2.** In case more complex interactions are to be integrated, combine gaze with other input methods like gestures or voice commands.

3.5. Testing Gaze Interaction:

- **3.5.1.** Play the scene in Unity's editor and simulate gaze interactions, ensuring the Vision OS SDK's gaze capabilities work as expected.

- **3.5.2.** Adjust any settings or parameters based on testing feedback.

- **3.5.3.** Build and test the scene on the Vision Pro device.

4. Implementing Gesture Recognition with Vision OS SDK in Unity:

4.1. Understanding Vision OS Input Mechanisms:

- **4.1.1.** Vision OS captures user intent primarily through 3D touch, skeletal hand tracking, and head tracking.

4.2. Setting Up 3D Touch:

- **4.2.1.** 3D touch is activated when a human gazes at an object with an input collider and performs the "pinch" gesture.

- **4.2.2.** Ensure objects responsive to 3D touch have a collider set to the PolySpatial Input layer.

- **4.2.3.** Use the PolySpatialTouchSpace Input device to capture this touch information.

- **4.2.4.** Integrate with the New Input System (com.unity. inputsystem) for handling touch inputs.

4.3. Implementing Skeletal Hand Tracking:

- **4.3.1.** Use the Hand Subsystem in the XR Hands Package for skeletal hand tracking.

217

- **4.3.2.** Add the Hand Visualizer component to the scene for visual representation of the human's hands.

- **4.3.3.** For advanced interactions, leverage the Hand Subsystem to measure distances between bones and joint angles.

4.4. Implementing Head Tracking:

- **4.4.1.** Head tracking is provided by ARKit through the VisionOS Package.

- **4.4.2.** Set up head tracking in Unity using the menu: Create ➤ XR ➤ XR Origin (Mobile AR). This setup is tailored for devices like Vision Pro that offer augmented reality experiences.

- **4.4.3.** Access pose data (position and rotation of the head) through the new input system using devicePosition [HandheldARInputDevice] and deviceRotation [HandheldARInputDevice].

4.5. Testing:

- **4.5.1.** Attach relevant scripts and components to game objects.

- **4.5.2.** Test in Unity's editor, using Vision OS SDK tools with the simulator.

5. Implementing Context Awareness with Vision OS SDK in Unity:
5.1. Understanding Context in Vision OS:

- **5.1.1.** Define the understanding of a human's physical environment, their current activity, or even their emotional state for the purpose of this project.

- **5.1.2.** Explore Vision OS tools or data that can be used to determine context.

5.2. Integrating Environmental Context:

- **5.2.1.** Open the Unity project tailored for Vision OS development.

- **5.2.2**. Navigate to the Vision OS SDK tools or settings within Unity.

- **5.2.3.** Look for features or tools related to environmental context detection, such as object recognition or spatial awareness.

- **5.2.4**. Implement these features in the application, ensuring they can detect and recognize key elements in the human's environment.

- **5.2.5.** Create the scripts to adapt application behavior based on the detected environment.

5.3. Integrating Activity Context:

- **5.3.1.** Within the Vision OS SDK tools in Unity, search for features related to human activity detection.

- **5.3.2.** Implement these features to detect activities like walking, sitting, or other human movements.

- **5.3.3.** Create scripts to adjust application behavior based on detected activities.

- **5.3.4.** Test these features in Unity's editor, simulating different human activities to ensure accurate detection and appropriate application response.

5.4. Personalizing Context:

- **5.4.1.** Explore the Vision OS SDK documentation to understand how it can provide insights into human preferences or emotional states.

- **5.4.2.** Implement these features in the application, ensuring they can gather and interpret human data accurately.

- **5.4.3.** Create scripts to adapt application behavior based on these insights. In this case, the goal would be that if the SDK detects a relaxed mood, it would be possible to change the application's visual theme to something calming.

- **5.4.4.** Ensure human data is handled securely and with respect to privacy concerns.

5.5. Testing Context Awareness:

- **5.5.1.** In Unity's editor, simulate various contexts to test the application's adaptability. This includes changing environments, simulating different human activities, and adjusting human mood or preference settings.

- **5.5.2.** Note any issues or inaccuracies in context detection and application response.

- **5.5.3.** Make necessary adjustments based on testing feedback.

- **5.5.4.** Once satisfied, test the application on the Vision Pro device in real-world scenarios to ensure accurate context awareness and appropriate application behavior.

6. Testing and Iteration for Vision OS in Unity:
6.1. Initial Testing in Unity Editor:

- **6.1.1.** Open the Unity project tailored for Vision OS development.

- **6.1.2.** Play the scene in Unity's editor by pressing the "Play" button.

- **6.1.3.** Use the mouse and keyboard to simulate human interactions, such as gaze, gestures, and context changes, with the Vision OS SDK simulation tool.

- **6.1.4.** Observe the behavior of the application, noting any glitches, unexpected behaviors, or performance issues.

6.2. Building for Vision Pro:

- **6.2.1.** Navigate to "File" ➤ "Build Settings."

- **6.2.2.** Ensure Vision OS is the selected platform.

- **6.2.3.** Click "Build" and choose a location to save the build.

- **6.2.4.** Once the build is complete, transfer it to the Vision Pro device using the method recommended in the Vision OS SDK documentation.

6.3. On-Device Testing:

- **6.3.1.** Wear the Vision Pro device and start the application.

- **6.3.2.** Interact with the application using natural gestures, gaze, and movements.

- **6.3.3.** Test the application in different environments and contexts to ensure context-aware features work correctly.

- **6.3.4.** Note any issues, such as lag, incorrect detections, or visual artifacts.

6.4. Gathering Feedback:

- **6.4.1.** Have other humans test the application on the Vision Pro device.

- **6.4.2.** Provide testers with a feedback form or method to report issues or suggestions.

- **6.4.3.** Observe testers as they interact with the application to identify any points of confusion or difficulty.

6.5. Iteration:

- **6.5.1.** Review the feedback and issues noted during testing.

- **6.5.2.** Prioritize the most critical issues or those that impact the human experience the most.

- **6.5.3.** Make necessary adjustments and improvements to the Unity project based on the feedback.

- **6.5.4.** After making changes, repeat the testing process, starting with the Unity editor and then on-device testing.

6.6. Performance Optimization:

- **6.6.1.** If performance issues are noticed during testing, use Unity's Profiler tool to identify bottlenecks.

- **6.6.2.** Optimize 3D models, textures, and shaders (if available, considering that shaders at this time are not fully supported yet) to improve rendering performance.

- **6.6.3.** Review the scripts and code for inefficiencies or unnecessary operations.

- **6.6.4.** Test the performance improvements in both the Unity editor and on the Vision Pro device.

6.7. Final Testing:

- **6.7.1.** Once the iterations are completed on the project and addressed feedback, conduct a final round of comprehensive testing.

- **6.7.2.** Ensure that all features work as expected and that the human experience is smooth and intuitive.

- **6.7.3.** Confirm that the application performs well in various environments and contexts.

7. Deployment for Vision OS in Unity:

7.1. Final Build Preparation:

- **7.1.1.** Open your Unity project tailored for Vision OS development.

- **7.1.2.** Ensure all assets, scripts, and scenes are finalized and ready for deployment.

- **7.1.3.** Navigate to "Edit" ➤ "Project Settings" ➤ "Player." Configure the player settings, such as company name, product name, version, and other relevant metadata.

- **7.1.4.** Optimize graphics, quality, and other settings for the Vision Pro device's specifications.

- **7.1.5.** Disable or remove any debug logs, test scripts, or unnecessary assets to optimize the final build.

7.2. Building for Vision Pro:

- **7.2.1.** Navigate to "File" ➤ "Build Settings."

- **7.2.2.** Ensure Vision OS is the selected platform.

- **7.2.3**. Click "Build" and choose a location to save the final build.

- **7.2.4**. Wait for the build process to complete.

7.3. Packaging and Signing:

- **7.3.1.** If Vision OS requires app signing for deployment, obtain the necessary signing keys or certificates from the Vision OS developer portal or equivalent.

- **7.3.2.** Use the Vision OS SDK tools or other recommended tools to sign the application package.

- **7.3.3.** Ensure the final package is correctly formatted and includes all necessary files for deployment.

- **7.3.4.** Verify the integrity of the application package to ensure it hasn't been corrupted or tampered with.

7.4. Deployment to Vision Pro Device:

- **7.4.1.** Connect the Vision Pro device to the computer using the recommended method.

- **7.4.2.** Transfer the signed application package to the Vision Pro device.

- **7.4.3.** On the Vision Pro device, navigate to the location where the application package was transferred.

- **7.4.4.** Install the application following the device's or Vision OS's installation procedures.

- **7.4.5.** Set any necessary permissions or configurations on the Vision Pro device to ensure the application runs without issues.

7.5. Testing the Deployed Application:

- **7.5.1**. Once installed, launch the application on the Vision Pro device.

- **7.5.2**. Ensure that the application runs smoothly, all assets load correctly, and there are no unexpected behaviors or issues.

7.6. Distributing the Application:

- **7.6.1**. Submit the application to the Vision OS app store or equivalent platform.

- **7.6.2**. Follow the submission guidelines provided by the platform, which may include additional testing, metadata provision, and other requirements.

- **7.6.3**. Await approval and, once approved, monitor human feedback and ratings.

- **7.6.4**. Regularly monitor human feedback, address any reported issues, and consider feature requests for future updates.

7.7. Updates and Maintenance:

- **7.7.1**. Based on human feedback, execute additional updates or fixes.

- **7.7.2**. Repeat the build, sign, and deployment process for any updates.

- **7.7.3**. If distributing through an app store, provide update notes and ensure humans are informed of the changes.

Tools and Resources Needed

- Unity 3D software

- Vision Pro SDK libraries

- Gesture recognition libraries compatible with Vision Pro

- Sample 3D assets for the Unity scene

- Documentation and guides related to Vision Pro's capabilities

Challenges and Solutions in Interfaceless Designs

One of the most interesting outcomes of the absence of tangible touchpoints is the potential overwhelming freedom that could lead to the effect of "decision paralysis." While some argue that actual "experience" cannot be defined, predetermined, and arranged, the scene of no guidance of any kind can also lead to confusion. Here, we observe different evolving expectations in the progressive nature of interfaceless designs, modifying baseline assumptions (Figure 7-5).

In terms of avoiding over-optimization, there is a potential risk of overlooking humans not familiar with the experience due to the data-driven insights as guidance for regular designs and its narrow optimization potential.

In an already invisible landscape approached with interfaceless principles, we pose the question of how to prevent human overwhelm due to the paradox of choice. A fine point also appears to become important when examining the balance between predictability and surprise, emerging from the appreciation of individuals at having systems that anticipate their needs but also ensuring space for delightful curiosity and serendipity.

226

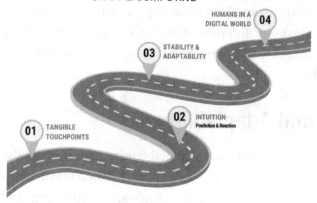

Figure 7-5. Challenges and Solutions for Interfaceless Designs

Intuition in Spatial Computing

In the context of interfaceless designs, intuition can be defined as predicting human actions, but in reality, this definition is limited. It extends to those actions that feel seamless and natural, reducing the cognitive effort to a minimum.

The prediction algorithm from regular 2D interfaces attempts to anticipate a human's next actions, for example, when a search engine generates suggestions based on text-based inputs or a music app suggests a song based on previous searches and saved lists. For interfaceless environments in spatial computing, this would look like using AR glasses and seeing relevant store displays as approaching it. On the other hand, the reaction system works by waiting to receive the signal of the human action, making a decision in real time, not anticipated as the prediction system. In traditional designs, this works, for instance, by swiping left and seeing the action outcome, for example, the next photo. In spatial computing, this works by the human performing the action of reaching out to an object and then the item being manipulated without any prediction of that specific action. This balance between prediction and

227

reaction is essential in spatial computing since the anticipation of needs
as well as the flexibility and responsiveness is part of the ultimate goal
of ensuring humans feel assisted and in control, allowing for individual
unpredictability.

Stability and Adaptability

Both stability and adaptability in spatial computing are equally
fundamental. When examining the importance of a set of parameters
for adaptability, we can see the need to avoid "overtraining" or "biasing"
specific human behaviors due to the potential loss of functionality.
Designers need to watch out to ensure that as a result of incorrect
predictions, this feedback loop gets incorporated back into the system,
minimizing the error rate, facilitating the fine-tuning of adaptability
mechanisms. Ideally, individuals should be able to reset adaptive
behaviors, empowering them to decide their comfort levels.

In case of uncertainties, having available safe modes is a practice that
can be implemented as standard, as part of the safety nets and fallbacks of
the internal mechanisms that can self-correct erratic system behaviors.

Humans in a Digital World

"Why would we try to maintain a balance between physical presence
and digital immersion? Why not just create the experience without any
type of limitations offering unlimited freedom?" one might think... This is
a question that at first glance might sound obvious to answer, but there are
also risks to contemplate about heavily skewed digital engagement.

It bears mentioning that the intrinsic value of mindful presence in the
physical and digital world still keeps the same level of importance in our
conscious design approach. Sensory experiences, emotional connections,
and tangible interactions are part of the experience of the world, and it is
still arguable at what point technology can fully replace a fully authentic
human communication experience with all its nuances and sometimes
mistakenly called "imperfect."

Extensive research has been performed in the field of cognitive function. To illustrate this further, let's take neuroplasticity as an example. Based on either external or internal stimuli, the brain has the intrinsic ability to modify itself and adapt, as it's the case when engaging in physical activity, encouraging neurotrophic conditions, which function to support the growth and health of neurons. This is already quite fascinating. In the same fashion, digital stimuli have been researched with basic tasks such as problem solving and critical thinking skills presented in spatial puzzles, aiding in cognitive development.

While temporary and limited digital resources and tools can help support some health-related functions, for the most part, research also indicates that the processes of focus and concentration are supported by digital downtime, rest, and reflection, supporting problem solving skills and memory formation.

In the age of social media, emotional impact has also been a target for many researchers in the world. It is well known that digital interactions cannot produce yet the same resonance and emotional depth from face-to-face encounters. I have participated in a variety of virtual reality events, and my observations confirm the most updated research: we are still in a nascent stage, and qualities such as tone of voice, physical touch, and nonverbal cues are still simulated without precision and as a placeholder rather than as a human, authentic communication sign, which are all essential for deep connections.

Consequently, it can be deduced that digital overreliance can at times lead to feelings of loneliness, as shown by studies about the excessive use of social media.

As a counterbalance for these risks, we might opt to design interfaceless solutions that motivate humans to real-world interactions and physical motion, including unobtrusive reminders prompting humans to the practice of mindful presence, breathing rests, nature walks, and modes that limit digital immersion, preventing digital overdependence.

And finally, for productive tools, establishing a balance between digital efficiency for productivity and tangible interaction for creativity can lead to higher levels of quality work, integrating physical breaks as the already tried and tested Pomodoro Technique, resulting in healthy living and mental health.

Automation and Inherent Risks

What does over-automation mean in interfaceless designs? Automation operates and exists in a spectrum that goes from zero automation to complete automation, and at different levels of this spectrum, human controls and intervention are established. When we talk about over-automation in spatial computing, what we are saying is that the system inherently contains the risks of execution of commands without human input, bypassing intentions or real needs, such as a voice assistant making decisions without the individual consent.

The consequences of working under a framework of assumptions are far-reaching. Consider the scenario where operational systems incorrectly order a product or service or it is found out using private information for other purposes than the support of the human experience.

To differentiate that balance of functional automation vs. over-automation, let's take a look at some examples.

- *Human Control*: Functional automation will offer the option to reset the system and intervene if needed; over-automation will eliminate the option, overriding human agency.

- *Accuracy*: Aside from the fact that no perfect system without error exists, over-automation could misread human intentions, whereas functional automation might demonstrate a higher level of fidelity.

- *Transparency*: Providing some feedback on its
  workings, functional automation can operate more
  reliable and accessible, and in turn, over-automation
  might perform as in a black box, meaning difficult to
  track down, to decipher.

- *Predictability*: It might come as a surprise, but to
  illustrate this point, let's ponder the current case
  with the latest trained generative AI systems. Upon
  surveying the researchers involved with their own
  evolution, the generative AI systems surpassed the
  level of expectations estimated by the researchers
  and sometimes even showcased totally unknown
  capabilities! Let's reflect on this... Without predictable
  systems, we are at their will.

Another current concern has been related with the dangers of mastery
in different skills, due to automated systems replacing human tasks,
putting a stifle in innovation and creativity. This aspect also directly
impacts the risk of job displacement and its broader social implications.

Implications of Universal Designs

Let's talk about the impact of culture on tech adoption. Starting with the
concept of universal design, its initial intent was to create solutions for
a wide range of individuals. There is a distinction that can be identified
with truly universal design methods and misinterpreted or broad-based
design. From here, we come to realize the impact that subtleties like voice
intonation, eye movements, and gestures have across different cultures.
As an example, we see certain nuances beyond translations posed by the
differences in context, idioms, and tone, creating additional complexities
for language processing. The same applies to ergonomic biases, where

cultural spatial behaviors differ from a traditional standard, for example, comparing preferences by a Japanese individual of sitting on a floor couch than on an elevated chair.

For these scenarios, offering customized or localized settings to provide humans with agency to adjust their experiences based on their own cultural preferences would be a resourceful approach to also foster respect for particular culture norms and values, navigating more carefully potential sensitivity controversies.

Legal Responsibility

The quest from preliminary tech products until today's multifaceted digital systems has set the pace of transformation for liability models as technology integrated more in our daily lives. One of the main reasons why older liability models might not be suitable for new technological setbacks is because unique practices that were valid in the past quickly get outdated with rapidly evolving technology. At the same pace, the public sentiment around technological responsibility has also evolved, and nowadays public opinion can have a direct influence on legal precedents.

Existing challenges in this field span the self-learning and executing capabilities of AI-based systems and the conundrum to trace back resolutions to human parameters; in the same fashion, the human determinations, in the dynamic of a team where different roles get involved, as designers, humans, developers, stakeholders, and manufacturers, make distributing responsibility a difficult undertaking.

Considering we have seen cases throughout history where ethical obligations are blurred when contrasted with legal responsibility, one might also see the other side of the story, that is, the role of corporations in this dichotomy. There are reasons to believe that beyond the intervention of solid laws, which usually take a long time to be established, other societal influential actors can exert earlier influence, such as, in this case, technology companies. This might look like in the form of corporate ethics new internal statutes, where clear directions are provided in place with defined ethical standards and obligations. How many times in companies have you seen their own ethics guidelines and everyone intrinsically compromised to them as an extension of themselves? If this is not a common practice seen currently, now is a good time to propose new initiatives and bring the discussion to the table.

Summary: From Theory to Practice— Implementing "Interfaceless" Designs

In this chapter, we set the practices that from XR are applicable to interfaceless environments for spatial design, beginning with a brief discussion about the background of the traditional UX practice, establishing a parallel between XR and the interfaceless approach for spatial computing, and studying factors to consider such as visual grammar, language and typography, and narrative design, along with special considerations for XR design.

A framework for interfaceless design is contemplated next, as a complementary thought process pointing out potential challenges, discussing human-centric analysis, environmental contextualization, natural interactivity, feedback mechanisms, adaptive and dynamic design, testing and iteration, and, finally, ethical and privacy considerations.

Potential use cases and examples were presented to understand the workings of these elements in real-world scenarios as well as some challenges and solutions, providing additional insights, aiming to open up a critical thinking, self-reliant approach.

Resources

Please refer to Appendix A, "List of Some Potential Ideas with a Conscious
and Mindful Approach," to check a more expanded list of potential mindful
interesting solutions for spatial computing.

CHAPTER 8

Ethical Design in an AI-Driven World

In the fields of quantum mechanics and general relativity, there is a term called "singularity." It refers to the theoretical phenomenon where gravitational forces cause matter to present infinite density, like the example of black holes, which are presumed to contain a singularity area that appears to break all the laws of physics. This is called quantum singularity. In the same way that we are uncertain about the actual happenings inside a black hole, it's also uncertain how AI surpassing human intelligence will behave and use its autonomous capabilities.

I remember studying in school some of the theories proposed by Stephen Hawking. Singularities challenge our understanding of physics and help us realize the nature of inventors of new models. In fact, when it comes to singularities, some scientists agree that to grasp the singularity phenomenon in quantum mechanics, the introduction of a completely new model of thinking needs to be considered.

Just as it happens with the singularities from black holes, we are faced right now with similar kinds of challenges. In the technology field, the point where technologies grow irreversible and exponentially away from human control is called a singularity. This idea was first proposed in the mid-20th century by the computer scientist and mathematician John von Neumann. He is remembered for having remarked that technological

D. Olynick, *Interfaceless*, Design Thinking, https://doi.org/10.1007/979-8-8688-0083-2_8

growth would accelerate beyond our human comprehension. And of course, famous futurist Ray Kurzweil, who wrote the book *The Singularity Is Near*, went so far to predict its occurrence by the year 2045. Our current understanding of ethics, the nature of intelligence, and even control mechanisms might be challenged in the process as AI continues with its exponential growth. This is a call for the proposition of new models and frameworks to understand, that invite us to help lead this generation, and upcoming generations of actors, through an uncertain technological landscape, and determining that which is compassionate and kind, and at the same time, that which is in tune with the reality of a paradigm shift and our role on it as the precursors.

Ethical Considerations in Tech

It happens that I haven't seen so many people speaking about this topic passionately between designers, engineers, product designers, creators, and technologists, and I believe that this is the result of a lack of understanding of what we are about to face as a collective society, so my aim in this chapter is to bring some light to the unknowns that perhaps we haven't been familiar with and open up a conversation that is insightful and necessary, especially during the current times (Figure 8-1).

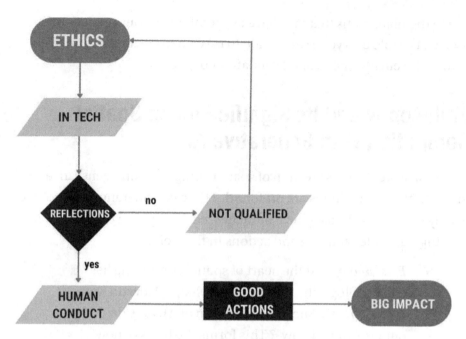

Figure 8-1. *Ethical Considerations in Tech*

We will be entering into the discussion of the origins of ethics because we hear this word and sometimes we are not very clear about what exactly it means. We will dive into the precedents and will have the opportunity to study some real-world cases that have been widely documented to spark a deeper reflection.

To begin with, according to Google and the definition from Oxford, ethics is defined as "The moral principles that govern a person's behavior or the conduct of an activity." It has all to do with our own behavior and display of conduct and, based on them, what type of consequences can happen. Like this, we begin to speak about standards, the group of guidelines that we can create around anything related to our own harmonious living, and the protection of rights because part of the ethics purpose is to help us navigate in safe scenarios, where we all can live as a community and we can all take care of each other. This foundation gives rise to the obligations that they have as members of communities, of a society, the role everyone can decide to take on protecting nature, the planet, the environment, and all its sub-ecosystems.

Philosophy and Its Significance in Spatial Computing with Generative AI

As we navigate the cross section of spatial computing and generative AI, the ethical considerations are profound. These considerations are rooted deeply in various philosophical branches, each playing a crucial role in shaping our understanding and actions in this field.

- *Epistemology*: At the heart of spatial computing lies epistemology, the theory of knowledge. How do we know what we know? In the realm of AI, how do our creations "know"? This forms the basis of how generative AI learns, processes, and generates content. The line between learned knowledge and generated knowledge becomes blurred in spatial computing, emphasizing the importance of understanding its roots.

- *Metaphysics*: The exploration of reality and being becomes particularly poignant in the age of spatial computing. As virtual realities become increasingly indistinguishable from our physical world, the line between the "virtual" and the "real" becomes ever so thin. This is where metaphysics shines. Metaphysics, originating from the Greek roots "meta" (beyond) and "physics" (nature), pushes us to explore the very nature of reality. Facebook's transition to "Meta" signifies a step into this expanded realm of existence. Aristotle's contemplation on the foundational and abstract aspects of reality now resonates deeply as we sculpt virtual worlds and AI entities. In essence, the study of metaphysics prompts us to question the realities we're creating and the entities we're emulating. It's a journey of self-discovery in a digital age, helping us understand our creations and, in turn, ourselves.

- *Ethics*: With the progression of spatial computing and AI, ethical considerations are paramount. Every line of code in AI, every spatial construct, holds ethical implications. From influencing user decisions to creating alternate realities, the ethical ramifications are vast. Ethics acts as our moral compass in this vast sea, ensuring that our innovations not only marvel but also respect the principles of right conduct. It's not about limiting creativity but guiding it in a direction that harmonizes with human values and rights. For instance, as we sculpt virtual realities, are we offering escape or entrapment? As generative AI crafts content, is it serving users or manipulating them? These are the questions ethics compels us to address.

- *Logic*: As we construct algorithms and AI entities, logic is our building block. It dictates how processes flow, how decisions are made, and how outcomes are determined. But beyond the code, logic also guides our reasoning and decision-making in the ethical and epistemological challenges we face. Ensuring that our spatial computing endeavors are not only technologically grounded but also logically consistent is essential for their success and acceptance.

In the dynamic intersection of philosophy and technology, these branches provide a holistic framework. Since our main focus has been the creation of intentional experiences, we can now reflect on how these creations are about understanding, reflecting, and ensuring that our technological innovations serve humanity in its fullest essence. As we continue our journey in spatial computing and AI, let's reflect on these philosophical pillars as a support to guide our path, ensuring a future that's not only innovative but also introspective and ethically sound.

Conscious Tech Commerce

In an attempt to avoid merely critiquing the current system we live in, providing a shallow assessment, I can see a potential application of a broader term that sometimes is brought to the economy field called "socially conscious entrepreneurship" or "sustainable capitalism." I came to call it "conscious tech commerce" as this new approach for tech companies focuses on awareness and intentionality of the technology that is created and its impact on humans. Corporations operating under this paradigm are aware of the environmental, societal, and ethical consequences of their actions or business operations. They are not in business merely to make money, but to make a positive and conscious difference in the world.

This paradigm and approach to business bring to the commerce field an additional layer to the way internal procedures are performed. They deliberately decided to focus on the metrics of positive impact and see the profits as the direct result of fair and transparent actions. They also cultivate this stance with their own employees, who as a domino effect will also create the remaining ripples in society. They speak in terms of societal impact, ethical considerations, and long-term sustainability.

As you might suspect, this approach requires another type of leadership, where the visionaries that are in the position of running this type of venture have a more advanced view of the world and themselves, and therefore they act from a higher aim than themselves. These types of leaders usually have a deeper standpoint, a developed sensitivity about their own role in the world as humans and the impact of their own decisions on others; usually, these humans are of a kinder nature.

Socially Conscious Corporations

To demonstrate how this is already in place and not a speculative approach, let's study a couple of successful cases walking toward a socially conscious future.

Toms Shoes

This company has adopted a model of supporting people in need of contribution while being in the field of business. Some of its philanthropic practices include donating one pair of shoes to a child in need for every pair sold. It also has expanded its giving to include sight saving surgery, safe birth services in countries in need, and clean water, among others, demonstrating why focusing genuinely on others first, rather than only profit and power, is a real and fair business model with the double benefit of making exceeding profits while impacting the world in a positive way without the use of dubious practices.

Salesforce

Its 1-1-1 philanthropic model consists of allocating 1% of its equity, 1% of employee time, and 1% of its products to exclusive philanthropic initiatives and community volunteering. It claims to be committed to full renewable energy sources used for its operations and support a focus on inclusivity rights with defined initiatives for racial and gender equal participation.

Trigger XR

I came to know about Trigger XR initiatives through one of the interviews for the XR Magazine podcast I conducted with its founder and CEO, Jason Jim. Trigger XR is an agency that has assisted widely recognized brands in the world, such as Sony, Disney, Warner Brothers, Fox Studios, and more, in their XR-driven projects. During the interview, it became clear that part of Tigger XR's priorities are kindness and charity at the forefront. This company is committed to making annual holiday season contributions to nonprofit organizations, such as The Marine Mammal Center, Habitat for Humanity, and The Dine National Youth Agency, and many more specific projects in the field of education, animal welfare, homes for people in need, and so on. This is a clear example of a corporation running a mission that demonstrates its compromise with a bigger cause than itself, therefore running on a foundation of greater purpose and impact for the world and society.

In summary, some signs of socially conscious entrepreneurship might include sustainable practices, ethical supply chains, transparent reporting, mission- and purpose-driven values and practices, commitment with philanthropy causes and charity, and employee engagement.

While we cannot always decide by choice in what company we want to work for and what type of corporation and values to align with, it's certainly something that makes us reflect on the sort of contributions we are making in society when we support organizations and leaders that don't seem to exert higher values with themselves, their employees, and society at large. A thought-provoking question is this: What type of company would you like to support in the future through your own work? This reflection not only applies to employees but also to freelancers and even owners of companies themselves. What type of values are you perpetuating through the relationships you are building on a daily basis? Whenever possible, we can come back to reflect on this and realign our values, redirecting our course of action as free human beings.

With this essential deliberation away, let's turn our focus to the four ethical theories to apprehend the influences of these roots in our current operative behavioral models (Figure 8-2).

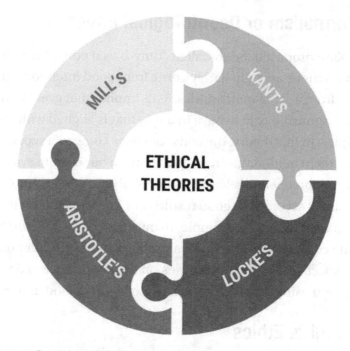

Figure 8-2. *The Four Ethical Theories*

The Four Ethical Theories

Mill's Utilitarianism

This ethical theory was proposed by John Stuart Mill, hence its name, and it describes a principle where the best action is the one that produces the bigger benefit for the majority. Looking at the current tech landscape, we can see that some companies frequently use a form of maximization of utility, arguing that their products are of direct benefit to the greatest number, even if there is harm to a minority. This can lead to overlooking the minority rights for perceived more significant gains.

Kant's Formalism or Deontological Ethics

Immanuel Kant proposed the so-called "duty-based ethics," which suggests that actions are right if they come from good intentions or will, coming from a set of moral duties. This implies that every human being has a responsibility to behave in a way that is aligned with their own principles. In this theory, the consequences come as a secondary effect to the intent behind the original actions. In our current system, the rapid development and release of potentially harmful technologies could potentially accomplish good results, but they are built on the basis of nontransparent intent, for example, using manipulative methods with the data collected, this becomes a problematic issue under the Kantian perspective. This theory focuses on the importance of designing, developing, and using tech with ethical protocols and good motives.

Locke's Rights Ethics

John Locke, an Oxford academic, proposed this theory on the basis of natural rights, especially property, liberty, and life. According to him, these rights are inalienable, or in other words, they cannot be surrendered. In our current tech landscape, we see issues with rights violations, particularly privacy. In this ethics approach, the infringement of fundamental rights supposes a case for stringent human rights considerations and stringent data privacy. As an example, technologies attempting to own our thoughts or mind pertain to the application of this ethical paradigm.

Aristotle's Virtue Ethics

Aristotle relied on the cultivation of virtuous character and attaining a "golden mean" between the opposites or extremes, excess and deficiency, placing a lesser focus on the consequences or rules. From this ethical perspective, corporations need to cultivate higher virtues like responsibility, transparency, and honesty, extending these practices reflected in their own products, which ideally would also aim to cultivate higher virtues in the individuals and clients using their products rather than exploiting them.

Granting the current issues and complexities of newest technologies and their consequences, not one theory can reframe the focus of the complete ecosystem. In turn, a holistic approach that applies all of these principles could offer better and effective lights to continue to build the path toward wise human evolution.

In light of the fact that ethics pertain to the foundations of human conduct, it has set the foundations for the principles of law. As a consequence, from law, the principles of justice came also to be set forth.

In justice, we have the tenets of protection of rights that in the field of technology requires a deeper study and definition: inherent morality, societal values that tend to adjust as technology advances and requires specificity and regulation; promotion of common good, an echo of the utilitarian principle explained earlier; and accountability, calling on tech companies to be responsible for their actions.

In brief, laws serve the society as living entities that protect individual and collective rights promoting the common good, but to manifest with justice, they need to be grounded in strong ethical foundations to achieve the ultimate goal of a greater good for all in the rapid pace of our current technologies.

Case Studies of Ethical Breaches: A Discussion on Spatial Computing with Generative AI

Modern Precedents of Ethical Concerns in Technology

In our journey through spatial computing and generative AI, it's essential to grasp the ethical quandaries born from technological leaps. Historically, each major innovation comes with unforeseen societal consequences.

By examining these, we can better anticipate and navigate the ethical landscape of spatial computing.

- *Biased AI Algorithms*: A more contemporary case would be the rise of machine learning algorithms in decision-making processes, which have been shown to possess unintended biases. For instance, AI-driven job recruitment tools that unfairly favored certain demographics over others due to biases inherent in their training data. These examples serve as a cautionary tale for the ethical deployment of spatial computing technologies, highlighting the importance of conscious design and the dangers of unchecked assumptions.

- *The Birth of the Internet and Unintended Societal Impacts*: The birth of ARPANET in the 1960s, which laid the foundation for today's Internet, was never coupled with an in-depth foresight into its massive societal implications. Much like how the pioneers of ARPANET couldn't entirely predict the societal transformation brought by the Internet, we must be cautious in presuming we can foresee all implications of spatial computing.

- *Social Media and AI-Generated Realities*: With the surge of social media in the 1990s, driven by the ubiquity of mobile devices, no one could have predicted the profound impact it would have on human interaction, psychology, and society at large. Delving deeper, when we integrate AI-generated content into these platforms, we're on the cusp of a new era where the lines between reality and AI-crafted experiences blur. The ethical concerns here aren't just about the reality we depict but also about the perceptions of reality we might inadvertently distort in our users' minds.

The unforeseen consequences of these technologies highlight the importance of our central theme: the conscious design of spatial computing applications. Reflecting on the foundational aspects of these platforms, many of their creators might not have envisioned the full range of their impact. The advertisement-driven models, leading to new societal challenges like the increased mental health issues in vulnerable individuals, stand testament to these undesired outcomes.

Modern Issues

Now, let's dive into some of the modern issues that have contributed to the rise of new ethical concerns around technology.

Deceptive and Addictive Design

With the rise of social media and the accessibility for most people to access a mobile device, other issues started to become evident. The most highlighted one is the practice of deceptive design and addictive consequences. This is exemplified through the creation and proliferation of misleading products and the main focus of companies of this kind in metrics such as click-through rate (CTR), saves, shares, likes, and comments; focus in platform retention indicators or engagement time, and daily active users (DAU). The problems that stem from these kinds of metrics pertain to the prioritization of short-term attention as an asset rather than long-term well-being, the urge toward addiction due to the emphasis on attention as a goal, and the promotion of sensational content that evokes strong emotions and psychological triggers, beside all the impacts of these mentioned priorities in society's and individual's mental health.

As we can see, since the approach for business operations is based on what I call "Obstructive Engagement Metrics" (OEM), they lead to the promotion of toxic behaviors and the manipulation of vulnerabilities, actively hindering the potential for healthier interactions and community well-being.

Social and Political Influence

Deriving from unethical uses of social media platforms and the asset of attention as the product, other societal actors have found ways to benefit from this phenomenon. This is the case of political entities and members looking to exert influence in interested segments of the population. At this level, we are no longer a consumer but the actual item or product they need to make high profits from, using misleading practices and manipulative information, to take entire communities toward a certain call to action.

Data Misuse

In order for companies to effectively capture our attention for as long as possible, deep psychological vulnerabilities in humans are used to achieve their goal. For the most part, borrowing from all the captured data from our created identity profiles and the reading of algorithms of our behaviors, their systems can track and read specific triggers to activate key emotional responses.

Using facial recognition algorithms has also been an issue for companies like Facebook, where the feature aims to tag individuals automatically in photos without proper consent or understanding of other potential uses of this data collected, which usually is not just for tagging individuals.

Data As a Commodity

The sharing of an individual's location information is another example that has allowed companies to sell the data to advertisers without consent. The access of third-party apps to human's data even if it's not directly breached by the company itself has also negative consequences when the information is not properly protected and secured, as the third-party apps can benefit and misuse these private identity profiles for a variety of unethical uses.

There are also reported claims of the creation of "shadow profiles" for individuals that are not part of the platform that get created through friend connections. This private and individual data is then used without the individual knowing that they exist in the platform with a profile, and the information is sold or used without agreement for consent.

Ethical Case Studies

Inspired by the documentary *The Social Dilemma* on Netflix, let's review some of the implications about design decisions performed in the past by some entities in the technological field.

The Like Button

According to open claims, the creation of this feature came to be as a tool for individuals to support others' posts or express appreciation. Behind its design goal, it was supposed to make interactions with the posts faster, therefore introducing efficiency. However, the actual consequences were unexpected. It became an instrument as a metric to get insights into validation and popularity. Its influence grew far-reaching to the point where it dictated human actions, the type of content creation, and, most importantly, the direction of the algorithm itself, giving priority to more engaging content, through the number of likes.

More specific outcomes of this feature include a wrong perception of self-worth and validation; the spread of a comparison culture; the activation of dopamine through addictive feedback loops; unauthentic content generation; mental health issues as a result of higher levels of depression, anxiety, and loneliness; individual identity distortion; misinformation and manipulation, children with self-esteem issues, and questionable economic/monetization methods.

Cambridge Analytica

As a watershed moment in the era of digital connections, this case comes with ethical issues in human data handling, data consent of use, and the implications of political influence and power.

Cambridge Analytica was a European political consulting firm founded in 2013, specialized in strategic communication and data analysis. As per the strengths of those specialized skills, they had a goal to influence voters' choice toward skewed candidates.

The main issue arose when the company obtained access to data of approximately 87 million individuals without their consent. The access of this data was acquired through participation in a quiz using Facebook that rippled the effects of information taken by capturing not only the respondents' profile data but also their friends without them knowing it. This was the raw material for Cambridge Analytica to begin creating psychological profiles and presenting manipulated information in front of them using vulnerabilities found to manipulate their decisions. This event had a direct effect on the 2016 elections and the Brexit referendum, creating a global concern of data privacy and the transparency of technological platforms with their collected human data.

AI-Biased Algorithms

This particular case occurred in the field of employment recruitment, showcasing a clear example of the impact of using artificial intelligence models with trained data containing biases, inheriting and exacerbating its performance outcomes.

250

In 2018, Amazon was reported using an AI recruitment tool with significantly skewed preference toward male candidates and rejection over females. The intended design was supposed to rank candidates based on their suitability for the position. Since the algorithm was trained on past recruitment data from the company itself, the results were biased toward males. The system automatically downgraded female candidates, and Amazon's corrective reaction proved to be more complex than expected. In fact, eventually, Amazon decided to abandon the use of the tool due to its high grade of uncertainty with the expected performance.

To properly wrap this section, let's reflect on a deeper question: What certainty do we have that past mistakes won't be extended in spatial computing? What would be our individual role in this?

We have as creators a huge responsibility in the process, in seeing the overall picture and the potential issues that may arise with the decisions that we make in terms of design.

Best Practices for Ethical Use of AI in Design

As explored so far, from predictive human experiences to dynamic adaptability, ethics in the field of AI for design purposes is a field worth to be explored by creators of experiences for spatial computing.

The current challenges remain to be around the balance between empowering humans and overstepping their own boundaries. Transparency in AI algorithms is a fundamental practice that is still being debated on what would be the safest practices, contemplating the inherent rights humans have to understand the design process and practices to design and develop their experiences and the methodologies and tools used for that purpose.

As illustrated in the previous section, the data where AI algorithms are trained on is sensitive and vulnerable to detrimental potential outcomes. Properly studying the datasets and making sure that the human input in these decisions is also transparent and free of discrimination, preferences, or particular tendencies could lower risks of exponential societal negative effects.

The Role of Designers and Developers in AI Ethics

As designers and developers, we play a role in addressing the considerations that come with our work. It is important for us to promote inclusivity and diversity in our data and design processes, prioritize user privacy, ensure transparency, and establish safeguards to protect user safety and well-being. Moreover, we should advocate for considerations at every stage of the design process from generating ideas to deploying our creations.

However, it's not enough to have intentions. We need to possess knowledge and skills in AI ethics, have an understanding of the implications of our design choices, and be committed to prioritizing ethics even when faced with challenges or inconveniences.

Above all else, we must see ourselves as more than designers or developers; we are also responsible for being caretakers of the AI systems we create. We hold the power to shape the landscape of AI in design, which comes with a responsibility.

Intellectual Property and Originality: A Discussion

The rapid progress in the field of intelligence and spatial computing has sparked discussions about intellectual property (IP) and what it means to be original. With machines producing artwork, music, and even literature, the concept of "originality" is becoming more complex and raising questions about its impact on intellectual property rights. Let's dive deeper into these concerns in relation to design and interfaceless environments.

The Dilemma of AI-Created Content

When a machine creates something, who owns the rights to it? Traditional notions of property are rooted in creativity, ingenuity, and labor. However, as AI algorithms generate creative outputs, the line between human and machine creation becomes blurred.

For example, Midjourney has produced artworks inspired by prominent artists. If these creations have value, who should benefit from them? Should it be the developers behind the AI technology or the users who utilized these tools? Perhaps nobody at all since machines lack legal personhood?

The concept of originality has evolved throughout history. In ancient times, originality was believed to be a gift, with art and creativity seen as blessings from the gods. During the Renaissance period, legendary figures like Leonardo da Vinci became symbols of genius. This era then brought focus on individualism, associating originality with uniqueness. Now, in the era of AI, we find ourselves at the brink of another transformation as we grapple with the idea of machine-generated originality.

One aspect that intensifies the debate on AI originality is design in environments without physical interfaces. As designers explore AI's potential to anticipate human needs, creating unique experiences and generating new design solutions, certain questions emerge: If an AI algorithm generates a design solution, who should claim ownership? How can we ensure recognition and compensation?

Moreover, interfaceless systems like voice assistants or holographic projections powered by AI have access to databases that enable them to create human solutions. When these solutions hold value, determining intellectual property rights becomes more complex, posing this panorama as an essential scenario for any creator to ponder and create their own individual work guidelines.

Unexpected Stakeholders: The AI Trainers

Should the individuals whose data was used to train the AI be entitled to a share in the rights to that property?

Let's imagine a scenario where an AI trained on thousands of indie music tracks creates a song that climbs to the top of the charts. While this song may appear "original" in terms of its combination of notes and rhythms, it undoubtedly bears influences from the training data it was exposed to. It becomes imperative then to acknowledge and compensate these contributors.

The convergence between AI and intellectual property in design and spatial computing presents us with both established principles and evolving challenges. While AI's creative capabilities challenge notions of originality, they also provide us with an opportunity to redefine property rights in an inclusive, fair, and collaborative manner.

Let's first define what we mean by property (IP). To protect these creations from use by others, we have intellectual property rights (IPRs) like patents, copyrights, and trademarks.

When it comes to design, IPRs play a role in safeguarding the output of designers. They ensure that designers receive recognition and compensation for their work and discourage others from exploiting their ideas without giving credit or compensation.

On the other hand, originality, as we have discussed, is a concept in design that holds significant importance. It involves creative thinking to come up with ideas and innovative solutions. Originality is highly valued among designers as a sign of talent and a driver of success.

Now, let's consider the intersection of AI, IP, and originality. When AI enters the scene, things become more complex. AI has the potential to generate designs, develop solutions, and in many ways imitate the process of human design.

However, these capabilities give rise to questions and challenges when it comes to property (IP) and the concept of originality.

When an AI system creates a design, these questions arise: Who should own the rights to that design? Should it be the developer who programmed the AI or the user who operated it? Should we consider that the AI itself has some claim? The current IP laws, which are built on the foundation of authorship, do not provide clear-cut answers.

Some argue that AI-generated designs should be credited to the AI system itself which would require a reevaluation of property (IP) laws. Others believe that the rights should belong to the developer or individual using the AI system, as they see it as a tool used in creating the design.

While AI can certainly produce combinations and variations, there is a debate about whether this qualifies as originality, which typically involves some level of creative intention or insight. With the line between human and machine creativity becoming blurred, we now have AI systems of generating works that many would consider truly original, becoming an increased sea of issues to navigate.

Widening the Ethical Horizon: Broader Considerations

At the end of the day, technology is always an extension of our own creations, so it's always working as a mirror, resembling our own humanity, our own level of understanding, and evolution. In this way, technology is not a separate entity we should fear, and in fact, there is no need for fear, but the actual desire for power that gets confused with the romantic idea of taking humans to a more elevated state. While we see great leaps of progress through history, we also see great mistakes, taking the lives away in extreme cases of millions of people. The extreme power of companies that have only as a driving force the desire for power and monopoly is a real problem.

Having abilities for control, platforms have the potential to be able to monitor and manipulate all aspects of our lives at a level that no other technology has so far yet enabled. When I speak about monitoring, I also speak about vigilance, having the power to monitor humans and their lives, in the same way that, as previously discussed, social media platforms have done it with our identity, our profiles, our history, our behaviors, our aims, and psychological tendencies, tracking where we click, what we buy, who our friends are, and more metrics.

To put it in perspective, for spatial computing we are at the same level of risk. In simulated environments, it will be as easy to track where we go, how we move, what we look at, and how we feel about it.

We are at the dawn of a new era with more uncertainties than solid paths of action for our own safety. This is very concerning. In the future, when augmented reality devices become mainstream, systems will be able to track our physical actions, walking pace, posture, expressions, emotions, and even vital signs, like pupil dilation, heart rate, and respiration rate; in short, they will track everything that we do in our daily lives. Right now, this is already happening to some extent with mobile devices; that's why we receive the advertisement we see on the screen, but in spatial computing this would take a more exponential risk.

As exposed so far, this is an imminent privacy concern, and as worrying as this reads, the whole picture is even beyond this. Think for a moment what could be done with all this data. As in social media, one of its uses could be for targeted advertising and better "user segmentation." At the cross section with artificial intelligence, the simulated environments could display all types of methods to manipulate humans toward biased decisions. Given that simulated environments replicate real experience and present it as if it were absolutely real, this is the perfect scenario to present misinformation and display it as veridical and genuine. Not being able to discern what is true and what is not, what is authentic, and what is fake is one of the main risks here as well.

We are running the sensitive risk that if we carry over the dangerous methods that have spread in 2D devices, in simulated spaces for spatial computing, for instance, with practices like targeting in advertising, chances are this also won't take the form of 2D interfaces in the way we see in videos or regular 2D ads, but with much more convincing and subtle methods.

We already see the phenomenon of *Roblox* and *Fortnite* where children and adults alike enjoy acquiring 2D assets like virtual clothes, accessories, and many other assets that pertain to identity. On the same line of experience, in simulated spaces for spatial computing, we will see virtual product placements and merchandise, offering more freedom and opportunity to platforms to appeal to individual's identity to satisfy new emerging virtual needs and exacerbate increasingly the desire to affirm a new virtual identity with new projected needs.

The types of experiences and practices we talk about in this book are free from this 2D toxic paradigm.

In a simulated environment, virtual objects could be used to manipulate humans based on what is known as their real preferences, so instead of seeing 2D advertisements where we know it is in fact an ad, in 3D spaces, this narrative might change altogether to use our preferences represented in objects, people, and spaces that we like, but with an underlying purpose: invisible manipulation.

If I access a simulated space and all of a sudden I see a living room with a beautiful song in the background and a candle and sweater lying on the chair of my preferred brand, I could see in this same scenario two possibilities: either the system knows me well and it's used for personalization in line with my own needs and preferences or it could potentially be a 3D object from a specific brand using retargeting, inserted in the space without my knowledge, albeit the psychological principle of "mere exposure effect," suggesting a product to create familiarity until it is trustable, therefore resulting in sales.

Virtual product placements will be targeted experiences injected into the spaces you visit by third parties for a fee. In this case, you could see products in your personal space that you think of as just natural parts of your experience, but they will be intentionally, and without your consent, placed there specifically for you to experience with a specific purpose.

Now, this is when it gets more interesting. The next level of this new and more sophisticated mode of advertisement could potentially be translated to inserting human-like beings, using more advanced generative artificial intelligence models, which could hold simulated natural conversations and look like any other individual present in the space. These digital beings will have access to all your data and will be used on the "surface" to help you guide your experience, but in different uses of these systems, this could be used to manipulate your preferences as well. Not only this could happen by means of you having direct conversations with these beings without you knowing their nature but also by seeing them around conversing with any other person about coincidentally things that you also like, as naturally as if it were another human being, completely unnoticeable. Maybe you overheard a conversation of a couple speaking across the table about a trip to France and the vehicle brand they rented, coinciding with an upcoming abroad trip you are planning and your previous thoughts of renting a vehicle. While you might think this is such a coincidence, the actions have been simulated to guide your actions toward a specific behavior. This is the next level of persuasion, and sadly we won't be able to discern what is true and what is not, what is genuine, and what is not.

Some experts say that we need to be careful about what we agree to when we click the button saying "I agree to the user Terms." Have you had that experience? Where the user agreement for data privacy is a long document that most of us, unless lawyers, don't fully understand? How often have you seen this working in a way where we are totally confident of what we are reading and gladly agree to those terms? Most of our acceptance of those terms is not even genuine, as most times we do it to get rid of that screen and start using the platform right away. So we still need to do more work on how transparent the process and the system created for humans is to know what we agree to.

So what can we do about it? It could be easy to say that stronger laws and regulations need to be in place, and although I agree, I sustain that the responsibility begins with each one of us, from our own mind frameworks, our own set of values, our own vision toward the future, and our understanding of our role as precursors of a technological new era that supports humanity, instead of extinguishing it.

Environmental Human Dynamics

While there are undoubtedly advantages such as increased efficiency and scalability, there are also concerns regarding job displacement and the potential widening of economic inequalities. In this regard, ethics compel us to consider developing AI systems that complement skills rather than replace them completely—striking a delicate balance between automation and maintaining the invaluable human touch.

Power dynamics also play a role. When it comes to AI systems, in design there is a chance that they can unintentionally reflect and exacerbate power imbalances. The questions arise: Who gets to define what is considered "normal" for AI? Who might end up being marginalized or left behind? It is essential that the evolution of AI-driven tools embraces principles with an effort made to prevent power concentration and promote equitable representation.

Furthermore, environmental considerations add a layer of complexity to our landscape. The energy-intensive processes involved in training and deploying AI models underline the significance of sustainability in design. Guided by these imperatives, we should strive for process optimization and waste reduction, a perspective not usually contemplated by creators and designers.

Emotion, which lies at the core of design, presents another challenge. As AI gains the ability to generate art, music, or other forms of design elements, there is a looming risk of diluting authenticity. In a time where deepfakes and AI's remarkable ability to create designs are prevalent, trust and transparency become crucial. Ethical design requires a distinction between what's created by AI and what is made by humans, along with the need for mechanisms to verify authenticity.

Education and lifelong learning play a role in upholding standards. As AI continues to reshape the design landscape, professionals must adapt accordingly. It is the responsibility of organizations and educational institutions to promote learning, ensuring that nobody gets left behind in the wake of new technological advancements.

Expanding our perspective, we also recognize the importance of accessibility, which goes beyond addressing disabilities. In the era of AI, ethical design should encompass other factors, educational opportunities, and digital inclusivity. Advancements should benefit not a few but society as a whole.

Lastly, due to AI's nature in design, ethical conflicts are bound to arise. It is crucial to establish frameworks and encourage dialogues that allow us to address these challenges constructively and come to harmonious resolutions. Every stakeholder's voice needs representation on platforms that foster respect and understanding.

Ultimately, when we incorporate AI into our design principles, our ethical responsibilities become more prominent. Our role extends beyond shaping products and services; we are actively shaping societies, cultures, economies, and human experiences of the future. The decisions we make today have far-reaching consequences that may be immediate or only reveal themselves over time. By embracing an individual responsible acknowledgment perspective, we not only protect the present but also establish the groundwork for a harmonious, inclusive, and fair future. Our moral compass should always point toward the good without wavering as we navigate through the landscapes of innovation.

Ethics Training for Designers

Currently, there seems to be a gap in ethics training within design programs. It's crucial for designers to have an understanding of ethics in order to navigate the evolving ethical landscape. Educational institutions need to adopt the inclusion of ethics in design curriculums, as well as encouraging designers to engage in further individual critical thinking toward these foundations for the ethical practice of the profession. As an engineer in Canada, in the process of practicing as a professional engineer and being able to sign and place stamps on designs, the engineer needs to undertake a stringent and strict process. To become one, after graduation, it is required to work for at least four years, submitting periodic reports of work to the association that grants the professional designation. The reports need to be availed by another already professional engineer with a designation. Before becoming an engineer, the individual needs to undertake and pass two tests, one about ABCs (Act, By-Laws, and Codes of Ethics) and a PPE (Professional Practice Examination), about law and ethical standards. This process ensures that upon receiving a designation for practice, the person is capable of navigating not only technical challenges according to the guidelines of the profession that aim to protect humans but also to correctly navigate ethical dilemmas when they arise. I have always wondered why other fields of practice that also have a great impact on society and every individual don't take the process of design to the level that needs to be observed. What I propose is the involvement of regulation entities to qualify individuals dealing with advanced technologies, based on more strict standards, to ensure that only qualified individuals that understand the impact of their work can create experiences that support the well-being and evolution of humans rather than detriment it.

To ensure that ethical practices in companies are consistently upheld, we can introduce the concept of assessments. These assessments would work similarly to safety audits commonly conducted by companies. By conducting these assessments, we can objectively evaluate the standards followed throughout the design process and promptly address any unethical practices that may arise.

In summary, it is essential for us as designers to acknowledge the nature and ranging impact of ethical considerations in AI design. By broadening our perspectives and knowledge base, we can develop AI systems that are not only technically proficient but also ethically responsible.

Ethical Roadblocks and Solutions

While technological advancements open up new possibilities, for experiences we must not overlook the profound and far-reaching ethical implications that come with these advancements.

This journey inevitably presents us with thought-provoking ethical dilemmas. Then viewing these challenges as mere obstacles, we should see them as opportunities for self-reflection, refinement, and collective growth in both design and technology.

The seamless integration of AI into our lives through spatial computing and an interfaceless approach has the power to make technology appear almost magical. However, a significant ethical challenge arises here: the concealment of AI processes. As interactions become more intuitive, it becomes harder to understand the underlying algorithms, decisions, and processes behind AI systems. This lack of transparency can inadvertently introduce biases, reinforce stereotypes, or mislead humans. For example, how can one determine the fairness or accuracy of an AI-powered system's recommendations or decisions?

Addressing this issue requires a twofold approach. To start, creators and designers have the option to adopt an "AI" approach, which ensures that systems can provide insights into their decision-making process when necessary. Additionally, it is crucial to foster a culture of learning and ethical education. By embedding an understanding of considerations from the design and development phase, we can take a proactive stance rather than a reactive one toward potential issues.

Nevertheless, transparency alone is not enough. The MSDF emphasizes conscious designs, which contemplates the possibility of excessive stimulation or unintended manipulation. Imagine a future where applications not only introduce and present information but also engage your senses in a dimensional way. If these sensory experiences are not crafted ethically, they could potentially impact human decisions or moods without their awareness on a health level.

The solution? Establishing a foundation based on respecting the autonomy of humans. Designers should commit to incorporating sensory cues, ensuring that they enhance human experiences rather than altering them. By engaging in feedback loops with humans, conducting evaluations, and conducting thorough testing, we can ensure that our designs align with this principle.

The ethical landscape becomes more complex with the amount of data that spatial computing and interfaceless interactions can accumulate. As these environments respond to our movements, gestures, and even emotions, it becomes challenging to maintain a distinction between personalization and privacy.

One way forward is through privacy designs. By emphasizing transparency, consent, and minimalist data collection practices, we can strike a balance between personalization and privacy. Additionally, leveraging technologies like blockchain, which adds a layer of protection by obfuscating individual data within a sea of statistical noise, it could ensure better encryption methods and safety measures.

Lastly, there's the challenge of dependency. As systems become more intelligent, integrated, and intuitive, there is a risk of becoming overly reliant on them. Relying heavily on these systems could potentially diminish our cognitive abilities in decision-making or even weaken our interpersonal skills.

To address this, the focus of design should shift toward empowerment of facilitation. The goal should be to utilize technology as a tool that enhances abilities rather than replace them. Regular breaks from devices, awareness campaigns, and designs that promote well-being practices rather than passive consumption can help us maintain control over technology rather than letting it control us.

When I speak with professionals in the field of interfaceless technology and spatial computing, the first ethical concern that often comes to mind is privacy. As these systems become more advanced, they have the ability to gather and analyze amounts of data about their subscribers and surroundings, as showcased earlier.

What measures are in place to safeguard this data from being misused or accessed without authorization? What happens to the data once it's no longer needed? Is it kept in a format that could potentially identify humans?

Another ethical issue that arises is the acquisition power and the access to technology from third-world countries, as there is a risk of leaving behind those who cannot access or afford them. This creates an imbalance where only a privileged few can access spatial computing experiences, further widening the gap between those who have access and those who don't.

To tackle these concerns, let's discuss some further considerations:

1. *Transparency in Data Policies*: It's important for companies to be open and transparent about how they collect, store, and use data. Humans should have the option to choose whether their data is collected and also have the right to request its deletion.

2. *Inclusive Design*: Technology without interfaces should be designed with accessibility and affordability in mind. It should cater to the needs of individual humans, considering factors like socioeconomic backgrounds, abilities, and digital literacy levels.

3. *Creating Balanced Experiences*: Designers should strive to create experiences that promote well-being for users. This could involve incorporating features such as reminders for usage or built-in breaks.

4. *Regulatory Guidelines*: Establishing guidelines can play a role in ensuring privacy and data security standards within interfaceless technology.

Addressing these considerations is a responsibility that demands collaboration among designers, developers, business leaders, regulators, and individual humans alike.

Summary: Ethical Design in an AI-Driven World

This chapter focused on the discussion of the main ethical considerations and ethical dilemmas associated with AI in design, starting with a fair background about what ethics mean, its history and precedents, as well as modern issues that have posed important breakthroughs about the way we undertake the evolution of technology. We explored the hidden layers that are not often explored in the field of ethical design using AI, due to a lack of set guidelines and trustable standards. Examples of particular cases were brought to illustrate the potential to replicate those same mistakes in spatial computing, and we discussed potential course of action to implement not only at an individual level but also the role of companies in it.

Wider considerations were presented to open up the discussion and invite active participation in our role as creators in the landscape of spatial computing.

CHAPTER 9

The Road Ahead: Predictions and Preparations

At setting the context for predictions, we see the inherent value of predictive analysis. Data has always driven important technological decisions and developments and still constitutes a source for shaping research and development directions. Although this has been a source of a level of confidence for discoveries and innovations in technology, in the past, visionary leaders have also steered the direction of important breakthroughs by leaning into the uncertain, as exemplified by how the rise of early personal computing was forecast by early computing scientists.

There are foreseeable limitations of linear extrapolations and potential pitfalls at the extension of current trends toward the future without contemplating conceivable paradigm shifts. History shows some examples of this risk, evidenced on instances with failure of linear thinking approaches, with the assumption about mobile phone devices remaining as a luxury item, as well as the Internet, not anticipating their ubiquity today.

© Diana Olynick 2024
D. Olynick, *Interfaceless*, Design Thinking, https://doi.org/10.1007/979-8-8688-0083-2_9

As we witnessed in the last years, black swan events like the last worldwide viral pandemic can exponentially change the evolution rate of adoption patterns and technological transformation. Unexpected leaps also play a role in unpredictable events accelerating innovation, which presents challenges for accurate predictions about prospective new technologies and the scenarios where they would unfold.

Conscious design and interfaceless environments are the consequence of a revolutionary step toward a more intuitive, seamless, and inclusive interaction with technology. At the convergence of this design philosophy, there are imminent opportunities to make real visions that once pertained to the field of science fiction. Consider the augmented reality tools and haptic methods used in *Minority Report* or the holodecks and communication methods from *Star Trek*.

We come to realize that the future of interfaceless design is not simply related to taking the current models and iterating from them, but to creating and embracing completely novel paradigms.

This leap in history requires from us a shift in perspective that invites us to look beyond the "how" of interfaceless design for spatial computing; it invites us to examine the broader opening of "why" and "what if," involving deeper reflection and critical thinking about economic, societal, and individual ramifications.

As we witness the unfolding of this journey of exploration, it's crucial to remember that the future isn't something that unfolds passively without our influence. It's a result of the choices we make and the actions we take today. The path ahead depends not on tomorrow's possibilities but on what we actively do today. Let's approach this path with curiosity, responsibility, and a collaborative mindset.

How Design Will Continue to Evolve

To truly understand the future of "interfaceless design and spatial computing," it is essential to recognize the evolution of design and how it has brought us to this point. Design has always been a reflection of our culture and our understanding of the world. It is influenced by our values, needs, and the tools available to us.

In its initial stages, design primarily revolved around finding solutions for basic problems. Our ancestors, who relied on their creativity and knowledge of the environment for survival, were essentially designers in their own right. They created tools for hunting and constructed shelters to guarantee their well-being.

As societies became more complex, over time we faced challenges that required other more sophisticated design solutions. The advent of agriculture 10,000 years ago led to the creation of tools and designed spaces specifically for farming. Similarly, as urban civilizations emerged in regions like Mesopotamia and the Indus Valley, architectural design evolved with planned cities, efficient drainage systems, and multistory buildings.

As we entered this century, with the Internet and mobile technology at our fingertips, there was an explosion of creativity and new design paradigms. The focus shifted toward creating human designs that provided deeper experiences. Designers started prioritizing empathy by conducting "user" research and incorporating feedback into their process. At the time, software tools like Photoshop and Sketch made it easier for designers to iterate and prototype efficiently.

Nowadays, we are witnessing an era in design that is being shaped by extraordinary advancements in AI and spatial computing as we enter this new decade. Design without interfaces is emerging as a frontier that blurs the boundaries of the reality of physical scenarios.

The new approach to design is undergoing a transformation shifting from focusing on humans to an effort between humans and machines. With the assistance of AI, designers are now able to generate and refine design concepts more effectively.

The emergence of fields like XR (extended reality) and spatial computing has opened up new opportunities for creating immersive and interactive experiences. Designers are now taking into account not just the 2D screen but also the entire 3D space surrounding humans. They are exploring ways to design for the senses, crafting experiences that respond to our movements, gestures, and where we look.

Moreover, generative AI is reshaping the role of designers from being creators to becoming curators. With AI generating a number of design options, designers can focus more on identifying the problem at hand, establishing appropriate constraints, and selecting the most suitable solutions.

As we stand at the cusp of an era in design characterized by interfaceless design, spatial computing, and generative AI, it is clear that our understanding of design and its societal significance will continue to evolve. It is vital for designers to embrace these changes wholeheartedly, constantly learn, adapt, and harness these tools and paradigms in order to deliver empathetic human experiences.

The Canvas of Design

In the past, traditional design found its expression on surfaces like paper, wood, stone, or metal. However, with the rise of interfaces in digital mediums, screens have become the medium for creativity. In a world without interfaces, our surroundings and the very fabric of reality become our canvas. Whether it's rooms, landscapes, or bustling cityscapes, these spaces will come alive with information and interactive elements.

The boundaries between design disciplines such as design, product design, sound design, and even architecture will start to fade away. An interfaceless environment demands a convergence of disciplines that give rise to fluid and ever-changing forms of design. Imagine a world where music transforms into a spectacle that responds in time to your emotions... picture spaces that reshape themselves according to your needs like something out of Salvador Dali's surreal paintings.

As we might suspect, the future of design will heavily rely on artificial intelligence. Without interfaces as we know them today, designers will utilize technology to tap into human emotions. Designs won't just respond to touch or voice commands, but will also resonate with our feelings, moods, and desires.

The beauty of scenic moments and the interplay of colors in watercolor paintings inspire a perspective on design experiences. Designs will no longer be static. They will transform into events that manifest once, never to be replicated in the same way again. This shift embraces the nature of life of the Japanese concept of mono no aware.

Amid our technology-dominated era, there will be a resurgence in seeking inspiration from nature. Biophilic design principles, which highlight our connection to nature, will play an important role in general design and even in the mix of real with digital experiences. Designers will draw guidance from the patterns, sounds, and rhythms found in the world to create harmonious experiences that transcend traditional interfaces.

Interestingly enough, as we delve further into spatial computing, there will be a renewed appreciation for physicality. Haptic feedback, augmented reality artifacts, and tangible interactions will bridge the gap between physical domains.

Ultimately, design will not simply progress; it will surpass expectations with new human considerations not thought of before, and conscious and mindful design will be the light to illuminate all this progress toward the right direction. New design standards will go beyond appeal and practicality to encompass a harmonious blend of experiences drawing inspiration from the diverse dimensions of art, philosophy, emotion, and technology. Just as Virginia Woolf once contemplated the future of literature by saying, "We must continue to explore," the same sentiment applies to design. The path that lies ahead holds potential presenting us with both opportunities and uncharted territories eagerly awaiting our courageous imagination and visionary ideas.

Upcoming Breakthroughs and Developments

Engineering designers have the ability to simulate the impact on a structure over a span of ten years in just minutes. They can also create models that take into account the tiniest of details, such as the changes throughout the day or how seasons affect things.

In the future, thanks to advancements in nanotechnology, we will have the power to design things at an unprecedented level. Imagine walls that can adjust their insulating properties depending on the weather or surfaces that can repair themselves by growing layers.

The next generation of augmented reality (AR) will be truly immersive. It won't just overlay information onto our surroundings; it will engage all our senses. We'll be able to step into buildings before they are constructed and experience everything from touching walls, smelling the environment, and hearing sounds of how it might look but also for historical buildings that don't exist anymore and experience them just as they were in those times.

Biodesign is another field that draws inspiration directly from nature's processes and organisms. With biodesign, we can expect to see living structures—buildings with walls made of materials that breathe artwork that evolves over time or furniture that grows and adapts based on its owners' preferences.

The rise of algorithms and the potential for self-creating designs is an upcoming further development from the capabilities we see right now in the current tools. By inputting criteria into AI systems, designers can now rely on the software to generate a multitude of design variations. These variations are not arbitrary, they are instead informed by deep learning insights extracted from collections of historical and modern designs. As a result, the role of a designer would transform from being the creator to becoming more of a curator, carefully selecting and refining these concepts generated by AI.

In 2014, a movie called *Transcendence* was released. At the time, this release caused some commentary on the potential of these technologies and the philosophical implication of artificial intelligence becoming completely self-regulated and autonomous. The search for immortality has, at the current moment, leaders in the industry like Elon Musk working on his Neuralink project. This project aims to supercharge humanity with the insertion of a brain interface targeting to help cure illnesses and improve the health quality of our current era. While this sounds promising, it also raises important considerations. Not only are there current works in that direction but also in a similar direction of the type of technology showcased in the movie *Transcendence*, where instead of inserting a supercomputer in the human brain, the aim is to download a human collection of experience into a supercomputer. Although research continues to be conducted in this field, it still remains speculative. Despite its conjectural nature, there is a possibility that in the future we will be able to see more accurate versions of human replicas, more than the ones we are seeing these days.

Let's take a look at some prospective upcoming developments:

Quantum Computing and Interfaceless Environments

As presented previously, quantum computers will continue to make their way toward superfast processing and expanded memory capabilities, along with enhanced cloud services. This will be fundamental for the evolution of interfaceless environments where the technology itself will take an invisible place, running in the background while getting unnoticed.

Neuro-adaptive Systems

For therapeutic interventions and medical diagnosis, new systems will emerge with the capability of adapting to cognitive states and neural signals. For instance, wearable devices could be used to send alerts through neural patterns detected for episodes of anxiety or depression, facilitating self-help procedures or in clinics.

Bio-integrated Interfaces

Pacemakers, defibrillators, and ventricular assist devices are examples of implants that have been in use for decades already. Just as with orthopedic implants, which are also not a new solution to bone fractures, implants of other types will arise to aid in other injuries and other health conditions.

Decentralized Spatial Web

As the increase in data privacy continues growing, decentralization and the evolution of blockchain technology will also continue to integrate in spatial computing environments along with artificial intelligence systems, enabling individuals greater control over their data, digital representation (avatars), and any other asset pertaining to safe and secure ownership.

Internet of Things (IoT)

Previously, we explored how spatial computing is more than experiences happening in head-mounted devices. It might include the sensor systems in smart homes, where no need for headsets is required, for example. IoT is set to transform from devices to interconnected ecosystems. Our homes, workplaces, and public spaces will communicate seamlessly anticipating our needs without us giving commands. Design will no longer focus on elements but on complete ecosystems.

Through workspaces, geographical barriers for designers will disappear. They can collaborate with peers blending insights, expertise, and visions into designs that are universally inclusive and resonating on a global scale.

Positioning Yourself for the "Interfaceless" Future

As we move closer to a future without interfaces, where conscious design, spatial computing, and AI take the main stage in spatial domains, we can realize the power on our hands to leave a legacy for the next generations and a mark in the field of our profession. Every decision we make continues to make waves and ripples, and every value we uphold contributes to shaping the interfaceless world that lies ahead.

At the core of this profession lies the importance of continuous learning. Nowadays, it's no longer enough to passively receive knowledge. We can see in educational institutions more and more, moving to project-based assignments and practical simulations of real-world problems because mere knowledge doesn't offer the guarantee of holistic understanding of real-world problems and solutions. We must delve into genuine exploration and deep questioning while constantly seeking answers that benefit humans.

Amid our immersion, in a landscape surrounded by algorithms, human touch becomes more indispensable. We are not just machines that write code; we are also infusing a part of ourselves, our values and our beliefs, into these entities. It is our responsibility to make sure that as we create these advancements, we do not forget the principles that guide us.

While technology often seems to be a one-way street, it's actually quite the opposite. The future of our current professions also continues to adapt with the new technologies, and what we call an "architect" today, tomorrow it might be called "buildesigner" or "architechneer," where various disciplines intersect. It compels us to break out of our spheres and engage with a range of voices—from artists to neuroscientists or from environmentalists to philosophers.

This focus requires the integration of the philosophy of adaptability, embracing an ethos of perpetual learning and unlearning. The future designers will broaden professional horizons beyond traditional design, exploring with curiosity and creativity fields like anthropology, neuroscience, and other human disciplines, integrating them in their practice.

The forming of these bonds with other disciplines would permit inter-cross-functional collaboration with other tech fields like nanotechnology and bioinformatics.

Additionally, cultivating AI literacy will contribute to facilitating more sophisticated creations and would elevate our worth and professional standard. As we have touched previously, the designers of the future will design with AI systems, which is also equally true for creators and developers, so keeping up with educational resources will continue to be fundamental.

However, our vision should not be limited to the present. It should be broad and encompassing, reaching toward positive horizons. By understanding trends and speculating about future risks, we ensure that our designs remain relevant and resonate not only in the present but also in times to come.

As we have previously emphasized, the road ahead isn't necessarily about a future technologically advanced. In raw terms, to express humanity with the best authenticity, technology is not even needed. This is a journey where each of us has the ability to contribute, creating professional and well-being opportunities for ourselves and others.

The following are some pointers toward a professional positioning in the landscape of AI and spatial computing as a creator, designer, developer, or tech enthusiast:

1. **Stay Ahead of the Ethical Curve**

   As we keep ourselves updated at the forefront of the latest developments and aim to pursue a higher professional standard, it requires the same approach with an ethical foundation to develop the capacity to resolve complex problems and ethical solutions. This could encompass advocating for ethical practices in your workplace or company, initiating discussions with your close circles or even becoming a leader in the field.

2.   **Master the Tools of the Trade**

While some traditional tools of design still continue to be used, it is expected to have new platforms in the market aiming to solve emerging problems for designers. Getting in touch with the tools, testing and finding out which ones adjust better to the task at hand, is an important practice that as a designer can be adopted. This includes tools for designing in 3D and for spatial computing, as well as tools for leveraging AI and other emerging technologies in design.

3.   **Collaborate Across Disciplines**

In today's XR landscape, designers need to collaborate with experts from a range of fields, from computer science to art and narrative to audio design. This supposes a continuous trend, and the fields for collaboration will even expand to other more specialized fields. As a result, developing strong collaboration and communication skills will be crucial.

4.   **Develop a Deep Understanding of Humans**

As we move toward an era of interfaceless design, the need for a deep understanding of humans becomes even more critical. The designers of the future need to dig deeper into the understanding of human mental states, emotions, and context, safeguarding these explorations from manipulative purposes and learning how to translate this understanding into ethical design decisions.

5. **Designing and Developing with Empathy**

Developing emotional intelligence is a paramount human trait for the creation of delightful and mindful experiences. As designers recognizing the demands of emotional, mental and physical integrations of technology, we can therefore take proper care of our individual mental health and self-care needs. On the surface, this pointer might sound irrelevant, but I would argue as the most important one, due to the fact that our work as creators is the direct reflection of our inner mental states and motives.

6. **Integrate Mindful and Conscious Design Practices**

Taking the initiative to incorporate conscious and mindful design practices in the workplace, educating others about the why, what, and how, can set you apart from other professionals and set you up for leadership responsibilities. The reason for this is because as the concern rates continue to increase around how we can lead implementations in a safer way, which is an important concern for companies that directly affect their business positioning, companies will look for professionals that can solve those kinds of complex problems in less costly ways, and whoever is prepared for this challenge will be invited to participate and take the lead. The other side of this pointer is the individual and personal understanding of our place in the world and how we can make a difference.

Let's take a look at a non-exhaustive list of skills required for spatial computing designers:

- Human research approach and empathy
- Spatial prototyping and testing
- Holistic design
- Cross-disciplinary collaboration
- Accessibility and inclusion
- Ethics and law
- Technical foundations of AI systems
- Data interpretation and trustable decision-making
- Interfaceless principles for spatial design
- Practical understanding of spatial computing devices

The Potential Impact on the Job Market and Skill Requirements

In the same way that the emergence of the Internet gave rise to new professions like digital marketers and web designers and developers, the era of interfaceless design and spatial computing with artificial intelligence brings to the evolving landscape of occupations a new job lexicon and new opportunities for specialization.

It is worth noting that at this point in time, we have already swiftly shifted beyond traditional design roles, with UI/UX design being redefined. The spectrum of design and all its canvas of creation has grown, bringing new tools and a reconsideration of what "users" and "experience" mean in the new evolving spatial mediums.

In this evolution of human-tech symbiosis, new roles will arise that will fit the technical complexities and challenges to solve for the upcoming implementations.

As a result of the global-wide pandemic, we witnessed the shift of organizations adjusting to the conditions of the time. It is expected that with even more enhanced communication technologies, people could tend to have more freedom to choose their preferred work model, therefore potentially adding more opportunities on how work is performed and delivered, amplifying channels for remote and global teams without geographic boundaries.

Moreover, the transition toward an interfaceless world highlights the significance of expertise. While specific problems would require specialization, there will also be a need for professionals who understand holistically the functioning of different systems. This holds true as it continues to work, where we see in every company specialists and general professionals alike. There is a potential for future design professionals to combine skills from various domains. For instance, a designer may need to grasp psychology, while a developer might explore the intricacies of behavior. Similarly, marketers could become proficient in analytics powered by AI. This blend of skills fosters solutions that are comprehensive and human focused.

Additionally, the MSDF puts emphasis on sensory, empathetic design and opens up opportunities for experts in various fields, like audio engineering, haptic technology, and even olfactory science. As designs become more immersive, professionals capable of crafting these dimensional experiences will be highly sought after.

Let's study some potential roles that could emerge out of this technological, social, and economic transformation. Bear in mind, those names might not be exactly the same ones, but potentially based on available expertise in the field and the analysis of emerging technologies and challenges, they could have similar scopes of practice.

Neural Interface Designers/Developers/Engineers

Out of the advances in brain cognitive states and neural signals, brain-computer specializations might begin to arise.

Spatial Design Ethicists

In some companies at the present time, such as Google, there is a role called "design ethicist," which is a person dedicated to evaluating the moral values and implications of various design decisions. This is expected to continue with the emergence of new technologies in spatial computing at the cross section with AI.

Bio-integrated Technologists

These are professionals taking care of the intersection between human biology and implant technology.

Spatial AI Data Scientists

As a result of the vast generation of 3D and 4D data, a specific need for analysis and interpretation of this information to derive correct decisions will arise in companies working with these systems.

Quantum Computing Architects

With an increased capacity of computers and their abilities to work with exponential data, experts who can navigate and understand the nuances of this field will be required.

Environmental AI Designers

As design incorporates more AI tools for creation, optimization will continue to get refined for the development of stylized or realistic virtual spaces and landscapes and digital individual representations in the virtual worlds.

Spatial Audio Engineers

Responsive 3D sound that adjusts based on other conditions will create a new need for audio engineers that understand the nuances of spatial computing.

Here's the positive aspect of it all. The future dominated by AI and lacking interfaces is not something to fear but an opportunity—an opportunity for growth, learning, collaboration, and creation. It serves as a reminder that change is constant, but growth is a choice. By embracing learning, seeking collaborations with others, and remaining grounded in ethics, we can not only navigate the upcoming shifts but also thrive amid them.

Summary: The Road Ahead—Predictions and Preparations

This chapter presented a space to dive deeper on the evolution of design tied to the symbiosis between interfaceless designs and spatial computing with AI systems, touching on the transition from form and function to empathetic experience.

A new wave of innovations in AI was studied, and potential new fields of development were presented for further research or study. In positioning yourself for the interfaceless future, we emphasized on the importance of keeping an ethical and professional standard and how this not only helps on an individual level but also on a societal macro level. Committing to continuous education and active participation, along with fully integrating conscious and mindful design practice, was also part of the main discussion in this chapter.

As part of a common concern about the prospect of AI and the job market, we touched on how new and unforeseen developments can bring new opportunities and the fundamental shift from task-oriented work to adaptability, creativity, and ethical decision-making.

CHAPTER 10

Concluding Thoughts and the Future Vision

That time in history when the Internet, computers, mobile devices, and social media didn't exist was marked by communicating through regular mail more often written either by hand or with typewriters or through phones in the streets enclosed in cabins, where we had to insert coins to make them work, making the message brief and concise, or our own home phones with the long cable attached to the wall, where we could just enjoy a long conversation without having to see the other person. One might wonder if life still went by, as a regular individual with our everyday life, if we were still doing in general the same routines we do today—waking up, going to work, coming back, having family time, and enjoying vacation times here and there—why did we need all these introductions to the world of communications anyways?

While life before these technologies was perfectly functional, their appearance in the world was not much about needing to exist, but a by-product of the natural progression of human innovation, which is always aiming to create something bigger than itself. Compared with a letter sent through regular mail, a message sent through email cut the speed of delivery from days, weeks, or months to seconds. Accessing information went from walking or driving to a library, consulting their extensive catalogs, and, if the desired book was not available or rented, days would

© Diana Olynick 2024
D. Olynick, *Interfaceless*, Design Thinking, https://doi.org/10.1007/979-8-8688-0083-2_10

have to pass before being able to obtain the answers to our questions. The economy saw its impact on globalization and the expansion from local commerce to global partnerships and new markets.

As a domino effect, new technologies open the path to new ones, and from computers to mobile devices, rather than only listening remotely to someone else, now we are able to see their image through video calls. Millions of jobs have been created as a result, and the economy has seen a direct impact of these innovations as well as society at large.

When looking back, humans have always pursued to create solutions to perceived or real problems related to efficiency, quality of life, and deep connection. The convenience these innovations have brought to our lives also has always come with its increased challenges, and we have always strived to create new resources or ways to solve the poised challenges. As with any innovation, it is about how it is used.

Why now?

As mobile phones continue to provide more innovative features and even the introduction of other wearables like smartwatches also refine more their features and capabilities, humans become increasingly tech-savvy, developing expectations for more intuitive and accessible ways to interact with devices.

Coupled with the latest AI advancements, it is naturally expected that platforms, devices, and tools of all kinds will have the ambition to integrate their systems with AI capabilities. This, along with the continuous and decreasing size of hardware allowing for integrated systems and an increase in speed, brings to the forefront the ubiquity of IoT with more intuitive ways to interact with the surroundings.

The advent of all these devices, including the rapid development of head-mounted devices, has brought the traditional methods of design to mediums that are not designed for it. Keyboards, touchscreens, and mice are a past form of input, and now the paradigm has changed again.

The recognition of modern generations juggling multiple devices, presenting a significant number of challenges related to their well-being and cognitive overload, draws the path for the natural unfolding of more streamlined, intuitive, and interfaceless experiences.

A Reflection on the Interfaceless Journey

When I got my first headset for virtual reality when it used to be called Oculus (Meta Quest), I was filled with excitement. I remember doing the initial setup and experiencing the first welcome walk-through. It was a unique experience. It felt like some of the sci-fi movies were starting to become real. The music was exhilarating, and I felt as if I had traveled to another universe. As I started to explore this device and its inside experiences, I started to realize the learning curve to figure out the commands in a pair of controllers for proper navigation. I saw the learning curve was unnatural to me, someone who was not exposed to video games and the controllers used since little. I tried hundreds of different experiences from the Meta Quest App Lab, Steam, SideQuest, WebXR, and the official store itself.

In some of those apps, I experienced headaches; in some, I didn't find them as intuitive and with a steep learning curve for which the platforms had dozens of tutorials to go through; and with other ones, the interfaces were confusing, and I couldn't find myself saying how easy the navigation was. To add to this complexity of the experience, I also found the devices extremely heavy and uncomfortable, and I felt my face skin dragging and had to increase the tightness of the headband very often, making it eventually unbearable to stay for long periods of time.

Another revealing experience has been to actively be part of user-generated content platforms in this field that allow anybody to create their own worlds. I find that, over the years, I have seen many different projects and experiences created by a wide variety of enthusiasts, designers, and other professionals who have been in the common learning process altogether. This observation, in addition to witnessing the direct knowledge-based and project-based outcomes from my own students, has taken me to important realizations.

Being an active participant in this field has also led me to create great connections, taking me to the creation of the XR Magazine podcast, bringing the leading minds in the field together, who have actually walked the path to create experiences for virtual mediums and who continue to share the biggest challenges that the current industry undergoes not only with the infrastructure available but also the talent required to solve complex issues.

The combination of all these sources has led me to extensive research, continuous expert consultations, and individual and client project developments, ultimately supporting and reaffirming further my initial observations of some of the fundamental design problems currently evidenced in the industry.

In line with Theodore Roosevelt's words, "Do what you can, with what you have, where you are," I acknowledge the variety of options we have at the moment in terms of tools, platforms, and resources of all kinds, opening up more opportunities for progress and refinement in our creations while at the same time implying the great responsibility of creating works for the medium that consider the health and well-being of every human who accesses those creations. Drawing upon Roosevelt's sentiment, we realize we are not just called upon to do what we can, but rather we are called to challenge the boundaries of the possibilities ahead, created from our present actions and decisions.

Contemplating the journey toward an interfaceless future evokes a sense of deep reflection on our standing beliefs about the essence of design, representing not simply a shift but a transition as well. In my experience, I have felt the urge to see beyond the surface level and dive holistically into the fields of cognition, emotion, and even spirituality.

Being connected to the world of art while working with technology has allowed me to borrow from artistic sensibilities to see other perspectives of technology. Let's think about Leonardo da Vinci for a moment. Da Vinci was a scientist, artist, and engineer, all in one during the Renaissance. Chances are he would not have seen the "interface" as simply a paint and canvas, but he would have described it as an interplay with light dynamics, shadows, perhaps scientific principles, and human emotions.

In the current times, the canvas has evolved to not just be a screen, and it comes as a surprise to think that not even a space, but the very fabric of the holistic human experience.

From this artistic reflection, we also realize how this interfaceless paradigm doesn't aim to subtract from the current model, but it adds dimension, dynamism, and depth. It is beyond the tangible touchpoints extending toward our daily lives, predicting, understanding, and responding, as an art and science in balance with human harmony.

From physical to digital interfaces, we are now at the outset of invisible ones. From automated doors to motion-activated lights, we are surrounded by the first signs in the direction of invisible technology.

With generative AI and other supporting technologies for data generation, conscious and mindful design for safe direction, and a medium that facilitates interfaceless experiences with spatial computing, we can say this interplay presents itself as a more holistic and supportive approach to this double fold, opportunity, and challenge we are facing.

Ultimately, it's clear to see that the paradigm of no interfaces is beyond the mechanism used for how humans interact with digital content. It is beyond symbols and even gestures. It is a natural extension of the physical space.

Until that space and time is here, we can continue to exert deeper reflections about our current systems and capabilities. It is necessary to also bring into context the reflection of how much a regular interface is really needed. This goes not only for spatial computing but also for other digital mediums. Let's take a look at some examples. At reflecting deeper on this, we might find instances where what a regular mobile app is doing now could be maybe not even needed or transformed in spatial computing. The case of smartphone apps for plant care could be translated in pots with built-in moisture sensors that release water and nutrients as needed or a meditation app with natural sounds vs. public meditation spaces near natural habitats. The conclusion of this is that the decision to include or not to include interfaces is very deliberate, and with enough introspection, we could find as well there is no need for the app at all if what we are trying to replace can be better performed already in the current circumstances.

This reflection takes us to contextualize the digital-physical balance of interfaceless designs, starting with understanding digital immersion, from passive screens to full interaction, combined with the intrinsic value of being present in the physical world, supporting the enhancement of cognitive functions and emotional well-being.

The concern for disconnection from the real world is a primary reason for this fundamental shift to happen. At the interfaceless level of experience, distractions are minimized, the ones traditionally caused by graphical user interfaces (GUI), leveraging other sensor inputs such as spatial audio, bringing both the best of the real and simulated worlds. Mindful interactions get introduced as an extension of the integration of contextual awareness, focusing on providing unobtrusive interactions that disrupt the human's presence in the physical world.

Addressing Common Criticisms and Misconceptions

It is only natural to face misconceptions at the transition of technologies especially at the revolutionary age we are now. The interfaceless design approach does not space this doubt and inquiry, for which it is crucial to address potential misunderstandings while seeking clarity amid the unfolding uncertainties.

Let's take a look at some of them:

1. **Interfaceless Design with AI Systems Is a Dream**

    Some traditional designers might agree that
    traditional interfaces have played a role in the
    progress that has been made going from early
    computers to mobile devices and even in headsets.
    While regular interfaces have been present in these
    mediums, and the common factor is a device that
    renders graphics, this does not mean that all of
    them have been designed for the same interface.
    In fact, the interface has been the element called
    to be redefined in every iteration, making it
    absolute or completely unnecessary for the spatial
    computing medium.

2. **It's a Threat to Privacy and Data Collection**

    The concept of "interfaceless" alone might seem
    unsettling, let alone at its intersection with AI. As
    exposed in our previous section about ethics, there are
    imminent risks that need to be counterbalanced, but
    the "interfaceless" future, as outlined in this book using
    the conscious and mindful design principles as well as
    the MSDF (Mindful Spatial Design Framework), is in
    fact our only way to progress in technology with a safe
    stance that our rights, our identity, and our integrity
    will be respected and protected.

3. **AI-Driven Designs Mean Loss of Human Uniqueness and Touch**

The reason behind this concern is that AI and spatial computing are meant to be tools, like any tool. Their main purpose is to enhance and support our abilities rather than replace them. They are designed to amplify our strengths, compensate for our weaknesses, and liberate us from tasks so that we can dedicate time to creative pursuits, empathy, and engaging in higher-level cognitive activities.

4. **"Is 'Interfaceless Design' Another Passing Trend?"**

With the evolution of technology, we've seen many trends come and go. Is it fair to dismiss "interfaceless design" as another short-lived fad? While it's important to approach developments with a dose of skepticism, it would be a mistake to view "interfaceless" design through the lens of temporary tech trends. Its essence lies in grounding technology with artificial intelligence, which is not a fad, founded in profound principles. This ground ensures that as technology evolves, it remains firmly rooted in addressing needs, aspirations, and overall well-being.

5. **"Interfaceless Design in Spatial Computing with AI Will Lead to More Technology Addiction"**

Because of a valid concern in this area, it is fundamental for designers and creators to prepare themselves for potential challenges on this front. Our attitude is not just about the system determining all the outcomes but what we are doing as autonomous individuals to lead the change. Rather than replacing our real world and completely detaching from it, we aspire to use the tools for a human-driven purpose and leave the tools when our goal has been accomplished away from defined dependencies. The set of principles proposed in this book helps with this aspiration, expressed through the implementation of conscious and mindful design and the MSDF (Mindful Spatial Design Framework).

In conclusion, embarking on the "interfaceless" journey comes with its share of obstacles and challenges.

Moreover, by acknowledging and addressing criticisms, continuously improving our comprehension, and remaining dedicated to putting humans at the center of our work, we are not merely defending a design philosophy. Instead, we are paving the way for a future that embraces inclusivity, intuition, and inspiration.

Expert Voices: Interviews and Insights from Leading Minds

Interview with Daniel Berrick, Policy Counsel, Future of Privacy Forum

XR Magazine: Daniel, what are the current risks and mitigations about privacy regarding immersive technologies?

Daniel's response: Today's XR technologies rely on the interplay of multiple sensors, large volumes and varieties of data, and various algorithms and automated systems, such as machine learning. But this comes with risks. XR technologies often depend on sensitive personal information, and the collection, use, and transfer of this data to other parties may pose privacy risks to both users and bystanders. In the future, integrating generative AI into virtual and augmented worlds also raises concerns around manipulation.

Many XR use cases capture or rely on data from which an entity may be able to learn deeply personal information about people, such as an individual's sexual orientation and medical conditions. This was recently corroborated by a study that demonstrated how personal attributes can be inferred from motion data captured in *Beat Saber*, a popular VR game. Using deep learning models, the study's authors learned about the user's background, demographics, environment, habits, and health from their hand and head motion data. This follows earlier research from 2023 finding that motion data can be used to identify individuals. Without proper safeguards, information inferred from XR data could give rise to discrimination and enable decisions that have negative impacts on individuals, regardless of whether this information is accurate. XR technology's novelty means that users may not recognize such risks, reducing the likelihood that they will take measures to protect their privacy in XR environments. This underscores the importance of educating users about threats to their privacy in XR and developing technical measures to mitigate these threats.

The quantity and variety of data captured by XR technologies also make it easier to track individuals across digital environments, a phenomenon known as digital fingerprinting. The more and varied data a person generates in an XR environment is, the greater its detail, and the easier it is for organizations to use it to single individuals out. At the same time, it may be very challenging to de-identify or anonymize XR tracking data for the same reasons this is the case for other granular non-XR data types, such as behavioral biometrics, historical geolocation, and genetic information. Digital fingerprinting may therefore undermine individuals' ability to maintain anonymity in XR environments, which may discourage users from fully expressing themselves or participating in certain activities due to worries about retaliation.

In addition to capturing information about users, XR technologies may also intentionally or inadvertently collect and use data about non-users. However, these bystanders often lack notice of this activity, including information about how the data is being used and with whom it is being shared, at the time of collection. Like users, bystanders also cannot control the unconscious behaviors that provide the sensor data inputs for XR experiences. Even if a bystander generally understands that a device is collecting data about them, the unconscious nature of some behaviors (e.g., pupil dilation in response to seeing an AR political advertisement) means that bystanders may neither be aware of the behaviors nor specifically understand that a device is processing data about these behaviors. Bystanders may therefore find it challenging to exercise control over the collection and use of data captured by XR technologies, undermining individual autonomy over privacy decisions.

In the future, companies may populate XR worlds with virtual agents powered by generative AI in order to improve gaming and training experiences and advertise goods or services. By adapting their interactions based on observations they make about users, these virtual agents could tailor their responses to a person's mood, personal history, and behaviors. The ability to calibrate responses in this way may enable virtual agents to influence an individual's decision-making processes and drive them toward a particular outcome, all without the individual's knowledge.

Manipulation in XR environments may also occur by changing virtual interfaces to influence individuals into giving up more information than is needed to provide a product or service. Before deploying these technologies in these contexts, stakeholders should consider how they affect users' decisions and, as relevant, make the necessary disclosures.

The aforementioned risks underscore the importance of designing and deploying mitigation strategies, which should be considered at the product or service's design stage and throughout its life cycle. Organizations should consider processing and storing data on a user's device, as opposed to remotely on a processor's server, to ensure that the data remains in the user's hands and is not accessible to others. They should also limit data collection, storage, and/or usage, including third-party use, to particular, specified purposes and require data controllers—the organizations responsible for determining the purpose and means of the processing—to provide notice to or obtain consent from users if they plan to use this data for a different purpose.

Certain technological innovations can also be useful tools for managing privacy risks. For example, advances in encryption and differential privacy can allow for privacy-preserving data analysis and sharing, and the use of synthetic datasets can alleviate concerns about data sharing or secondary data use. Finally, organizations should design XR devices to ensure that bystanders' data is not unduly collected. This could include automatically blurring bystanders' faces or using a system of lights on a head-mounted display to signal to non-users that the device is on and potentially collecting data.

Interview with Gabriele Romagnoli, Shapes XR

XR Magazine: Does the fact of the 2D paradigm or flat screens to 3D interactions change in some way the fact that people are not familiar with them? How has that transition been happening?

Gabriele: Familiarity is important. So you cannot make something that is completely alien to people because then they wouldn't understand. The fact is that finding the right balance is really the key, right? So I want to give you an example. In our case, people always ask us how do I delete an object? Because that's not immediately intuitive, but what happens is that when they discover that to delete an object, they throw it away, they have a laugh, a smile, and then they appreciate the experience. So then throwing an object away is an analogy of how you would throw away an object in the real world, and yet it is still somehow resembling.

It is also about guiding the user to understand those interactions and to make the experience that is in VR something that is more delightful, that is more memorable. So yes, something that is completely alien is tricky, but this is the moment that we are defining those interactions in the future. So I think it's important to be open-minded and keep exploring with this and not always be afraid. That's why there is prototyping software that allows you to understand and start creating those interactions and not always relying on 2D.

XR Magazine: Where do you see the future of design going?

Gabriele: I think that we are always talking and designing for VR, but we also know right now that there is a lot of interesting things—this new generation of mixed reality headsets that are coming: for example, Project Cambria and Apple glasses; and at that point, would you want to see just 2D panels floating in your room? You don't, right? You don't want that. You want maybe something that is more playful or something that is more sleek than just 2D panels with a toggle. And how do you do it? Well, that's one of the things we also have to put in even more effort. So we are improving our pass-through features; for you to be able to toggle pass-through, see your real surroundings in color, and then within that environment, you can start to create. You can start adding digital content; maybe you can add portals to really augment the space around you. So it's not just about 2D panels anymore, it's really about creating a room and a scale experience literally where the room and the physical space meet, so it's key at that point that we should be able to design around it. So it's for VR, it's for mixed reality, and it's for the future that is ahead of us.

Interview with Thomas Van Bouwel, Cubism

XR Magazine: Why did you choose the minimalist style for developing your application?

Thomas: When I made the first prototype, I was sort of surprised that there's a lot of complexity you can put into a VR game, in a VR prototype, because you're immersed. I was surprised there weren't that many minimal games in VR, and the starting point of thinking about the concept of Cubism was what could a minimal game in VR look like, and where it makes use of the best affordances of VR, and where it could only work in VR, but where you strip away all the fat, all extra things.

So it felt like it was a game mechanic that really fit VR well, but where you could also just strip away all the context and just have you in the puzzle as this minimal setup. With this first prototype I made over weekends, all these sort of core concepts of the minimal design were already there. It was really just a gray environment with the puzzle there and just these little triangles as hands and you were solving a puzzle, and that was it. So from the get-go, the idea was to make a minimal game and figure out what a minimal design could look like, but there's also a part of the consideration of making a game that's easy to pick up and play.

And that's definitely something I wanted to have for Cubism as well, to have a game that could really be picked up and played by anyone, even if they haven't played games before or if they weren't that familiar with VR. This was something I didn't have in the first prototype, where the first prototype was using all the buttons on the controllers. That was sort of a lot of the process of the work that I was doing in the years developing it; it was simplifying the control scheme and making it easy to learn and to really just be able to put the headset on someone and get them to solve a puzzle within the first 15 seconds to make the game accessible and easy to use. So that's also a big part of the idea behind the minimal interactions and aesthetic.

Interview with Nanea Reeves, TRIPP VR

XR Magazine: As we are discussing mindfulness in XR, how did you get started with TRIPP?

Nanea: I am excited to be building what we like to call the mindful metaverse. I believe that we're on the verge of a major technology shift of computing, moving from the hand to the head and enabling a whole new interface for spatial computing. How do you experience content in ways as opposed to just interacting with it in a 2D format? And it's been really exciting to lean into that in these early days, to create something that can promote wellness, a deeper connection to self. And as an entrepreneur and also as a team, we are really excited to show up for that mission every day.

It originally started out with me asking the question, what is the product that I want to bring to the world? This idea to actually take some of the things I love the most, I have benefited the most in my life: from playing video games. It helped give me a sense of control over my environment. I really, as a young person, found a lot of mental health benefits from playing video games. And then also I have very much benefited from a mindfulness practice from a long time that I was given by a mental health professional when I was 15 years old. And it really changed the course of my life.

When we had this idea to create these beneficial experiences, and it was less really about meditation and VR, it was more about a catalog of moods that you could check and then see how we would design an experience to make you feel more focused or make you feel calmer. And that really opened our minds up to think a little bit outside the box. So with building the environments, it's important to get something out there with real people using it so you can start to get feedback. We had a lot of concepts about AI creating the experiences for you. And then what we found once we got live was that same thing that I felt as a young person playing video games: people wanted more of a sense of control over how the experience unfolded for them.

XR Magazine: How were you able to incorporate mental health into your VR experience?

Nanea: We are really excited with how we're doing that with AR because one of the things with a mental health product is you have to be very careful that you don't put the person on a self-improvement plan. I'm very good friends with Amy Jo Kim, who's a wonderful voice in the game industry, and she's also worked with how to gamify mental health apps. And she and I always laugh because I like to call some of these implementations I see as lame-ification instead of gamification; your resiliency score is not motivating enough! It's really got to get people on a path of self-acceptance, which will lead to self-care as an act of self-love, right?

If we only focus on self-improvement and mental health, it can be an ongoing constant communication that you're not okay the way you are right now in this moment. It's the risk, and so we thought, well, how do we innovate from that? If you look at gaming communities that are really active, you have the community contributing to the build-out of the platform. We want people to have a sense of purpose that they're also able to support others with their experience.

Interview with Julian Park, CEO at Bezel

XR Magazine: Speaking about designers, what in your opinion are some of the most common mistakes that designers make when approaching 3D?

Julian: I think one thing that people miss a lot is that when they're experiencing a design content, especially on a headset for AR/VR purposes, it's easy to overcomplicate the user flow or the number of options that the user can take. But if you can remember the early days of mobile phones like the iPhone one, it was difficult to convey complex user flows and complex application logic because there weren't a lot of industry standards or design patterns established for the platform yet. So you would often end up with single button actions or things that are simple enough for people to understand and that became used a lot. I think there's a similar sentiment within the XR industry where a lot of times people come from the game industry backgrounds, or people are trying to set up something that might be a bit too complicated to get the job done inside 3D. So, I think having an almost oversimplifying perspective to the number of things and the number of actions you expose to the user in the 3D content is super important so that people don't get lost when they start the experience or they just don't know what to do from here.

XR Magazine: One thing that I think is part of the future of UI or designing in this field is voice. What do you think?

Julian: I think voice is going to be, has been, and will be an important part of input to these machines. I think, that being said, there will always be a non-voice way of interacting with these apps just because whether it's from an accessibility standpoint or a speed standpoint, from a productivity day-to-day perspective, I would just want to type in something as opposed to talk to my computer. I think there are some fine lines between what's really interesting to imagine, which obviously is important, and, at the same time, what people usually end up doing sort of day to day. So I think that's where we're really trying to balance the two and trying to figure out what is really cool and different, but at the same time something that people can stick to and really use every single day.

Interview with Valentino Megale, CEO at Softcare Studios

XR Magazine: How are you using VR in hospitals and how is it used to help kids specifically?

Valentino: Virtual reality is an experiential technology. It's all about providing the opportunity to feel yourself present in another space than the physical one where you are. And thanks to virtual reality, we have the opportunity to take the patients beyond the walls of the hospitals.

I started to discuss with colleagues the opportunity to explore the potentialities of new technologies, of digital technologies such as virtual reality, to improve the experience of patients in the hospital because we understood that when you talk about therapy, it's not only about medical procedures or the administration of drugs, it's a 360-degree holistic experience that is all about emotions, all about social connections. It is also about loneliness and all the stressful feelings that patients experience within the clinical context. So all these aspects are able to deeply and also negatively impact the outcomes of therapy.

We had this idea of helping children in the hospital using virtual reality. So we decided to launch Softcare Studios using virtual reality as a way to improve the therapy experience of patients, but especially to change the way we manage pain and anxiety in patients undergoing very stressful medical treatments. So we started with pediatrics with a first project called Tommy. We started with pediatric oncology, and we are now using Tommy as a virtual sedation tool. It means that normally children undergoing very painful and stressful treatments like vascular access, in most of these cases, are totally sedated. It's total sedation because it's very painful, very stressful in the 90% of cases where we are using our solution with them. With children, we can avoid the need to administer drugs, to administer sedation. So we are using virtual reality as an alternative, which is digital and drug-free sedation; it's virtual sedation. Thanks to this, you are able to reduce and limit potential adverse effects coming from drugs. You are able to also save time and cost for the medical specialist and improve the experience, the overall experience of the therapy and the medical procedures for children.

XR Magazine: How does a virtual reality experience influence the brain?

Valentino: Our brain takes all the inputs from the external world, it processes them, and the results are our actions and interactions—our behavior. So the problem is that when it comes to pain, it's only partially a physical sensation, a physical feeling; a meaningful part of pain is all in our mind. So it's a psychological aspect, and virtual reality is a cognitive technology. It is a technology made to engage our brain and also minimize potentially the perception of pain, because if you want to define virtual reality, it is a digital technology designed to simulate the sense of presence in another space.

So suddenly you can be in a jungle even if you are just comfortably sitting on your couch. And after a couple of minutes, even if you know that you are in virtual reality, your brain starts reacting to virtual stimuli as if they were real. This is the sense of presence, even if you know that you are in virtual reality; this is the magic of virtual reality. So when a patient undergoes a painful treatment, in most of the cases, all the pain that they perceive is also determined by the clinical settings, by the fear, the anxiety, all the medical specialists coming around, and so on.

Around the end of the 1990s, Dr. Hunter Hoffman and David Peterson used virtual reality for pain management of war veterans. And that was an amazing first case. They even made medical imaging of the brains of people, and they saw that the brain areas that perceive pain were shutting down when people were immersed in virtual reality. That was something amazing because it's not only about distraction, it's about how our brain starts working differently when we are in virtual reality. The objective reality is that you can minimize pain using a digital tool instead of using drugs.

XR Magazine: What are the risks and ethical considerations to consider with virtual reality?

Valentino: Virtual reality is amazing. It's a projector for virtual scenarios, but it's first of all a sensor. So you can collect a huge amount of data, and from collecting data, you can do good things like personalizing the scenarios, but you also can do bad things sometimes, not just breaching, but collecting data about the privacy of people. So all these technologies have huge potential, but the huge potential comes if we are able to understand and recognize what the potential risks are. Especially, I'm dealing with child safety, and we are discussing with a lot of stakeholders, policymakers, educators, and families about the risks and the challenges of virtual reality for children from content, which is not appropriate to a specific age, to the possibility to meet people in their avatars who are not who they're saying to be. There are many challenges. So the challenge right now is to recognize the benefits but also the risks and try to balance to maximize the first and minimize the second.

Virtual reality is a tool that can replace reality sometimes. It can be used for children during a specific medical treatment and before a medical treatment to relax them during long-term hospitalization to reduce all the anxiety, especially in pediatric oncology. So this is a tool that well-trained medical operators can use to better manage patients, help them relax, and also help them manage pain without drugs. A lot of people say, "Hey, children are wearing virtual reality headsets and it's about isolating children." In this case, it's not about isolating children, it's about reconnecting children with their needs in a very stressful clinical context where they are limited or isolated from the world. Suddenly, a tool which is theoretically isolating children is reconnecting people across realities. And this is something major that happened during the years. And yes, virtual reality is isolating the person, but if well designed and well used, it can reconnect people even beyond the walls of the hospitals or beyond the screen they use in virtual reality.

Interview with Nick Busietta, PsyTech VR

XR Magazine: From the point of view of psychology, why do you think we need to induce and augment emotional and cognitive estate? In other words, what are the benefits of this?

Nick: I think there's many benefits and it spans many different motivations and use cases for not just VR as a technology and not even technology, just life. You can see people want to optimize themselves and upgrade all the time; they want to perform at a peak level. People like feeling different things. There's just an intrinsic quality about the human experience that really it's the reason we experience content. It is the reason we watch television, we watch sport, we play sport, we go to the movies, we go to the theater, we listen to a song. It's all about these feelings that can be generated by content in general. There are obvious use cases when it comes to, okay, well what if we make someone feel a certain thing for a very specific purpose? So if you are a highly strung, anxious individual, or you're going through some stresses in life, the ability to reliably calm yourself down in the moment, on demand, with minimal effort and training, has obvious benefits.

If you are experiencing chronic pain, virtual reality can distract you from that pain so that you don't feel it anymore, or at least you've got analgesic effects that are very large, so it's not as pronounced as it would've been without the technology. You've got this non-pharmacological intervention that can alleviate people's pain or maybe another use case; if you are looking at creating a training experience, where you want people to perform under pressure, then making people feel pressure has obvious benefits in that training session when you want to simulate scenarios. So there's lots and lots of different reasons why we'd want to do this. I would almost go to the extent that any content creator and any content consumer are doing it, whether knowingly or unknowingly, creating or using these experiences explicitly for that purpose. So in some ways, what we're doing is not overly new, it's just that our goal is to build a sense of rigor and framework and collect data to help optimize the design of these experiences to get better and better and more effective in the way that we do that.

So we've got a design guide, which I guess summarizes a lot of our key research as a web-based resource, which we call the psych docs. And the psych docs come with two different sections. We've got a quick start guide, which is basically all the quick and easy dos and don'ts of how to design a calm experience, how to design an awe experience, a pain relief experience, and so forth. And then we've got a more detailed explore section where we're breaking down our research into different categories of design, be it color motion, mindfulness, interactivity, sound, music, or whatever it may be; there's quite a lot in there. So that is a more detailed deep dive into VR design.

XR Magazine: When you're speaking about collecting the data based on all the research that's been done, what are some of those very important lessons that you've learned in terms of designing these types of experiences?

Nick: One obvious thing that developers use is color. So we know now when people think about colors, they typically think about blues and greens for calming experiences and maybe reds and yellows for more uplifting, energizing experiences. And that's true; those sorts of color palettes do have an effect. But what's more important than the actual color selection is the color saturation level. So you can have sort of soft muted colors that are more likely to be interpreted by users as being in a calming environment, or you can have very loud, sort of saturated, colors that are going to be more energized—or very saturated blue or very soft pinks, where the soft pink is more likely to be calming than the saturated blue.

XR Magazine: How do you envision change, if any, in the way that we're experiencing wellness experiences now, but with new devices upcoming in the future?

Nick: I think in a way the distinction between VR, AR, the real world, and even more other traditional gaming devices is a very short-term distinction. In the future and potentially in the near future, we're going to see an increasing blend between these technologies, and that's where this metaverse word comes from that everyone's talking about now. It's not necessarily virtual reality vs. augmented reality. Which one's better, or which one's going to take hold? They're both going to take hold, and they're both going to take hold at the same time, and in all likelihood, they're going to be the same device that takes hold. So the way I see it going is, you've touched on it, the form factor of virtual reality is currently a little bit cumbersome from the point of view that it can feel heavy if you're using it for long periods of time. That's all being addressed, and what we're seeing is this convergence of a lot of different technologies. We've got 5G technologies coming to the fore. These headsets that we currently have are going to be getting smaller and smaller and then eventually becoming glasses that can switch between virtual mixed reality and the real world in different blends. And so I think that is at a hardware level where it's all going, and it's just a matter of time when that's going to happen.

Interview with Alex Fink, CEO of the Otherweb

XR Magazine: Now that we have the ability to create even more information quickly with these generative AI tools, how do we try to address the temptation of just creating for the sake of generating huge amounts of content that is already established in our current Internet ecosystem?

Alex: Everybody will try to create more content to at least achieve the same number of clicks and views that they achieved before everybody else started using this, right? The only way that I think we can change that incentive for everybody is by actually changing how advertising pays to the people who create this content. So the crude method is to filter on the consumption layer, right? So if many people filter a certain type of content out, that content no longer pays; therefore, the creator has an incentive to not create it or to create something else. Instead, a slightly more complicated approach, but it might be more granular, granular and better in some sense, is to actually change how advertisements pay based on what content they appear on. So if it's a pay-per-click advertising, then perhaps instead of the number of clicks times cost per click, the payout should have a third factor in the formula that is called quality of the underlying page.

I think we need to spend some thought on what that looks like to create good incentives for people. You mentioned, I guess, (what is) the equivalent of clickbait in VR. We already see the equivalent of clickbait in YouTube, let's say, when the thumbnail for a video often includes some very attractive woman that does not appear in the video itself, right? So that is also a form of clickbait. I assume VR will have an even more advanced version of the same thing, maybe a very attractive woman in 3D. It happens all the time. I'm sure it'll happen there as well. The question is how do we create a disincentive for it?

XR Magazine: What do you think are actual things that we could do to help ourselves with this issue?

Alex: We just need to develop our own routines to filter things out, right? Choose where we consume information, how we select what we consume, and maybe introduce some third-party tools to try to filter out what we are consuming. And in many ways, it shouldn't just be limited to how we select what we consume on a particular platform. The first question we can ask is, should we spend this much time on a particular platform? Even once we're there, the question is how do we select the content that we are consuming online? There needs to be some conscious planning in this; otherwise, the company that runs the platform we're on is going to select for us. And their incentives are pretty different from our incentives. Typically, every one of these platforms is developed to maximize our time on site and our engagement, right? But your goal is not to spend as much time as possible on social media, right? Your goal is to get as much value as possible and in as little time as possible. And so clearly your goals are not aligned with any platform goals, right? Unless you plan it, if you let that algorithm decide what you see next, the algorithm is going to be really good at maximizing your time on site, which is not what you want. The question is can we not just help ourselves but can we help the entire ecosystem somehow?

Can we create an incentive for creators to create better content for social media, to show us the best content available and not the ones that we are just most likely to click. And it seems to me like for this to happen, many of us need to start filtering junk out because if many different users filter junk out, that creates a disincentive for creators to create junk. They know that people will not actually see it if users are going to filter it out. And so we want to create tools to do this for as many people as possible.

XR Magazine: From a design point of view, we are actually supposed to help create apps or experiences that are human centric. As you've said, it makes more sense from that real human-centric approach where we are the ones who decide, and we have the freedom to actually decide through filters.

Alex: You talked about human-centric systems and how they're trying to maximize the decision-making of people to decide what they consume or at least what they're supposed to. I want to caution you also to consider that at different time horizons, people decide different things. Like, I might decide that I want to eat salad every day for the next year, but if you offer me cake right now, I might decide to eat the cake anyway. And so our decisions in the moment are very different from our decisions in the long run. In the long run, we try to maximize our higher self, so to speak, whereas in the moment we don't have much willpower and we make really bad decisions. So our approach has been to try to let people control what they will consume in the long run because that's what they think is good for them, whereas what a social media platform would do is try to measure what you react to in real time and just give you more of that. So if you react to cake and not to kale, you'll get cake all the time. In contrast, we're going to actually ask you what proportion of cake to kale you want in your diet. And if you say at least 80% kale, then we will try to get you that.

Final Thoughts: Embracing the "Interfaceless" Promise

As individuals involved in design and development or as consumers, it can be tempting to stick to what we know and play it safe. Venturing into the territories of interfaceless technology and conscious design might seem intimidating. However, throughout history, there have always been pioneers—those who bravely explore territories armed with their vision, passion, and resilience, shaping the future. Today, you are faced with a choice: to passively observe or actively contribute as an architect of this transformative era.

As learned so far, the concept of "interfaceless" is not simply about the absence of interfaces but about something more profound—a more intuitive, humane, and enriching way for us to interact with technology. As we find ourselves at this point in time, let us reflect on the words of visionary Steve Jobs that deeply resonate: "Technology alone is not sufficient. It is the combination of technology with arts and humanities that produces results that truly touch our hearts."

So as we conclude this journey together, let's not just embrace the promise of interfaceless technology but champion it. Let's remember that amid all the advancements and innovations, our ultimate goal remains unchanged: to enhance the experience.

I encourage you to embrace this era of design with curiosity, optimism, and an open mind. Explore, experiment, learn, grow, and—above all else—enjoy the process along the way. The future without interfaces awaits us—a future brimming with opportunities and challenges that will push you to become a better designer. Let's wholeheartedly embrace AI and work together to shape a kind future.

As you finish reading this book, I hope you are filled with the passion to not anticipate what lies ahead but to play an active role in shaping it. Let's make sure that as technology progresses, we never lose sight of the importance of humanity.

APPENDIX A

Resources and Tools for "Interfaceless" Design

As "interfaceless" design continues to gain traction in the technological and design worlds, the need for relevant tools and resources becomes increasingly evident. These tools, primarily software platforms and frameworks, facilitate the implementation of such designs, enabling professionals to transform theoretical principles into practical solutions. This appendix aims to provide an extensive list of valuable resources and tools, essential for those eager to delve deeper into the world of "interfaceless" design.

1. **Design Platforms and Frameworks**

    *   *Framer X*: Renowned for its innovative approach to design and prototyping, Framer X offers unique tools specifically tailored to creating and testing "interfaceless" environments.

    *   *Unity with ARKit/ARCore*: Unity, a widely used game engine, combined with Apple's ARKit or Google's ARCore, becomes a formidable tool to develop augmented reality applications emphasizing spatial computing.

© Diana Olynick 2024
D. Olynick, *Interfaceless*, Design Thinking, https://doi.org/10.1007/979-8-8688-0083-2

- *A-Frame*: An open source web framework for the creation of VR experiences. Its simplicity and wide adoption make it perfect for budding "interfaceless" designers.

- *Unreal Engine*: Also used in the filmmaking and gaming industry because of its great rendering capabilities, it allows any developer or creator to deliver 3D experiences that are of the highest visual quality.

2. **Sensors and Hardware Kits**

- *Leap Motion*: This hardware tool captures the movement of hands in 3D space, allowing for precise gesture recognition—a cornerstone of "interfaceless" design.

- *Microsoft's Azure Kinect DK*: This developer kit integrates AI sensors in a single device, making it an excellent tool for spatial computing endeavors.

- *Meta Quest 3/Pro*: A mixed reality device from Meta that supports the blend of the physical world with the digital environment, facilitating immersive experiences.

- *Vision Pro*: Apple's mixed reality device that seamlessly blends digital content with the physical space facilitating remote interactions, allowing navigation with your eyes, hands, and voice.

3. **Voice and Sound Design Tools**

- *Descript*: This is an audio/video editor that works like a document. It features a screen recorder, full multitrack editing, publishing, and some AI tools.

- *Sonic Pi*: A unique tool to code music and design sound. Sonic Pi makes the process of sound design for "interfaceless" environments a lot more accessible.

4. **AI and Machine Learning Platforms**

   - *TensorFlow*: Google's free open source platform, which has been at the forefront of integrating AI with various applications.

   - *IBM Watson*: Offers a plethora of services, but its Assistant feature can be instrumental in creating smart "interfaceless" applications.

   - *RunwayML*: A unique platform that bridges the gap between AI and creative professionals. It allows creators to use the power of machine learning without the need for extensive coding knowledge.

   - *Midjourney*: An advanced graphic image generator with an embedded editor that works on Discord.

   - *Adobe Firefly*: The generative AI tool from Adobe that facilitates the creation of assets to be used in other Adobe Suite Products.

   - *Stable Diffusion*: DreamStudio is a graphic text to image generator that outputs realistic or stylized images

5. **Online Communities and Forums**

   - *Spatia*: A dedicated community for spatial computing enthusiasts where one can share projects, seek guidance, and discuss the latest in "interfaceless" design.

- *Voiceflow Community*: This forum is all about voice design, hosting numerous experts in the field who share their experiences and solutions to common problems.

- *AR/VR Journey*: A Medium-based publication with articles, tutorials, and news centered around the augmented and virtual reality domain.

6. **Webinars and Tutorials**

- *Udacity's VR Developer Nanodegree*: Though not solely focused on "interfaceless" design, this course provides a strong foundation in creating applications for VR, a key component of the "interfaceless" approach.

- *Coursera's AI For Everyone*: Hosted by Andrew Ng, this course is a gentle introduction to the concepts of AI, demystifying the process for designers and developers alike.

By incorporating these resources and tools into your toolkit, you'll be well prepared to tackle the challenges and opportunities presented by "interfaceless" design. It's essential to remember that this list is not exhaustive, and the field is rapidly evolving. Therefore, continuous learning and exploration remain pivotal.

Other Resources

- *OpenAI GPT API*: This is the engine that powers ChatGPT. It can help you create AI models for a wide variety of language tasks. It's a fantastic tool to create dialogue for interfaceless applications. You can access the OpenAI GPT API here: `https://openai.com/blog/openai-api`

- *Microsoft Cognitive Services*: These services are powered by machine learning and cover a wide range of capabilities from speech recognition to emotion detection, making them highly useful for building intuitive, empathetic interactions in your designs. You can access Microsoft Cognitive Services here: `https://azure.microsoft.com/en-us/products/ai-services/?activetab=pivot:azureopenaiservicetab`

- *Dialogflow by Google*: A natural language understanding platform that makes it easy to design and integrate a conversational user interface into your mobile app, web application, device, bot, and so on. Access Dialogflow here: `https://cloud.google.com/dialogflow`

- *Amazon Alexa Skills Kit*: This set of tools, APIs, and documentation allows you to create voice-based interactions for Alexa. It's a great place to start when designing voice user interfaces. You can access the Amazon Alexa Skills Kit here: `https://developer.amazon.com/en-US/alexa/alexa-skills-kit`

- *Apple's Human Interface Guidelines*: Apple's Siri section provides guidance on designing great voice interaction experiences for Siri and your app. Access the guide here: `https://developer.apple.com/design/human-interface-guidelines`

- *Google's Actions on Google*: This platform allows developers to create actions for Google Assistant. Its design guide provides valuable insights into designing conversational experiences. Access the guide here: `https://developers.google.com/assistant/console`

- *AR.js*: A lightweight library for augmented reality on the Web, with a very low barrier to entry and great performance. Access AR.js here: `https://ar-js-org.github.io/AR.js/`

- *A-Frame*: A web framework for building virtual reality experiences. A-Frame simplifies VR and AR development and is compatible with most web-based AR and VR libraries. Access A-Frame here: `https://aframe.io/`

- *Rasa*: An open source machine learning framework to automate text- and voice-based conversations. It's an excellent tool for developing conversational AI applications. Access Rasa here: `https://rasa.com/`

- *Online Learning Platforms*: Websites like Coursera, edX, Udemy, and Khan Academy have a wealth of courses on AI, ML, AR, VR, design thinking, and more. They can provide the foundation and deepen your knowledge of the concepts discussed in this book.

- *Books*: There are countless books that offer in-depth knowledge on the topics of AI, ML, design thinking, UI/UX design, ethics in design, etc. Some notable titles include *Designing with the Mind in Mind* by Jeff Johnson, *The Design of Everyday Things* by Don Norman, and *Designing for Emotion* by Aarron Walter.

Please note that while all these resources provide a solid foundation for your exploration and implementation of interfaceless design, the most valuable learning will come from hands-on experience. Don't be afraid to experiment, prototype, and iterate. The future of interfaceless design is in your hands.

Tools

In this section you will find a guide for creating your own framework, a design guide for experiences in spatial computing (Table A-1) and for experiences in games (Table A-2).

Guiding Questions Checklist for Crafting Your Personal MSDF (Mindful Spatial Design Framework)

1. **Empathetic Approach**

   - What considerations will you make to guarantee your understanding and give a diverse range of human experiences?

   - How will you make sure that your designs encompass the psychological and emotional needs of humans?

2. **Understanding Humans**

   - How would you describe the ideal human who would interact with your designs? What are their needs, challenges, preferences, and habits?

   - How do you estimate your ideal human interacting with the spatial computing landscape?

3. **The Role of Mindfulness**

   - How do you define mindfulness in the context of spatial computing design?

   - In what ways do you foresee humans to be present and conscious at the interaction with your design?

4. **Feedback and Iteration**

   - What processes will you follow for continuous iteration, adjustment, and reflection of your own framework?

   - How will you obtain insight on your designs to the objective of making sure that it matches your MSDF principles?

5. **Personal Values**

- Which of the mentioned MSDF universal general principles resonate with you the most, and why?

- What values and beliefs are important to you regarding design for spatial computing?

6. **Future Vision**

- How are your designs facilitating the interactions for humans five years from now? What does it look like?

- How will the principles in your MSDF guide this preceding vision?

Table A-1. *Design Guide for Conscious and Mindful Design Experiences for Spatial Computing*

CONSCIOUS DESIGN GUIDE						
Design Domain	**Key Factors**	**Caution Points**	**Desired Outcomes**	**Score (Initial)**	**Score (Midway)**	**Score (Final)**
Spatial Sensitivity	Ambient Awareness Human Comfort Virtual Boundaries	Overloading senses Inducing disorientation Ignoring real world spatial constrains	Environments that resonate with human spatial understanding and comfort			
Engagement Dynamics	Human Focus Immersive Depth Interaction Fluidity	Fragmented attention Overstimulation Redundant interactions	Seamless, immersive experiences that captivate and maintain human attention			
Information Architecture	Contextual Relevance Spatial Data Presentation Human Orientation	Decontextualized info Overwhelming data displays Ambiguous spatial cues	Clear, intuitive information structures that aid spatial understanding and decision making			
Human Autonomy	Spatial Choices Interaction Freedom Intuitive Controls	Over-guidance Restrictive interactions Misleading cues	Empowering humans to navigate and interact with agency and clarity in the spatial medium			
Community Cohesion	Collaborative Spaces Shared Experiences Group Dynamics	Isolating experiences Disrupting group interactions Lack of communal norms	Foster collaborative and harmonious group interactions withing the spatial environment			
Spatial Social Interactions	Authentic Avatars Relationship Dynamics Social Presence	Impersonification risks Superficial social metrics Forced social engagements	Genuine, meaningful social interactions that respect and enhance human relationships in the spatial context			
Scoring System	0 - 3 Needs Improvement 4 - 6 On trackk 7 - 10 Excelling					

Note   Using this tool, designers can evaluate their spatial computing designs at different stages (initial, midway, and final) based on the indicators presented. The scores range from 0 to 10, with 10 indicating optimal alignment with the conscious and mindful design principles. Feedback loops would be required to bring the experience to more optimal levels depending on the project priorities.

Table A-2. *Design Guide for Conscious and Mindful Design Experiences for Games*

CONSCIOUS DESIGN GUIDE FOR GAMES	
Measurement Area	**Methods and Metrics**
Wellbeing and Satisfaction	☐ Surveys and feedback focusing on emotional wellbeing ☐ Longitudinal studies on long-term impacts
Ease of Interaction	☐ Task completion rate ☐ Error rate
Depth of Engagement	☐ Time spent in meaningful engagement ☐ Mindfulness metrics from surveys
Inclusivity and Accesibility	☐ Diverse human testing ☐ Feedback from various demographics
Environmental and Ethical Impact	☐ Carbon footprint measurement ☐ Regular ethical reviews or audits
Cultural sensitivity and respect	☐ Feedback from different cultural groups ☐ Cultural assessments
Holistic Safety	☐ Incident reports ☐ Safety surveys
Genuine Value and Meaning	☐ Human testimonials ☐ Depth Interviews
Adoption and Retention	☐ Human growth metrics ☐ Retention rates
Community and Social Support	☐ Community feedback ☐ Social Impact Assessments

The following checklist is a design resource for developing minimalist experiences (Table A-3).

Table A-3. Design Checklist for Minimalist Experiences

MINIMALIST EXPERIENCES DESIGN CHECKLIST

Criteria	Objective	Mechanism to Judge	Pass / Fail
Purpose Clarity	Ensuring the design's primary goal is clear	Does the primary function stand out immediately?	☐ Pass ☐ Fail
Human-Centric Approach	Design should cater to the target human individual rather than the demographic	Does it meet the needs of both novice and experienced humans in the space?	☐ Pass ☐ Fail
Efficiency Evaluation	Achieve goals with minimal steps	Are all steps essential, without redundancies?	☐ Pass ☐ Fail
Visual Harmony	Aesthetic consistency and hierarchy	Is there a balance in the use of colors, fonts and elements?	☐ Pass ☐ Fail
Functionality Depth	Adapting to various human scenarios	Can the human customize their experience to some extent?	☐ Pass ☐ Fail
Flexibility and Adaptability	Design depth without overwhelming	Are advanced features accesible without cluttering?	☐ Pass ☐ Fail
Feedback Mechanisms	Clear feedback for human actions	Are human actions met with appropiate and clear feedback?	☐ Pass ☐ Fail
Consistency and Predictability	Uniformity across the interface	Are design elements consistent in appearance and behaviour?	☐ Pass ☐ Fail
Learning Curve	Ease of understanding for new participants	Can a human become comfortable quickly? Are there tooltips or guidance mechanisms?	☐ Pass ☐ Fail
Future Proofing	Ability to adapt to future changes	Is it easy to modify or update the design with new tech or human needs?	☐ Pass ☐ Fail
Iterative Review	Periodic updates based on feedback	Is there a system in place for regular human feedback and iterations?	☐ Pass ☐ Fail

The following is a summarized comparison of a traditional design funnel to one of spatial computing (Table A-4).

Table A-4. *Comparison: Traditional vs. Spatial Computing Design Funnel*

TRADITIONAL VS SPATIAL COMPUTING DESIGN FUNNEL

Phases	Traditional	Spatial Computing Design Funnel
Requirement Gathering	Stakeholder meetings	Immersive meetings in 3D spaces
	User surveys and interviews	Human experience journeys in 3D environments
	Market analysis	Gathering of spatial interactions and feedback
Conceptualization	Brainstorming	Ideation in 3D spaces
	Sketching and wireframing	Storyboarding, bodystorming, acting in real and 3D simulated spaces
	Concept boards	Layered experiences
Design	Mock ups	Mindful and intentional 3D model creation
	Prototyping	Prototype development in 3D simulated spaces
	Design reviews	Design audits and tests in immersive environments
Testing	Usability testing	Human testing in immersive environments
	A/B testing	Real time feedback collection in 3D spaces
	Feedback iteration	Iterative design based on spatial feedback
Implementation	Development	Development with iterative immersive testing
	Quality assurance	Quality assurance evaluations in 3D spaces
	Deployment / Feedback	Deployment and feedback in XR platfoms / mediums

List of Some Potential Ideas with a Conscious and Mindful Approach

- *Eco-Friendly Reminders*: Homes with sensors that adjust to environmental conditions saving energy.

- *Compassionate Communication*: AI companions as holographic avatars that support humans when sensing stress.

- *Animal Welfare Alerts*: Highlights of cruelty-free products in shopping AR experiences.

319

- *Smart Vegan Recipe*: Repurpose of remaining ingredients in the fridge to avoid waste.

- *Yoga Posture Corrector*: Holographic trainer that helps with guidance on yoga postures to avoid injuries.

- *Walking Meditation Guide*: AR-guided meditations in parks with visual cues and instructions.

- *Community Service Finder*: Digital AR boards that highlight volunteering opportunities.

- *Mindful Shopping Consumption*: Transparent data and sourcing of products in AR shopping experiences, inviting you to reassess if you really need the product and why.

- *Animal Rescue Alerts*: Holographic and geolocation information about animals in need and how to contribute.

- *Mindful Travel*: Eco-friendly attractions and events about community and social impact.

- *Plant Care Reminder*: Spatial sensors read the plant health and modify conditions of light and water to keep it healthy for prolonged winter places.

- *Yoga at Home*: Sensors adjust the ambient conditions with music, temperature, and light for the specific theme of the yoga session.

- *Mindful Community*: Personal and group spaces where people can join to discuss community projects or to share their resources.

- *Mindful Eating*: AR experience or smart bowl that senses the speed of eating and the amount, helping you practice consistently.

- *Digital Detox*: AR experience using sensors or AR devices to suggest breaks and activities for wellness.

- *Mindful Driving*: A sensor system or AR device that helps the driver wake up in case of falling asleep, avoiding fatal outcomes. It could also help with relaxing music if sensing stress.

- *Relationship Aid*: AR and sensor system that reminds you to come back to yourself and reconnect when sensing disagreements or potential confrontations, inviting you to breathe mindfully.

- *Work-Life Balance*: After extended hours of work, a system suggests breaks and alternate activities to promote well-being and balance.

- *Emotion Helper*: An AR device and experience that detects levels of anxiety, depression, or other mental states and encourages you to breathe mindfully.

- *Mindful Learning*: An AR device and experience that helps you discuss the topic of study to assess learning and understanding.

APPENDIX B

Glossary of AI and Spatial Computing

- *Algorithm*: A set of rules followed by a computer to solve a problem or complete a task. In machine learning, algorithms are used to discover patterns in data and make decisions or predictions based on these patterns.

- *AI (Artificial Intelligence)*: A field of computer science that aims to create systems capable of performing tasks that require human intelligence. These tasks include problem solving, understanding natural language, perception, and decision-making.

- *Augmented Reality (AR)*: An interactive experience where digital elements are superimposed onto the real world through devices like smartphones or AR glasses.

- *Bias in AI*: The systematic error introduced by the choice of data or the way the algorithm processes it.

- *Biometrics*: Technologies used for measuring and analyzing human body characteristics, such as fingerprints, eye retinas and irises, voice patterns, facial patterns, and hand measurements.

D. Olynick, *Interfaceless*, Design Thinking, https://doi.org/10.1007/979-8-8688-0083-2

- *Chatbot*: An AI software designed to interact with humans in their natural language. These interactions can occur in messaging apps, websites, or over the phone.

- *Conscious Design*: A design philosophy that emphasizes mindfulness, sustainability, and the holistic consideration of end-user needs, societal impact, and environmental footprint.

- *Context-Aware Computing*: A mobile computing paradigm in which applications can discover and take advantage of contextual information (such as user location, time of day, nearby devices, and user activity).

- *Data Privacy*: The practice of ensuring that the data shared by users is only used for its intended purpose.

- *Data Mining*: The process of discovering patterns and knowledge from large amounts of data. The data sources can include databases, data warehouses, the Internet, and other information repositories.

- *Deep Learning*: A subfield of machine learning that models its computations after the human brain with structures called neural networks. It's particularly useful for tasks like image and speech recognition.

- *Ethics in AI*: The aspect of the AI field concerned with ensuring AI technologies are designed and used in a way that respects the rights and dignities of individuals.

- *Generative AI*: A type of artificial intelligence, more specifically a type of machine learning, which allows computers to generate creative outputs on their own.

- *Gesture Recognition*: The mathematical interpretation of human gestures via computational algorithms, allowing for interaction with machines without any mechanical devices.

- *Haptic Feedback*: Feedback provided to the user through touch, often by vibrations or other physical responses from a device.

- *Intellectual Property in AI*: The legal and ethical considerations around ownership and usage rights of AI-generated content.

- *Interfaceless*: A design approach that seeks to minimize or eliminate traditional graphical user interfaces, emphasizing more natural interactions, like voice, gesture, or thought.

- *Interfaceless Design*: The design philosophy of creating intuitive and immersive user experiences that do not rely on traditional graphical user interfaces.

- *Machine Learning (ML)*: A subset of AI that involves the scientific study of algorithms and statistical models that computers use to perform a specific task without using explicit instructions, relying instead on patterns and inference.

- *Mindful Design*: An approach to creating user experiences that focuses on awareness and understanding of the user's cognitive, emotional, and physical needs.

- *Mindful Spatial Design Framework (MSDF)*: A conceptual model emphasizing mindfulness in spatial computing and "interfaceless" design. MSDF prioritizes the user's cognitive and emotional needs, ensuring that designs are intuitive, immersive, and ethically crafted.

- *Mixed Reality (MR)*: A hybrid of both physical and digital worlds where real-world and digital objects coexist and interact in real time.

- *Natural Language Processing (NLP)*: A field of AI that gives the machines the ability to read, understand, and derive meaning from human languages.

- *Neural Network*: A series of algorithms that endeavor to recognize underlying relationships in a set of data through a process that mimics the way the human brain operates.

- *Originality in AI*: The concept of unique, novel outputs generated by an AI system, often discussed in the context of generative AI.

- *Spatial Computing*: It refers to a range of ideas for how humans could interact with computers in the future, primarily involving the integration of physical environments and digital interfaces.

- *Tactile Interface*: An interface that relies on touch or physical interaction as a primary mode of interaction.

- *User Experience (UX) Design*: The process design teams use to create products that provide meaningful and relevant experiences to users, including aspects of branding, design, usability, and function.

- *Virtual Reality (VR)*: A simulated experience that can be similar to or completely different from the real world. It typically requires specialized equipment such as a headset.

- *Vision OS*: An operating system designed for devices that interpret and respond to visual input.

- *Vision Pro*: A professional suite of tools for creating, managing, and deploying vision-based applications.

- *Voice Recognition*: Technology that can recognize and respond to spoken commands, commonly used in "interfaceless" designs.

- *Voice User Interface (VUI)*: A voice or speech platform that allows users to interact with systems through voice commands.

- *XR (Extended Reality)*: A term encapsulating AR, VR, and MR. It represents a spectrum of experiences that blend the physical and virtual worlds.

This glossary serves as a concise reference to some of the pivotal terms discussed in this book. As with any rapidly evolving field, new terms and concepts emerge regularly. It's vital to stay updated, continuously expanding one's vocabulary in the domain.

APPENDIX C

Additional Resources for Further Learning

In addition to the content of this book, there are a multitude of resources available for designers and developers interested in deepening their understanding of AI and "interfaceless" design. Here is a curated list of recommended resources:

Online Courses and Tutorials

- *Introduction to Artificial Intelligence (AI)*—Microsoft, edX: This course provides an overview of AI concepts and workflows, machine learning and deep learning, and performance metrics.

- *Machine Learning*—Stanford University, Coursera: This course by Andrew Ng, the cofounder of Coursera and a computer science professor at Stanford, is widely recognized as one of the best introductory courses on machine learning.

- *The Elements of AI*—University of Helsinki: This free online course aims to demystify AI and its implications, with no complicated math or programming required.

- *Google AI Hub*: A platform where developers, data scientists, and enterprises can access AI tools and resources.

D. Olynick, *Interfaceless*, Design Thinking, https://doi.org/10.1007/979-8-8688-0083-2

- *AI For Everyone*—deeplearning.ai, Coursera: This course gives a nontechnical introduction to AI technologies and the impact of AI on society.

- *Deep Learning Specialization*—deeplearning.ai, Coursera: A series of courses developed by Andrew Ng to help students understand deep learning, build neural networks, and lead successful machine learning projects.

Books

- *Artificial Intelligence: A Modern Approach* by Stuart Russell and Peter Norvig: This is a comprehensive text that provides an up-to-date introduction to the theory and practice of AI.

- *Deep Learning* by Yoshua Bengio, Ian Goodfellow, and Aaron Courville: This book offers a comprehensive introduction to the field of deep learning.

- *Human + Machine: Reimagining Work in the Age of AI* by Paul R. Daugherty and H. James Wilson: This book explores the impact of AI on businesses and jobs.

Websites and Blogs

- *Towards Data Science*: A Medium publication that offers a wealth of articles on data science, AI, and machine learning.

- *arXiv*: A repository of scientific papers in fields that include statistics, computer science, and artificial intelligence.

- *AI Alignment*: A blog focused on aligning AI systems with human values.

- *OpenAI Blog*: A blog by OpenAI, an artificial intelligence research lab, featuring their latest research and insights.

Conferences and Events

- *NeurIPS (Conference on Neural Information Processing Systems)*: This is one of the most prestigious annual events in the field of machine learning.

- *ICML (International Conference on Machine Learning)*: This conference is one of the leading conferences in the field of machine learning.

- *AI & Big Data Expo*: This expo brings together key industries for top-level content and discussion on AI and big data.

Podcasts

- *Artificial Intelligence Podcast*: This podcast features discussions with some of the most interesting minds in artificial intelligence and related fields.

- *The AI Alignment Podcast*: A podcast that explores the ways in which we can ensure that AI systems are beneficial for all.

- *Data Skeptic*: A podcast that explores topics related to data science, statistics, machine learning, and artificial intelligence.

These resources offer a wealth of information, but the most important resource is your curiosity and willingness to continue learning. As AI continues to evolve, it's critical for designers and developers to stay up to date with the latest developments and discussions in the field.

APPENDIX D

References

The following is a representative list of the types of resources that indirectly contributed to the information in this book:

- *Artificial Intelligence: Structures and Strategies for Complex Problem Solving* by George F. Luger

- *Artificial Intelligence: A Modern Approach* by Stuart Russell and Peter Norvig

- *Designing for Emerging Technologies: UX for Genomics, Robotics, and the Internet of Things* by Jonathan Follett and the UX Design team at O'Reilly Media

- *Human-Computer Interaction: An Empirical Research Perspective* by I. Scott MacKenzie

- *Information Visualization: Perception for Design* by Colin Ware

- *AI Superpowers: China, Silicon Valley, and the New World Order* by Kai-Fu Lee

- *Weapons of Math Destruction: How Big Data Increases Inequality and Threatens Democracy* by Cathy O'Neil

- *The Ethical Algorithm: The Science of Socially Aware Algorithm Design* by Michael Kearns and Aaron Roth

D. Olynick, *Interfaceless*, Design Thinking, https://doi.org/10.1007/979-8-8688-0083-2

- Various papers, blogs, and articles by leading technology companies such as Google, IBM, Microsoft, and OpenAI

- Key online resources such as Medium, Towards Data Science, AI Alignment, and the OpenAI blog

- Several case studies such as Facebook's "Like" button, Google's DeepMind AlphaGo, IBM Watson, OpenAI's GPT models, and others

- Popular documentaries and shows exploring AI and ethics such as *The Social Dilemma* and *The Great Hack* on Netflix

- Russell, S. J., & Norvig, P. (2010). *Artificial Intelligence: A Modern Approach.* Prentice Hall.

- Maeda, J. (2006). *The Laws of Simplicity.* MIT press.

- Norman, D. A. (2013). *The design of everyday things: Revised and expanded edition.* Basic books.

- Saffer, D. (2013). *Microinteractions: Designing with Details.* O'Reilly Media.

- Raskin, J. (2000). *The Humane Interface: New Directions for Designing Interactive Systems.* Addison-Wesley Professional.

- Buxton, B. (2007). *Sketching User Experiences: Getting the Design Right and the Right Design.* Morgan Kaufmann.

- O'Reilly, T. (2011). *What Is Web 2.0.* O'Reilly Media.

- Kurzweil, R. (2006). *The Singularity Is Near: When Humans Transcend Biology.* Penguin.

- Gibson, W. (1984). *Neuromancer.* Ace.

- Harari, Y. N. (2017). *Homo Deus: A Brief History of Tomorrow.* Harper.

- Mann, S. (2001). *Wearable computing: A first step toward personal imaging.* IEEE Computer, 34(2), 25–32.

- Fogg, B. J. (2002). *Persuasive Technology: Using Computers to Change What We Think and Do.* Morgan Kaufmann.

- Schwartz, R., & Collins, C. (2016). *Implications of Augmented Reality in Design: A Transcendence from Experience to Engagement.* Journal of Design and Science, 5.

- Rawlinson, K. (2015). *The Conscious Design Method: The Underlying Philosophy of Total Design as a Paradigm for Total Way of Life.* Design Journal, 18(2), 193–207.

- Johnson, S. (2001). *Emergence: The Connected Lives of Ants, Brains, Cities, and Software.* Simon and Schuster.

- Vinge, V. (1993). *The Coming Technological Singularity: How to Survive in the Post-Human Era.* Vision-21: Interdisciplinary Science and Engineering in the Era of Cyberspace, NASA, 11–22.

- Casado, E. & Derakhshan, M. (2019). *Mindful Spatial Design: Balancing the Digital and Physical Worlds.* Journal of Human-Computer Interaction, 36(4), 380–399.

- Satyanarayanan, M. (2019). *The Emergence of Edge Computing.* IEEE Computer, 50(1), 30–39.

- Wigdor, D. & Wixon, D. (2011). *Brave NUI World: Designing Natural User Interfaces for Touch and Gesture.* Morgan Kaufmann.

- Kaku, M. (2011). *Physics of the Future: How Science Will Shape Human Destiny and Our Daily Lives by the Year 2100.* Doubleday.

- Krishna, G. (2015). *The Best Interface Is No Interface: The Simple Path to Brilliant Technology.* New Riders.

- https://blog.unity.com/engine-platform/unity-support-for-visionos

- https://docs.unity3d.com/Packages/com.unity.polyspatial.visionos@0.0/manual/GettingStarted.html

- www.midjourney.com/app/

- https://dreamstudio.ai/

- https://stability.ai/stablediffusion

- www.adobe.com/ca/sensei/generative-ai/firefly.html

Index

A

G

Printed in the United States
by Baker & Taylor Publisher Services